Tell Them Who I Am

THE LIVES OF HOMELESS WOMEN

Elliot Liebow

PENGUIN BOOKS

PENGUIN BOOKS

Published by the Penguin Group

Penguin Books USA Inc., 375 Hudson Street, New York, New York 10014, U.S.A.

Penguin Books Ltd, 27 Wrights Lane, London W8 5TZ, England

Penguin Books Australia Ltd, Ringwood, Victoria, Australia

Penguin Books Canada Ltd, 10 Alcorn Avenue, Toronto, Ontario, Canada M4V 3B2

Penguin Books (N.Z.) Ltd, 182–190 Wairau Road, Auckland 10, New Zealand

Penguin Books Ltd, Registered Offices: Harmondsworth, Middlesex, England

First published in the United States of America by The Free Press,
a division of Macmillan, Inc., 1993
Reprinted by arrangement with The Free Press
Published in Penguin Books 1995

1   3   5   7   9   10   8   6   4   2

Lyrics to "Paper Doll," by Johnny Block, are quoted by permission of
Edward B. Marks Music Company.

THE LIBRARY OF CONGRESS HAS CATALOGUED THE HARDCOVER AS FOLLOWS:
Liebow, Elliot.
Tell them who I am: the lives of homeless women/Elliot Liebow.
p.   cm.
Includes bibliographical references and index.
ISBN 0-02-919095-9 (hc.)
ISBN 0 14 02.4137 X (pbk.)
1. Homeless women—Washington (D.C.) Region—Case studies.
2. Shelters for the homeless—Washington (D.C.) Region—Case studies.
3. Homelessness—Washington (D.C.) Region—Case studies.   I. Title.
HV4506.W2L54   1993
362.83´08´6942—dc20   92–39453

Printed in the United States of America
Set in Fenice

Critical acclaim for *Tell Them Who I Am*

"Mr. Liebow lets the women's voices shape the book. . . . *Tell Them Who I Am* should be required reading for anyone who wants to understand women who are 'defined by where we sleep at night.'"
—*The New York Times*

"Liebow is masterly at depicting the women in the shelters as individuals, while keeping his focus on their collective life . . . With *Tell Them Who I Am* he has illuminated one of the most important problems of our time by bringing an invisible population to the attention of the American people."
—*Chicago Tribune*

"Here is a morally awake social science utterly free of jargon, pomposity and self-importance, those abiding contemporary sins that confront so many of us readers in our search for social truths. Here is a brilliant, and yet humble effort to understand and render an aspect of our humanity, however down-and-out our condition." —Robert Coles

"Skillfully blending a social scientist's objectivity with humanitarian concern . . . probing and morally honest . . . *Tell Them Who I Am* reveals hard truths about the humanity and inhumanity of us all."
—*Publishers Weekly*

"The purity of Liebow's intention to 'put [him]self in the place of homeless women' is manifested in a crystalline clarity of perception. The women's stories are told in limpid prose free of social science jargon . . . [and] everything he reports, in a series of engrossing portraits, rings true."
—*San Francisco Chronicle*

"Liebow's deeply compassionate book invites us to pay attention, and perhaps in the end, the homeless men and women in our community will tell us who we truly are." —*The Philadelphia Inquirer*

PENGUIN BOOKS

TELL THEM WHO I AM

Elliot Liebow was chief of the Center for the Study of Work and Mental Health of the National Institute of Mental Health, and also Cardinal O'Boyle Professor at the National Catholic School for Social Service of the Catholic University of America in Washington. In addition to *Tell Them Who I Am*, Dr. Liebow wrote *Tally's Corner*, an ethnographic study of black urban streetcorner society. The book had a profound influence in its field, and it earned Dr. Liebow the C. Wright Mills Award of the Society for the Study of Social Problems.

Dr. Liebow died in September 1994.

To Harriet

Contents

Preface

A Soft Beginning

This is a participant observer study of single, homeless women in emergency shelters in a small city just outside Washington, D.C. In participant observation, the researcher tries to participate as fully as possible in the life of the people being studied. Of course, there are obvious and severe limits to how well a man with a home and family can put himself in the place of homeless women. One simply goes where they go, gets to know them over time as best one can, and tries very hard to see the world from their perspective.

It is often said that, in participant observation studies, the researcher is the research instrument. So is it here. Everything reported about the women in this study has been selected by me and filtered through me, so it is important that I tell you something about myself and my prejudices as well as how this study came about. Indeed, I feel obliged to tell you more than is seemly and more than you may want to know, but these are things that the women themselves knew about me and that had an important if unknown influence on my relationship with them.

In a real sense, I backed into this study, which took shape, more or less, as I went along. In 1984, I learned that I had cancer and a very limited life expectancy. I did not want to spend my last months on the 12th floor of a government office building, so at 58 I retired on disability from my job of 20-some years as an anthropologist with the National Institute of Mental Health.

I looked well, felt well, and had a lot of time on my hands, so I became a volunteer at a soup kitchen that had recently opened. I worked there one night a week. In the early part of the evening, I helped serve food or just sat around with the men and women who had come there, usually eating with them. In case of trouble, I tried to keep the peace. Later I went upstairs to "the counselor's office," where I met with people who needed assistance in getting shelter for the night. For the next hour or so, I called around to the various shelters in the county or in downtown Washington, D.C., trying to locate and reserve sleeping space for the men and women who needed it.

I enjoyed the work and the people at the soup kitchen, but this was only one night a week, so I became a volunteer at The Refuge, an emergency shelter for homeless women. This, too, was one night a week, from 6:30 to 10:00, and involved sleeping overnight twice a month. I picked this shelter because I had visited there briefly the year before and liked the feel of it. Here, along with three other volunteers, my job was to help prepare the food (usually just heat the main dishes and make a salad); help serve the food; distribute towels, soap, and other sundries on request; socialize with the women; keep order; and keep a daily log that included the names of all the women present and their time of arrival.

Almost immediately, I found myself enjoying the company of the women. I was awed by the enormous effort that most of them made to secure the most elementary necessities and decencies of life that the rest of us take for granted. And I was especially struck by their sense of humor, so at odds with any self-pity—the ability to step back and laugh at oneself, however wryly. One evening, soon after I started working at the shelter, several of us remained at the table to talk after finishing dinner. Pauline turned to me and said, in a stage whisper, making sure that Hilda would hear her, "Hilda has a Ph.D."

Hilda laughed. "No," she said, "I don't have a Ph.D., but I do have a bachelor's degree in biology." She paused, then began again. "You know," she said, "all my life I wanted to be an MD and now, at the age of 54, I finally made it. I'm a Manic Depressive."

Seduced by the courage and the humor of the women, and by the pleasure of their company, I started going to the shelter four and sometimes five days a week. (For the first two years, I also kept my one-night-a-week job with the soup kitchen.) Probably because it was something I was trained to do, or perhaps out of plain habit, I decided to take notes.

"Listen," I said at the dinner table one evening, after getting permission to do a study from the shelter director. "I want your permission to take notes. I want to go home at night and write down what I can remember about the things you say and do. Maybe I'll write a book about homeless women."

Most of the dozen or so women there nodded their heads or simply shrugged. All except Regina. Her acceptance was conditional. "Only if you promise not to publish before I do," she said. Believing that neither one of us, for different reasons, would ever publish anything in the future, I readily agreed.[1]

Over the next two, three years, my health was great. I had been led to a new drug available in Canada, and I went to Quebec every three months (after a year or so, every six months) for a supply of the drug and tests of one kind or another. The women knew about the trips, of course, and they knew why I made them. Meanwhile, in the same town, a day shelter had opened up in 1985 and two new emergency night shelters in 1986. The day

---

[1] Let the record show that now, some seven-plus years later, I have her permission to go ahead.

shelter was open from 2:00 P.M. to 6:30. From there, the women went to their respective night shelters, all three of which opened at seven o'clock. Sometimes I spent mornings with the women, sitting around in a park or coffee shop, or driving them somewhere, but my usual working day was from 2:00 P.M. till 10:00 at night, when the shelter lights went out.

When The Refuge was open (November 1 to March 31), I usually went there from the day shelter. When The Refuge was closed, I went to one of the other two shelters. I remained a volunteer at The Refuge, and was careful to make a distinction between the one night a week I was an official volunteer and the other nights when I was Doing Research (that is, hanging around). Occasionally, I also filled in as a volunteer on an emergency basis at the day shelter as well. In general, I identified myself with the women as much as possible, and tried to distance myself from staff and management of the shelters.

It is difficult to be precise about how I was perceived by the women. I am 6'1" and weigh about 175 pounds. I had a lot of white hair but was otherwise nondescript. I dressed casually, often in corduroy pants, shirt, and cardigan. The fact that I was Jewish did not seem to matter much one way or another so far as I could tell.

Most of the women probably liked having me around. Male companionship was generally in short supply and the women often made a fuss about the few male volunteers. I would guess that there were as many women who actively sought me out as there were women who avoided me. The fact that I had written a book that was available at the library (three or four women took the trouble to read it) enhanced my legitimacy in their eyes.[2]

Principally, I think, the women saw me as an important resource. I had money and a car, and by undertaking to write a book, I had made it my business to be with them. I routinely lent

---

[2] *Tally's Corner: A Study of Negro Streetcorner Men.*

out $2, $5, $10 or even $20 on request to the handful who asked.
I told them I had set aside a certain amount as a revolving fund
and I could only keep lending money if they kept returning it.
This worked fairly well.

There were a few women, of course, who would never be in
a position to return the money, and this made for a problem. It
would have been patronizing simply to make a gift of the money;
they wanted to be borrowers, not beggars, and I was just as eager as they to avoid a demeaning panhandler/donor relationship. But I did not want them to be embarrassed or to avoid me
simply because they couldn't repay a loan, nor did I want to
shut them off from borrowing more. My solution was to reas-
sure these women I had no immediate need for the money and
could wait indefinitely for repayment.

Some of the women would perhaps characterize me as a
friend, but I am not certain how deep or steadfast this sense of
friendship might be. One day, Regina and I were talking about
her upcoming trial about two months away. I had already
agreed to accompany her to the courtroom and serve as an ad-
visor, but Regina wanted further reassurance.

"You will be there, won't you?" she said.

As a way of noting the profundity that nothing in life is certain, I said, jokingly, "It's not up to me, it's up to The Man
Upstairs."

"Well," she said, "if you die before the trial, you will ask one
of your friends to help me, won't you?" I looked hard at her to
see if she was joking, too. She wasn't. She was simply putting
first things first.

One or two of the women did say something like "If you weren't
married, would you give me a run for my money?" Neither "yes"
nor "no" was a suitable response, but it usually sufficed for me
to say (and mean), "I think you are a very nice person."

I tried to make myself available for driving people to Social
Services, a job interview, a clinic or hospital, a cemetery, to
someone's house, to another shelter, to help them move their

belongings, or on other personal errands. With my consent, several women used my name as a personal reference for jobs or housing, and a few used my home as a mailing address for income tax refunds or other business.

Several of the women got to know my two daughters, both of whom came to The Refuge a few evenings each during the winters. One daughter was engaged to be married and her fiancé also came a few times. These visits helped strengthen my ties to those women who knew my daughters by face and name. They could ask me how my wife, Harriet, or Elisabeth and Jessica and Eric were doing, and my subsequent participation in discussions about family or child-rearing was much more personal and immediate as a result.

It is difficult to exaggerate the importance of this kind of familiarity. It is essential, I believe, in this kind of study—a participant observer kind of study—that relationships be as symmetrical as possible, that there be a quid pro quo; the women needed to know as much about me as I knew about them.

My association with the women was most intense during the winter of 1984–85, all of 1986, much of 1987, and the winter of 1987–88. Thereafter, I backed off a bit, partly for health reasons and partly because I had already collected more notes than I knew what to do with.[3] I continued to go to the shelters intermittently, and several of the women called me regularly at home. It was also at this time that I started playing around with the notes to see how I might eventually make sense of them.

•　•　•

In general, I have tried to avoid labeling any of the women as "mentally ill," "alcoholic," "drug addicted," or any other characterization that is commonly used to describe—or, worse, to

---

[3]For the same reason, I stopped taking life histories. After the women had known me for a few months, I took about 20 life histories on tape, often at the request of the women themselves and over a period of two years or so. Some of these lasted several hours over two or three sessions and I found myself accumulating more information than I could handle.

explain—the homeless person. Judgments such as these are almost always made against a background of homelessness. If the same person were seen in another setting, the judgment might be altogether different. Like you, I know people who drink, people who do drugs, and bosses who have tantrums and treat their subordinates like dirt. They all have good jobs. Were they to become homeless, some of them would surely also become "alcoholics," "addicts," or "mentally ill." Similarly, if some of the homeless women who are now so labeled were to be magically transported to a more usual and acceptable setting, some of them—not all, of course—would shed their labels and take their places with the rest of us somewhere on the spectrum of normality.

The reader may be puzzled by the short shrift given here to mental illness. This was no oversight. I have no training as a mental health professional so it is not always clear to me who is mentally ill and who is not. There were always some women who acted crazy or whom most considered crazy, and the women themselves often agreed with the public at large that many homeless people are mentally ill.

From the beginning, however, I paid little attention to mental illness, partly because I had difficulty recognizing it, and partly for other reasons. Sometimes mental illness seemed to be a "now-you-see-it, now-you-don't" phenomenon; some of the women were fine when their public assistance checks arrived, but became increasingly "symptomatic" as the month progressed and their money (security?) diminished, coming full circle when the next check arrived.[4] Others had good or bad days or weeks but with no obvious pattern or periodicity,

---

[4]"Many schizophrenics are completely lucid for long periods of time, and their thoughts and behavior are completely indistinguishable from those of normals. Even Bleuler . . . asserted that there were certain very important cognitive processes . . . that were frequently identical among schizophrenics and normals. *In many important respects, then, an insane person may be completely sane"* (emphasis added). Morris Rosenberg, "A Symbolic Interactionist View of Psychosis," *Journal of Health and Social Behavior,* 25, no. 3 (September 1984), p. 291.

although one woman linked her down period to her menstrual cycle. With a little patience on my part, almost all the women with mental or emotional problems were eventually and repeatedly accessible. Even on "bad" days, perhaps especially on "bad" days, these women sometimes said things that seemed to come, uncensored, from the depths of their emotional lives.

It seems to me that those women who may have been mentally ill (or alcoholic or drug addicted) by one or another standard were homeless for exactly the same proximal reason that everyone else was homeless: they had no place to live. Similarly, their greatest need of the moment was the same as everyone else's: to be assured of a safe, warm place to sleep at night, one or more hot meals a day, and the presence, if not the companionship, of fellow human beings. Given this perspective and my purposes, which and how many of the women were mentally ill was not a critical issue.

Whatever one's view of mental illness, it is probably true that the more one gets to know about a person, the easier it is to put oneself in that person's place or to understand his or her viewpoint, and the less reason one has for thinking of that person or treating that person as mentally ill.[5]

This perspective—indeed, participant observation itself—raises the age-old problem of whether anyone can understand another or put oneself in another's place. Many thoughtful people believe that a sane person cannot know what it is to be crazy, that a white man cannot understand a black man, a Jew cannot see through the eyes of a Christian, a man through the eyes of a woman, and so forth in both directions. In an important sense, of course, and to a degree, this is surely true; in another sense, and to a degree, it is surely false, because the logical extension of such a view is that no one can know

---

[5]In a symbolic interactionist view, "insanity is not a matter of . . . impaired functioning or social maladjustment. . . . It is unequivocally an interactional concept that is distinguished by an *observer's* inability to take the role of the actor" (emphasis in original). Rosenberg, "A Symbolic Interactionist View," p. 291.

another, that only John Jones can know John Jones, in which case social life would be impossible.[6]

I do not mean to say that a man with a home and family can see and feel the world as homeless women see and feel it. I do mean, however, that it is reasonable and useful to try to do so. Trying to put oneself in the place of the other lies at the heart of the social contract and of social life itself.

• • •

In the early months, I sometimes tried to get Betty or one of the other women to see things as I saw them. One night Betty waited half an hour in back of the library for a bus that never came. She was convinced this was deliberate and personal abuse on the part of the Metro system. Metro was out to get her, she said. "But how did Metro know you were waiting for a bus at that time?" I asked. Betty shook her head in pity of me. "Well for Christ's sake, Elliot, I was there on the street, right there in public, in the open! How could they not see me waiting for that damn bus?"

Fairly quickly, I learned not to argue with Betty but simply to relax and marvel at her end-of-the-month ingenuity. ("End-of-the-month" because that's when her public assistance money ran out and when she was most bitter at the way the world was treating her. At that time, a $10 or $20 loan could dramatically reduce or even eliminate her paranoid thoughts.) Once, when her food stamps had not come, even two days after Judy had received hers, Betty dryly observed that this was further proof that Richman County was trying to rid itself of homeless

---

[6]Those who romanticize history and heroes are especially likely to close their minds to the possibility of people "understanding" one another. Allan Bloom, who does not let his brilliance get in the way of drawing wrong conclusions, is one such person. After separating "thinkers" from "doers," he argues that the thinker cannot understand the doer, then proceeds to a spectacular nonsequitur: "Does one not have to be akin to Caesar to understand him? To say that one does not have to be Caesar to understand him is equivalent to saying that one does not have to be anything to understand everything." *The Closing of the American Mind,* p. 303.

women. "They give Judy Tootie her food stamps so she'll eat herself to death [Judy weighed 300 pounds]. They won't give me mine so I'll starve to death." She got no argument from me. I had learned to go with the flow.

Sometimes I annoyed or even angered some of the women. When Louise told me that some of the women were following her around all day and harassing her, I asked her why they did these things. "You're just like the state's attorney," she said, "always asking for reasons. Whenever I tell him that someone assaulted me, he always asks me why they did it. People with criminal minds don't need a reason to do something. That's what makes them criminals."

• • •

I think of Betty and Louise and many of the other women as friends. As a friend, I owe them friendship. Perhaps I also owe them something because I have so much and they have so little, but I do not feel under any special obligation to them as research subjects. Indeed, I do not think of them as "research subjects." Since they knew what I was trying to do and allowed me to do it, they could just as well be considered collaborators in what might fairly be seen as a cooperative enterprise.

In introducing the women, and perhaps elsewhere, I may seem to have placed undue emphasis on their physical appearance—pretty, fat, skinny, and so on. That may be true. But ours is a sexist society (though less sexist than most) and almost everyone, including women themselves, emphasizes physical appearance. Moreover, since homeless women are not likely to have formal credentials, social status, money, or useful social or business connections, they confront potential employers, landlords, indeed the whole world, with little more than themselves to offer for evaluation. For this reason, and more than for most of us, the way homeless women present themselves—how they look, speak, and carry themselves—makes a great difference in how they are treated by the rest of the world.

Originally, I had asked three homeless women and the director of a shelter to write comments on the manuscript. One of the women, after reading a draft of the manuscript, and for reasons not clear to me, angrily decided she did not want to be in the book at all. She did agree to allow herself to be quoted (but not described) in a couple of places. All other references to her were deleted at her request. Similarly, in the second year, one of the more distinctive and more troubled women told me she wanted nothing to do with me or anything I might write. (Given her ethnicity and life history, "Madama Butterfly" would have been a perfect pseudonym for her.) We had gotten along well until the day she saw me in earnest conversation with a woman who had become her enemy. On the theory that "the friend of my enemy is my enemy," she refused to talk to me thereafter (as she had refused to talk to some of the women as well). Also, from that day on, to her I was no longer "Elliot" but "Idiot," as in "Here comes Idiot again to seduce all the women." I continued to include her in my notes in the hope our friendship could be revived. Hers was a colorful and strong personality that contributed importantly to the atmosphere of the shelters, year after year. Unfortunately, she appears only fleetingly in the book.

Two homeless women—Kim and Grace—and Rachel, director of one of the shelters, agreed to comment on the manuscript. Their comments had to be edited for length, but none of the language has been changed. Many of the unused comments from all three were anecdotal confirmations of assertions and interpretations in the text. I tried to include especially those comments that disagreed with the text or with one another, or that offered a different perspective. These comments appear in italics on the relevant pages.

Inevitably, in the pages that follow, I had to make small compromises with the literal truth (as I saw it). Most of these were omissions, as in omitting, at one woman's request, any reference to her mild physical disability (not obvious to others), and in omitting another woman's selected references to her family members, also at her request. These compromises were necessary because it is impossible to ensure total anonymity. In those cases where I took life histories, I asked the women to pick their own pseudonyms. Several women chose their mothers' names. Other names were taken or assigned arbitrarily.

One other point about names. I have given names to women who appear only once or twice in the book in order to keep the individuals separate from one another. Attributions of word or deed to unnamed persons would, I felt, be more confusing than a lot of names.

African-American women called themselves "black" and referred to one another that way, so I have done the same. Similarly, I would have preferred to use "disabled" rather than "handicapped" throughout, but fidelity to others' usage made that impossible.

Although the names of the women, the shelters (except those in D.C.), and many place names were changed for obvious reasons, most of the women will be known to one another and perhaps to others as well. Where a faithful physical description would be likely to identify a woman to family or friends or others, as in Elsie's case (only one external ear, no ear canals, a weight of over 300 pounds), I sought specific permission to use it. In two cases I substituted one disabling characteristic for another. With these minor exceptions, the people here are intact and presented as I saw them.

• • •

In addition to the homeless women and the staffs at the three shelters, I owe a great deal to many people, but first I must acknowledge the extraordinary institutional support I received from the National Institute of Mental Health and The Catholic University of America.[7] When I retired, I had been working in

---

[7]Neither the National Institute of Mental Health nor The Catholic University of America should be understood to sanction the views expressed in this book. Responsibility for what is in this book is mine and mine alone.

NIMH's Laboratory of Socio-environmental Studies. Melvin Kohn (now at Johns Hopkins) and Carmi Schooler, his successor as head of the laboratory, made it possible for me to stay on in the laboratory as a "guest researcher"—an official status as an unpaid worker that allowed me the use of a desk, a telephone, and a computer terminal. A short time later, Fred Ahearn, Dean of the National Catholic School of Social Service (NCSSS) of The Catholic University of America, offered me an endowed chair.

I received much valuable assistance from both of these institutions, but far and away the most important came in the way of collegiality and emotional support. At NIMH's Laboratory of Socio-environmental Studies, Carmi Schooler, who disagreed with many things in the manuscript, especially my handling of mental illness, did not let that disagreement stand in his way. He and Carrie Schoenbach and Leslie Caplan read all or most of the manuscript and made many insightful and important suggestions. Melvin Kohn and Carles Muntaner read one or more draft chapters and also made several useful suggestions. The recommendations of Marta Elliot, a Johns Hopkins graduate student in sociology who worked at NIMH part-time, were crucial to the final product. Virginia Marbley, the laboratory secretary, patiently listened to my stories and helped make work-life easier in many ways. Other members of the laboratory—Paula Darby Lipman, Jason Lee, Bruce Roberts, Marjorie Lewis, and Douglas Herrmann—did the same. Stephen Fiore, another student, solved my computer problems as they arose.

At Catholic University, Fred Ahearn, Joseph Shields, Philip Schervish, and Joan Mullaney gave me encouragement whenever I needed it, which was often. Janet Rosenkrantz paved the way for me with the staff, and Sheila Kelly produced a remarkably faithful transcription of dozens of hours of taped life histories, right down to "uh's" and intonations.

Other friends pitched in, too. Neal Herrick, Arlene Kaplan Daniels, Diane Doherty, Burt Saxon, and Herbert Gans all made important suggestions. My sister, Bernice Lee, and Maria Foscarinis, founder and director of the National Law Center on Homelessness and Poverty, were important personal resources, as was Michael Schuchat, counsel to the American Anthropological Association, who gave me needed legal advice and made substantive suggestions as well.

Another friend, John Kitsuse, generously gave me the title to this book. "Look here," he said, when we were at some meeting or other, just about the time I started writing. "I'm not going to write any more books and I have a title left over. You can have it if you want it. It's 'Tell Them Who I Am.'" I think that's a fine title and I can only hope the book is worthy of it. Michael Ames, editor-in-chief of Temple University Press, was an early and enthusiastic supporter of the manuscript, and I benefited greatly from the comments he solicited from an anonymous reviewer.

I took much inspiration from Kim Hopper, that rare combination of scholar and activist (researcher and currently president of the National Coalition for the Homeless). I learned much more from him and his publications than is suggested by the few citations I included.

The heaviest hand in the manuscript, besides my own, is that of Adam Bellow, senior editor at The Free Press, who made many critical suggestions, chapter by chapter and line by line, about presentation of the material. He proposed different ways of looking at some of the issues and also saved me from several lapses in judgment and good taste. I hope he caught all of them. Loretta Denner, also of The Free Press, with patience and imagination shepherded the manuscript through production.

I can't name the homeless women or the people who staffed the various shelters, but they know who they are and I am grateful to them for allowing me to look over their shoulders and even, on occasion, to participate in their lives.

I also thank Gottfried O. Lang, professor emeritus of anthropology, University of Colorado, who had nothing whatever to do with this book and everything to do with it. For more than

35 years, first as mentor, then as friend, he has put his stamp on everything I have thought and written.

My wife, Harriet, and my daughters, Elisabeth and Jessica, read the manuscript and made valuable suggestions. I owe all three of them, as well as my daughters' husbands, Scott Feeser and Eric Astran, much more than I can say in brief and in public for their support over these years. Final thanks to my literary agent, Ann Edelstein, who helped me in so many ways.

Introduction

The Women, the Shelters, and
the Round of Life

Tell Them Who I Am focuses on the dynamics of shelter life.[1] Initially, my aim was to write a straightforward description of shelter life and, ideally, to try to see the world of homelessness as homeless women see and experience it. Later, when trying to make sense of my notes, I realized that another of my aims was to explain both to myself and others how these women remained human in the face of inhuman conditions. I had come to see how inadequate it was to think of them in one-dimensional, stereotypical terms such as "mentally ill" or "alcoholics," as incomplete persons deficient in morals or character, or even as "disaffiliated" persons, go-it-alone isolates no longer connected with family or friends.

---

[1] There is no claim that the women or the shelters here are representative of homeless women and shelters elsewhere. I do believe, however, that the problems the women face, and the dynamics of their relationships with one another and with others, do have relevance for other homeless women and for homeless men as well.

1

Some homeless people might seem to fit one or another such category. There are many highly visible people on the street, their goods piled all around them, who live, more or less, by scavenging the detritus of the rest of us. One of the most startling things about them is that from city to city and region to region, they look so much and act so much alike. Such persons seem to have lost dimensionality. They may indeed be "mentally ill," "disaffiliated," and otherwise different from the rest of us, but they tend to be different in the same way, hence their likeness to one another. However much each of them seems to be going his or her own way, they are all following the same road. They are social products no less than everyone else.

A most important fact about these dramatically visible homeless persons on the street is that, their visibility notwithstanding, they are at best a small minority, tragic caricatures of homelessness rather than representatives of it. For every one of them, there are 10 or maybe 20 less visibly homeless persons on the street or in emergency shelters.[2] A few of the women I met in the shelters or on the street may have been on their way down to join the caricature population. To my knowledge, I never met anyone on the way up from there. This is not to say that some do not recover nor that some will not do so in the future, but the cards are stacked against them.

It is, perhaps, all too easy to fall into homelessness, but being there is not easy at all.[3] In the pages that follow, I have tried to document some of the hardships of homelessness and the struggles of the women to surmount them. I have tried to show that only through extraordinary efforts can a woman work her

---

[2] "Those whose homelessness is apparent . . . who . . . fit the long-held stereotypes of bums, derelicts, winos, or the insane, are only the tip of the iceberg." Richard H. Ropers, "The Rise of the Urban Homeless," *Public Affairs Report: Bulletin of the Institute of Governmental Studies* (University of California, Berkeley) 26 (October–November 1985), p. 1. See Appendix C for a brief discussion of the statistics of homelessness.

[3] "Being homeless . . . takes effort and work. It requires collaboration with circumstance." Kim Hopper, Ezra Susser, and Susan Conover, "Economies of Makeshift: Deindustrialization and Homelessness in New York City," *Urban Anthropology* 14, no. 1–3 (1985), p. 215.

way unaided out of homelessness, and sometimes not even extraordinary efforts are enough. Many homeless women work or look for work, knowing they will not find jobs they can live on.

The humanity of the women is under constant threat and by no means easy to preserve. Most homeless women are engaged in an unremitting struggle to remain human in the face of inhuman conditions. Many look to the social service system—public assistance, food stamps, medical care—for help in physical survival. Some want help but cannot get it. Others will not submit to what they see as demeaning treatment and refuse to purchase public assistance at the cost of their self-respect. Still others find they cannot deal with what to them is the arbitrariness and irrationality of social service systems. For them, there is not nearly so much craziness among homeless persons as there is in the systems ostensibly designed to help them.

As the social service system looks at the women, however, and tries to separate the deserving poor from the undeserving, the difficulties are seen to lie with the women. It is the homeless women who are demanding and unreasonable, the women who are ungrateful and uncooperative, and the women who don't appreciate the fact that the people who make the system work are understaffed and overworked and must go by the rules, or else there'd be chaos.

In addition to exclusionary eligibility criteria, a major problem with social service programs is that many homeless people do not have the strength to reach out for them or the persistence to keep trying. Others decide to take their chances without them. Together, those who can't and those who won't comprise a majority of homeless persons.[4] For others, public assistance in one or another form is crucial. But whatever it is, it is not enough. In 1990, *combined* SSI, food stamps, and medical and housing assistance totaled $5,016 for single persons or

---

[4] "Over half of all homeless persons are eligible for some type of benefit under these [Social Security] programs. Yet only a small fraction—in some areas fewer than 10%—actually receive them." National Law Center on Homelessness and Poverty, "Social Security: Broken Promises to America's Homeless," March 1990, p. 3.

84.3 percent of the poverty level.[5] By themselves, assistance
programs might not lift you out of poverty; they might not even
keep you off the street.[6]

It is no wonder, then, that most homeless women—those who
receive public assistance as well as those who do not—look to
shelters to provide that minimum security, nourishment, and
sociability that begin to make life possible. It is there that the
women put together the physical basis for life in a city: food,
protection from (human) predators and the weather, safe sleep,
clean water for washing oneself and one's clothes, toilets, and
a few creature comforts as well. Shelters also serve as a home
base for women who have no homes, and provide a pool of persons from which they may choose acquaintances, associates,
comrades, and friends.

The Shelters *Rockville / Bethesda ? Montgomery / Fairfax ?*

The Refuge, which opened in the city of Upton in 1982, was the
first emergency shelter for single women in Richman County.[7]
When I began this study in the winter of 1984–85, it was still the
only one. In 1986, however, two more night shelters opened up
(Bridge House and New Beginnings). A day shelter, which had
opened in 1985, was patronized by women from all three night
shelters. Since the women often went from one shelter to another, my focus broadened to include these new shelters as
well.

All four shelters are within walking distance of the Richman
County office and courtroom buildings that anchor downtown

---

[5] Committee on Ways and Means, *Background Material and Data on Programs within the Jurisdiction of the Committee on Ways and Means*, Section
9 (1989). Cited by the National Law Center on Homelessness and Poverty,
"Social Security," p. 6, n. 8.

[6] "Even if all homeless people participated in every benefit program available to them, the net benefit they would receive would, in many cases, still
not keep them off the streets." James D. Wright, *Address Unknown: The
Tragedy of Homelessness in America*, p. xiii.

[7] The names of the shelters, the city, the county, and the women are
fictitious.

Upton. Perhaps half of Upton residents consider themselves to be living in a bedroom satellite of Washington, D.C. The other half, who live and work in Upton, consider Upton their hometown with its own unique history and personality, completely independent of Washington. Indeed, some see Washington as alien territory to be visited only on special occasions, if ever. Now that their city is tethered to Washington by subway, however, even hardcore Upton boosters would concede that Upton is, in reality as well as administratively, an integral part of the Washington metropolitan area.

Perhaps half the women in these shelters come from Upton or nearby towns in the same or a neighboring county. Perhaps a third or more are from Washington itself. The remainder are mainly from within the state or from neighboring states, with only a handful passing through, to or from faraway places such as Houston or Chicago or Los Angeles.[8]

Staff persons at the shelters might be paid or volunteer, trained or untrained. Volunteers are mostly local; paid workers are more likely to commute from D.C. or other nearby communities. Although paid staff may be working class or middle class, black or white, those who hold these low-pay, low-status jobs are more likely to be black and working class; volunteers are more likely to be white and middle class.[9]

The Refuge—Fellowship Hall is an auditorium on the top (third) floor of the church school associated with Mainline Church One. The school and the church are connected by a breezeway at ground level. For 10 years now, every November 1, the chairs are put away, the stage is cleared, cots and blankets are brought

---

[8]The homeless persons in Peter Rossi's Chicago study were also predominantly local: almost half were born in the state of Illinois and almost three-fourths had lived in Chicago for 10 years or more. Peter H. Rossi, *Down and Out in America: The Origins of Homelessness*, p. 126.

[9]I am not certain of the difference it makes, but it is often the case that the poorest paid, least trained, and least experienced staff are on the front lines. The better-trained and more experienced persons are miles and miles away and they are called supervisors or professors.

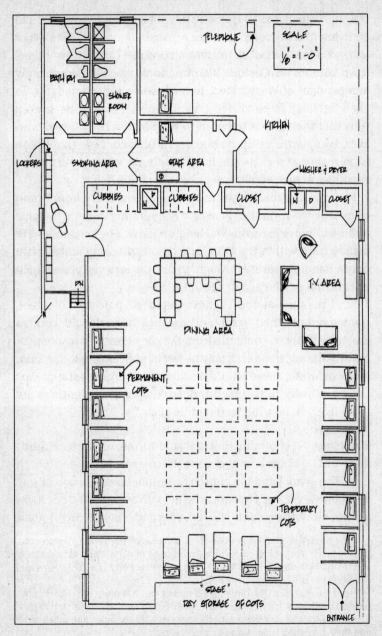

Floor Plan of The Refuge

out, and Fellowship Hall is transformed into The Refuge, an emergency shelter for 25 to 30 homeless women. Exactly five months later, on April 1, the cots, blankets, and tables are put away, the stage and other storage places are emptied out, the women disperse, and Fellowship Hall once again reclaims its name and function.[10]

The main room of The Refuge is 55 feet long, 50 feet wide, and 14 feet high. The floors are alternating squares of black and gray asphalt tiles, waxed and buffed to a shine. The cinder-block walls are painted a pale yellow. The three eight-foot tables arranged in a U-shape near the entrance to the office and kitchen are the heart of the shelter. Here the women eat breakfast and dinner, and here is the center of social life as well. Under the steady growth of population pressure, the men's restroom (two toilet stalls, one useless urinal, no shower, two basins) was also given over to the women.[11]

For the first five years of its life, The Refuge was an all-volunteer operation. Each evening, four volunteers arrived at 6:15 to prepare dinner and generally ready the shelter for the seven o'clock arrival of the women. At 10:00 P.M. when the lights were turned out, two volunteers left and two remained overnight. To prevent burnout, volunteers were limited to a maximum of

---

[10]The organizers of The Refuge decided on a women's shelter because they thought this "least frightening population" would have the best chance for community acceptance. The Refuge is open only during the winter months for two main reasons. One is that, in the initial negotiations with the church congregation and with neighborhood representatives, the organizers of the shelter committed themselves to operate the shelter only during the five months of cold weather. The second reason—closely related—is that the organizers did not believe they could sustain an all-volunteer operation throughout the year, year in, year out.

[11]The first shower was installed in 1983. Despite sign-up sheets and other attempts at control, there was constant friction around its use. A second shower was installed in 1990, in place of one of the two remaining toilet stalls (requiring that the men's restroom be opened to the women). Clearly, the introduction of a scarce but highly desirable resource is not without costs. Not surprisingly, when there was no shower, there were no problems around its use. The introduction of the first shower created discord where none had been before. The introduction of a second shower sharply reduced it.

three evenings (6:00 to 10:00 P.M.) and one sleepover a month, permitting them to come to the shelter fresh and eager to serve. Overall, more than 120 volunteers were required, half to staff the shelter, the other half to supply the food. A few staff volunteers were husband-wife teams, and perhaps 10 percent were men. Most of the volunteers had regular jobs.[12]

The operating philosophy of The Refuge contributes powerfully to its atmosphere and feel. Staffed with volunteers, it makes few demands on its residents. Its modest goal is to provide the women a safe, warm place to sleep at night, a hot meal, and a few other comforts to make their lives minimally decent. It is a low-pressure, laissez-faire operation that keeps rules to a minimum, ensuring health and safety while allowing the women to be what they are.

Bridge House — Bridge House, an emergency shelter for some 15 women, opened its doors in late 1986. It is run by a national organization on contract with Richman County.[13] The shelter itself is a one-story cinder-block building in a light industrial area very close to downtown Upton and the subway. To the left and right of the entrance hall are staff offices, one of which doubles as a kitchen. As one walks the length of the building, the women's rooms—four of them, each about 12 feet square— are lined up one after another on the right. Each room has a

---

[12]In 1987, the shelter began to accept county money for assistance with utilities and supplies, and to begin paying the two sleepover staff $60 a night (6:15 P.M. to 7 A.M.). The following year, sleepover staff were paid $70 a night, and each now receives $75. Some staff persons continue to serve as volunteers (6:15 to 10:00 P.M.) on some nights and paid overnight staff on others. Significantly, some staff members—by no means affluent—donate their pay back to the shelter.

[13]For the first six months of its life, while its permanent home was being readied for occupancy, this shelter was as homeless as the women it served. Anywhere from 10 to 15 women "occupied" this No Name shelter, moving every week or two from a church to a parochial school (Easter vacation) to another church to a public high school (summer break) to another church to a senior citizens center, and so on, much like an old-time floating craps game. When it took up permanent residence, it also took its name.

three-drawer dresser, a mirror, and three cots or two bunk beds. Opposite the rooms are general-purpose open spaces for eating, socializing, and holding meetings. On that side too are two restrooms, each with a toilet, washbasin, and shower.

In sharp contrast to The Refuge, Bridge House is operated by paid staff, all of whom, with the exception of the director, are women. The shelter director—who had other organizational duties as well—had a master's degree in social work. Similarly, some of the more senior staff had some training, if not degrees, in social work, but overall, the staff àre poorly paid and often undertrained and underexperienced. Most of the food is brought in by volunteers from churches and other organizations, but volunteers are otherwise discouraged from participation in shelter operations. Unlike the Refuge volunteers, who work one night a week, the paid staff at Bridge House have to face the women night in, night out. Daily stress and poor pay make it especially difficult for staff to radiate sweetness and light in their dealings with the women. They also make for high turnover.

At Bridge House, the staff see themselves as professionals whose job it is to help the women out of homelessness and to weed out those who do not want to be helped.[14] In addition to observing the usual injunctions against alcohol, drugs, carrying weapons, fighting, and using abusive language, the "regulars" (long-term residents) are often required to sign contracts promising to modify their behavior by going into therapy, applying for public assistance, looking for a job, getting up promptly in the morning, or simply "showing that you want to improve yourself." Where The Refuge tends to be relatively relaxed and laissez-faire, Bridge House tends to be directive and authoritarian.

---

[14]The differences between volunteers and paid staff are not always this simple and clear-cut. In large, municipally operated shelters, for example, many of the paid staff serve as security guards. At other shelters and some soup kitchens, security is provided by volunteers.

New Beginnings — New Beginnings was also started in 1986. It was founded by a nearby black church, which operates the shelter with no outside support. One paid staff person works a 6:30 P.M. to 7:00 A.M. shift five nights a week. She is respected and liked by the women. She has no formal training but has years of experience with homeless and incarcerated women. The church supplies a volunteer to assist her every evening and volunteer coverage on her days off. Church members also supply all the food.

New Beginnings is a neat, three-bedroom brick bungalow in a residential working-class neighborhood adjacent to one of the largest open-air drug markets in the area. To my knowledge, there have never been any problems because of this neighbor, but some of the women have been afraid to walk back to the shelter alone after dark. Normally, there are three women in each of the three bedrooms, but unlike The Refuge and Bridge House, New Beginnings will sometimes take in a woman with small children. What would normally be a living room has been converted into a bedroom for the overnight staff person. Meals are prepared in the kitchen. The women carry their plates of food to the finished basement, which is also set up as a lounge and laundry room.

The atmosphere at New Beginnings is somewhere between that of The Refuge and that of Bridge House. New Beginnings does not take outside money and is therefore accountable to no one. It enforces the same injunctions about weapons, drugs, abusive language, and fighting as the other shelters do, but because it has a maximum of nine women, everything is much less formal, and each one has a personal relationship with the director. The director decides who shall be allowed in, who shall go and who shall stay, and under what conditions. She is quick to point out that she is the sole and final judge of what is acceptable behavior in the shelter. She exercises this arbitrary power with an eye toward the particular needs of each woman as she sees them.

The Day Shelter — The day shelter was opened in 1985, only one block from The Refuge. It was formerly the Teen Lounge in Mainline Church Two and is managed by an all-woman board of directors who are members of that church. The board contracts with the same national organization that operates Bridge House to provide two staff persons daily (sometimes the same women who staff Bridge House). Some days, a board member also serves as a volunteer. Day shelter hours are from 2:00 to 6:30 P.M. six days a week. The homeless women ring a bell for admission and wait for a staff person to come downstairs and escort them through two locked doors at the entrance. Another locked door on the second (top) floor leads into a hallway that opens up into a warm, bright room, about 25 feet square. At the entrance is a desk with a telephone and a log book for the staff. The asphalt tile floor is covered with two bright-colored shag rugs. In the center of the room is a six-foot game table for jigsaw puzzles and general use, surrounded by half a dozen folding chairs. There are also a console TV, a sofa, and several upholstered chairs. On one wall is a bookcase that offers religious and self-improvement literature and a variety of romances and mysteries. On another wall is a small table with a hot-water urn and the makings of hot drinks and finger foods along with day-old doughnuts and cookies. On the same wall is an old upright piano. A large, round electric clock hangs above it. A door next to the piano opens onto a small, modern kitchen.

The atmosphere at the day shelter is at once relaxing and sti-fling. Inside the shelter, things are easy and relaxed, but every entry or exit—even to the locked bathroom, for which the women have to request a key—is documented in the log book. If you want to go out for a smoke or just fresh air, you must in-form a staff person who escorts you down the stairs and locks the three doors after you. This procedure is reversed for re-turning to the shelter.

The Daily Round

At The Refuge, the lights come on at 5:30 A.M. The women must be out of the shelter by 7:00.[15] A few are already up and dressed at the 5:30 wake-up, thereby avoiding the rush for toilets and washbasins. Other women awaken quickly and hurry to wash up. Still others remain in bed, waiting for the rush to subside or trying to squeeze in another few minutes of sleep. By 5:45, a make-it-yourself breakfast is ready and the women help themselves to frozen orange juice, milk (usually fresh, sometimes powdered) for packaged cereals, and hot water for cocoa or instant coffee, regular or decaffeinated. Bread, jam, margarine, and peanut butter are also on the table. Most of the time a staff person will make toast on request.

The morning atmosphere is usually quiet and businesslike as the women wash, dress, eat breakfast, make up their cots (most of the women most of the time), and sort their belongings, deciding what they will take with them for the day, what leave behind. Occasionally an argument will flare up in the washroom or at the breakfast table, but these tend to be short-lived.

There is typically more going on between the women and the staff than among the women themselves as the staff try to hurry them out by seven o'clock. Some women move especially slowly because they are on drugs of some sort, and some because they are not. The staff—many of whom must leave by 7:00 in order to get to their own jobs or see their children off to school—plead, cajole, or threaten that those who are not out on time will not be allowed to return that night. Bag lunches prepared by volunteers the night before (a cheese or lunch meat sandwich, a piece of fruit, and a granola bar) are on the table for the taking. In ones, twos, threes, and fours, the women shuffle out.

They fan out in different directions. Many will use public transportation to get to their jobs or to the Department of

---

[15]The daily routines at the other two emergency shelters are almost identical to those at The Refuge. Unlike The Refuge, however, both of these shelters are open year-round, and both require the women to do housekeeping chores.

Social Services, to a doctor's office or a shopping mall. On any given day, about half will remain in the immediate downtown area, sitting around in coffee shops or the lobbies and cafeterias of the county office buildings. In good weather, some will congregate on park benches. Many go to the public library when it opens at 9:30. ← *Gotta be Presbyterian Church on CW, Mart, + Public Library*

At two o'clock, the day shelter opens. A dozen or so women—mostly from The Refuge and Bridge House, two or three from New Beginnings—doze, watch TV, write letters, play cards, do jigsaw puzzles, snack, look at help-wanted and room-for-rent ads in the newspapers, read, and socialize. At 6:15, the food is put away and the staff clean up, often with the volunteered assistance of the women, who also begin to pick up their belongings and walk back to their respective night shelters. The Refuge is only five minutes away; Bridge House about 10 minutes; and New Beginnings about twice that.

By 6:30, the daily in-gathering at the night shelters is under way. Several women from the day shelter are already waiting for the 7:00 P.M. opening of The Refuge. Soon they are joined by women returning from their jobs or other activities. A bench that seats three is long filled. The other women stand or sit in the breezeway that connects the church to the school building, protecting themselves as best they can against the elements. Some staff persons will let the women in early, others will not, and still others allow the weather to be the determining factor. When the door is finally opened, the women file in and climb the three flights of stairs to The Refuge. Once inside, there is a small-scale rush as some hurry to sign up for the shower or washing machine, to get to the toilet or coffee pot, or just to get to their cots, put down their bags, and stretch out.[16]

---

[16]Each woman is assigned her own cot, two cubbyholes, and a small metal locker. With prior notification, these are reserved in her name for an absence of up to three days. After three days, the cot and storage sites are forfeited. If the forfeited cot happens to be in a preferred location (i.e., against a wall and with a moveable partition), a lottery is held to determine its next occupant.

A few women may go straight to bed for the night, with or without getting out of their street clothes, but for most this is a period of peak activity. The women take showers, wash clothes and iron, and get ready for dinner and bed. Most of the women come to the shelter with their own night clothes. The others are issued pajamas or nightgowns by the shelter. A handful will sleep in their clothes.

By 7:30, dinner is ready. The tables are set with paper napkins, plastic knives and forks, and laminated placemats made by a Sunday School class—signed drawings on colored paper covered with clear plastic. Individual portions are served on paper plates. The main course is often a casserole of some sort, commonly meat and rice, but spaghetti, macaroni and cheese, chicken dishes, and sloppy joes are also common. Typically, each plate contains a serving of peas or other canned vegetable. Fresh carrot and celery sticks are always on the dinner table, and most meals include a fresh salad or cole slaw. Servings are modest, but the women may ask for more as often as they like. It is not unusual for an exceptionally tasty main dish to run out, but most of The Refuge staff go to great lengths to find an acceptable substitute in the pantry or refrigerator. The elegance of the dessert tends to vary inversely with the elegance of the meal. A macaroni and cheese dish is more likely to be followed with cake and ice cream than, say, a meat and potatoes dish.[17]

---

[17]This menu compares favorably with the findings of a national study of shelters and soup kitchens commissioned by the U.S. Department of Agriculture: "The meals typically available to the homeless . . . provide substantial variety. A majority of lunches and dinners . . . contained at least four of the five core food groups . . . The average meal provided over 50% of the Recommended Dietary Allowance (RDA) for both men and women for 7 of 11 nutrients studied [but, for women, only 39 percent of the RDA for iron]. . . . The average caloric content per meal was 1023 . . . 38 percent of the 2700 calories a day recommended for men and 51 percent of the 2000 a day recommended for women." Martha R. Burt and Barbara E. Cohen, *Feeding the Homeless: Does the Prepared Meal Provision Help?* p. x. One major problem was that "the average number of meals eaten daily [by homeless persons] was 1.9, compared to 3 or more meals a day for the average American. . . . Their diets also lack certain core foods, mainly milk and milk products, fruits and vegetables" (p. xiii).

Seating at the dinner table tends to reflect faintly the socialization patterns that hold elsewhere during the day. Perhaps one-third of the women choose to sit opposite or next to friends or acquaintances; one-third keep to themselves; and another third allow themselves to be drawn into conversation with one or two staff people who join them for dinner after everyone has had a first serving.

By eight o'clock, some of the women have begun to peel away from the table. Some go to bed for the night. Some resume the grooming and personal chores interrupted by dinner. Some leave the table to watch TV. Some retreat to the smoking area in the hall. Groups of two or three may return to a cot for some private conversation, and another group remains to talk with one another or with staff over coffee (at night, decaffeinated only). A woman with her hair in curlers may sit on her cot or at the table and do her nails, and two others may do one another's hair or nails. At almost any place and any time, an argument might flare up suddenly and die down just as fast, with or without mediation. Occasionally the argument persists, and staff have to dig deep into their repertoire of peace-making skills.

At 10:00 the lights go out. Almost half the women have been asleep an hour or more. Most of the others go to bed at this time, but there are three, four, or five who want to sit in the hall—some to smoke, drink coffee, and talk; others to smoke and be alone with their thoughts; some to cry. Before the night is over, two or three more women may ring the doorbell looking for a place to sleep. The police may call first and bring someone to the shelter, or a woman may come on her own, unannounced, and ring the bell as late as 2:00 or 3:00 in the morning.

Once the lights go out, a noisy restlessness takes over, but the nights become progressively calm as the women give themselves up to dreams or the deep, noisy sleep of exhaustion.

Thus it is that shelters begin to make physical life possible. But these supports alone are not enough to stave off the devastation and despair of homelessness. For that, the women must finally look to themselves—to their native optimism, their sense of humor, their modest wants, and their faith in God.

The Women

For the great majority of the women I came to know, life had never been easy. Their childhoods were often punishing and painful. They came into homelessness by many different paths, almost all of which, one way or another, had to do with being poor and powerless.

Seen from a distance, the women appeared to be a fairly homogeneous group.[18] They were mainly from lower working-class and lower-class families. With few exceptions, they were poor and did not have many marketable skills beyond domestic and clerical work. But as one moved closer to the women— close enough to see them as individuals—they appeared to be strikingly different from one another, more different, perhaps, than their more successful non-homeless counterparts. Our society is more accepting of people who conform, people who are, in an important sense, very much like one another—like the students in a college classroom or workers and managers in a bureaucracy. Many homeless women have tried to conform but have failed, often for reasons outside themselves, and many are still trying. Still others, perhaps for physical or mental reasons, are less able to conform to society's models. Their non-conformity takes many different shapes. There are many ways of being different, and the women I knew showed exceptional individuality.

At any given time, there were perhaps 50 women in the three night shelters included in this study. They ranged in age from 18 into their 70s. Some had been homeless for years, and some

---

[18]In 1984–85, about 10% of The Refuge women were black. Although both white and black women increased in absolute numbers over the years, the number of black women increased more rapidly; by 1991 about half the women in The Refuge, and even more than half in the other two shelters, were black. I do not know if this reflects changes at the national or regional level or if it was simply a local phenomenon.

were going to be. A core group of women, perhaps a dozen or so, remained in one or another of the three shelters year-round and year after year. Others went to shelters in downtown Washington, and some came from Washington to Upton. Others stayed at The Refuge for the winter months, lived mainly on the streets the rest of the year, and returned to The Refuge when it opened again for the winter. Some women stayed weeks, months, or years. Still others disappeared after only a night or two.

The overall image is that of an inner core of regulars surrounded by concentric circles of women with successively shorter stays. The whole system was in a state of flux as incumbents moved in and out, some to return later, some to move into a different set of circles in this or another shelter, some who had come into homelessness for the first time, and still others who managed to escape homelessness altogether.

Some Prominent Women

Brief biographies of some 20 women, abstracted from their (taped and transcribed) life histories, are presented in Appendix B. For the dozen or so women who appear most prominently in this book, short sketches—modified versions of the first paragraphs of their life histories—are presented here to introduce them, alphabetically, to the reader. Here and throughout the book, the years 1985, 1986, and 1987, when most of the life histories were taken, are all to be considered the historical present.

Betty is white and 50 years old. She is of medium build, but her upper arms are exceptionally fat, forcing her to wear a cape and loose-fitting blouses rather than tailored garments. She wears rimless glasses and looks very distinguished. Her appearance, together with her assertive carriage and way of speaking, suggests to newcomers that she is, at the very least, an important visitor if not the director of the shelter. Despite heavy drinking in the past, Betty has not had a drink in more than four years. She is exceptionally outspoken about the rights of homeless women and is seen as their champion and spokesperson by some women, as a loudmouth and bully by others.

DeeDee is white and in her 40s. She is stockily built, dwarf-like, with disproportionately short arms and legs. She has a speech defect and is also retarded.[19] DeeDee came to the shelter after being evicted from a live-in program for the developmentally disabled where she had been for five years. Before that, she had been in the state psychiatric hospital for 10 years. She is an outspoken racist and is also fiercely competitive with some of the less competent women (but all more competent than she). Fortunately for her, most people make wide allowances for her condition.

Elsie was born in an Appalachian farming community in 1941. She is white and about 5′4″. Her normal weight is about 300 pounds, but she has weighed as much as 327. Her gray-streaked hair is cropped just long enough to cover where her ears would be, thereby concealing her hearing aid and the fact that she was born without ear canals and with only one external ear. Elsie was also born with a palsy that shows itself most prominently when she is under stress, curling one side of her lip and pulling down the same-side eyelid. She became homeless when she lost her job and her housemate got married and wanted their apartment for herself. Elsie is lively and sociable. It is no accident, however, that all of her friends are white.

Ginger is white and 24 years old. She is taller than average, thin, almost lanky, with dark hair and fair complexion. Ginger is retarded, but her eyes are bright and some people think she's very pretty. Ginger is in the shelter because she cannot get along with her father and stepmother. She is very much at ease with the other women and her social skills are such that no one has to make allowances for her.

Grace is white and 44. She is 5′4″ with fair skin, blue eyes, and blonde hair that most people take to be natural. Most of the

---

[19] I do not have life histories for DeeDee or Queen, below.

time, Grace wears tailored suits that she makes herself. She is a graduate of a Baptist Bible college. She came into homelessness when she refused to acknowledge the authority of the courts to judge her as a mother and a wife. "Only God can do that," she said. The courts disagreed and awarded her husband custody of their children, their townhouse, and their two automobiles. Grace is seen as an especially devout woman who stands up for her rights and speaks forcefully on behalf of homeless women. Patty and Brenda think Grace the most beautiful woman they have ever met. Patty wants to name her baby after Grace and hopes she will grow up to be like her namesake.

Judy is white and 23 years old. She is of low-average height but very heavy, normally about 250 pounds but up to 300 at times. Officially, Judy is a "borderline personality" with emotional and learning problems, and is perhaps retarded. Unofficially, she is quick-minded and knowledgeable, the person to go to for expert information on welfare/social services or the bus/subway system. She is homeless because she and her parents find it impossible to live together and she has no other place to go.

Kim is white and 32. She is 5'3", medium build, with red (Vita-Wave Brite Red) hair. Kim is extraordinarily bright and quick-witted and a great storyteller. She is powerfully attracted to teenage boys and allows this attraction to dominate her life. She confesses: "I am a very self-centered person. I am a selfish person. I'm a person that is out for myself more than most people that know me realize. Everything I usually do is for ulterior motives. I'm concerned with my own game." At least, so she would have you believe. Kim is very popular with the women, black and white, especially the younger ones. She is also a "vegan," a fierce vegetarian.

Lisa is a black woman of average height. She has dark skin, a round face, and an infectious laugh. She is 27 but looks older, mainly because she is so big: well over 300 pounds, say some women; almost 400, say others. Lisa is very bright and easily dominates a conversation when she chooses to. She is often the

center of attention and takes a special delight in Kim's stories.
She can be intimidating physically and few women dare argue
with her. She exudes competence and confidence. It is not clear
to me or others why she is homeless.

Louise is white and 42 years old. She has blue eyes and fair
skin. Her long blonde hair is parted in the middle and gathered
into a bun at the nape of her neck. Louise spends a lot of time
combing her hair and grooming herself, amazing everyone with
her talent for looking not only well-dressed but even stylish,
whether she is living in her car, in a shelter, or on the street.
Louise is essentially a loner who shies away from most personal
contacts. She is quick to snap at others, and few people get along
with her or like her. She became homeless after her husband divorced her and the courts forced the sale of their house.

Peggy is white and 51 years old. She is about 5′2″ with medium
brown hair and fair skin. She was born and raised in a small
town near the Pennsylvania-Maryland border. Peggy is seen
as a warm, friendly person. She is close to Phyllis, who is 71
and white, and Evelyn, who is 33 and black. Peggy became
homeless after a string of welfare spells and unemployment
compensation ran out. She has made some half-hearted attempts at suicide.

Phyllis is white and 71 years old. She is a fairly big woman,
taller than average. She has white hair and fair, splotchy skin,
with many "age spots" on her hands and neck. Her walking is
labored, as if her feet hurt (they do). Phyllis stands tall and
erect and seldom speaks unless spoken to. She carries herself
with great dignity and is respected and liked by all the women
Phyllis came to shelters after being discharged from the state
hospital. Her life goal is to return to the same apartment she lived
in before she was hospitalized. Nothing more. Nothing less.

Queen is a black woman, small to average in size, who looks
much younger than her 40-odd years. She is at once tough,
sweet, and smart. She spends a great deal of time sewing on a
sheet or blanket, sometimes a chenille bedspread, and wears

them as floor-length robes. She wears a towel or other piece of cloth as a turban. Queen's short hair is sometimes orange, sometimes blue. Her fingernails are two inches long and the different color on each nail is usually set off by glitter. Sometimes she wears glitter on her cheeks as well. Her speech is as colorful as her dress. She is popular with many women and a few of the staff as well.

Odd class

Regina is white and 48 years old. She is of medium height, thin and wiry, with short reddish-gray hair. Her speech announces her working-class English background. She became homeless when she lost her job as a live-in housekeeper. She was often engaged in examining herself and assessing her future, and especially enjoyed deeply personal and religious conversations with other women or staff.

Lost job

Sara is 31. She is a black woman, short and stout, with a round, pretty face. She is working most of the time she is in the shelter. She moves and dresses with a flair, not afraid of calling attention to herself. There is an air of self-confidence about her, a purposefulness that commands instant respect from everyone in the shelter, including the staff.

Jobs

Vicki is in her late 20s. She is a small, thin white woman, with dark bushy hair and a withered arm. She is very bright. She is bitter about her lot but avoids people like Betty, who "is always complaining and always putting people down." Vicki lives for the day when she can get a "regular" job. None of that "make-work, workfare, welfare bullshit" for her.

Disabled

• • •

None of the women ever said "Tell Them Who I Am" in just those words, but they demand to be seen—and have a right to be seen—as they are, with many warts and human frailties, but fully human nonetheless. For our own sakes as well as theirs, we must pay attention to them.

PART ONE

Problems in Living

1

Day by Day

O n the street or in a shelter, homelessness is hard living. At
first sight, one wonders why more homeless people do not
kill themselves. How do they manage to slog through day after
day, with no end in sight? How, in a world of unremitting grimness, do they manage to laugh, love, enjoy friends, even dance
and play the fool? How, in short, do they stay fully human while
body and soul are under continuous and grievous assault?

Simple physical survival is within the grasp of almost everyone willing and able to reach out for it.[1] As the women thrash
about, awash in a sea of need, emergency shelters, along with

---

[1] "Almost" is crucial because the issue is life and death. Some homeless
people are killed by homelessness. Some die quietly and others die violent
deaths. Some die from untreated disease or injury, some freeze to death, and
still others lose digits or limbs. Here is the sworn testimony of a doctor who
treated homeless patients in several Washington, D.C., shelters: "During the
winter of 1987/88, I have personal knowledge that approximately 30 homeless
persons . . . had one or more fingers, toes, feet, or legs amputated as a result
of gangrene following frostbite. . . . I have been informed that during the winter of 1987/1988, at least 10 homeless persons froze to death." Janelle

public assistance in the form of cash, food stamps, and medical assistance, make it just possible for many of the women to keep their heads above water.[2] Through the use of shelters, soup kitchens, and hospital emergency rooms, it is even possible for most homeless people who do not get public assistance to survive at some minimal level without benefit of a structured assistance program.

At their very best, however, these bare-boned elements of a life-support system merely make life possible, not necessarily tolerable or livable. Serious problems remain. Homelessness can transform what for others are little things into insurmountable hurdles. Indeed, homelessness in general puts a premium on "little things." Just as some homeless women seem to have learned (more than most of us, perhaps) to value a small gesture of friendship, a nice day, a bus token, or a little courtesy that others might take for granted or not notice at all, so too can events or circumstances that would be trivial irritants to others approach catastrophic proportions for the homeless person.[3]

For homeless women on the street, the struggle for subsistence begins at the animal level—for food, water, shelter, security, and safe sleep.[4] In contrast, homeless women in shelters

---

Goetcheus, MD, *Affidavit (W) in Support of Plaintiff's Memorandum* . . .

In mild-wintered San Francisco in 1988, the death rate for homeless persons was 58% higher than that for the general population. National Coalition for the Homeless, *Safety Network* 8, no. 2 (February 1989), p. 1.

[2] See Appendix D for a brief description of the major social welfare programs.

[3] It was from the women that I learned to juxtapose good little things and bad little things in this way. It puts "little things" in a fresh perspective and supports Otto Jesperson's observation that the world is made up of little things; what is important is to see them largely. Cited by Geoffrey K. Pullum, *The Great Eskimo Vocabulary Hoax and Other Irreverent Essays on the Study of Language,* p. 68.

[4] Contrary to popular belief, homeless persons do not have secret, ingenious, and sometimes easy ways of getting along. In fact, homeless people on the street have precisely those terrible problems that one would guess them to have. Kathleen Dockett, in her interview study of street homeless persons in Washington, D.C., reports that "a lack of access to bathing (68%) and laundry facilities were the most difficult needs to satisfy. The . . . need for sufficient

usually have these things; their struggle begins at the level of human rather than animal needs—protection of one's property, health care, and avoidance of boredom. The struggle then moves rapidly to the search for companionship, modest measures of independence, dignity, and self-respect, and some hope and faith in the future. These needs are not particularly sequential or hierarchical. One can just as easily be immobilized by hopelessness and despair as by hunger and cold. Body and soul are equally in need of nurture and the women must grab whatever they can get when they can get it.[5]

∙ ∙ ∙

For some of the women, day-by-day hardships began with the problem of getting enough sleep. A few women complained they could never get any sleep in a shelter. Grace was one of them. "There's no getting sleep in a shelter," she said. "Only rest."

There was indeed much night noise and movement. There was snoring, coughing, sneezing, wheezing, retching, farting, cries from bad dreams, occasional weeping or seizures, talking aloud to oneself or to someone else who may or may not have been present, and always movement to and from the bathroom. Grace was complaining about noise, and she found a partial remedy in ear plugs. But ear plugs could not help those women like Kathleen who were kept awake not by noise but by questions: Is this it for me? How did I end up here? How will I get out? But eventually, as the night wore on, there was a lot of snoring, and that meant that, Grace and Kathleen notwithstanding, there was a lot of sleeping, too.

---

sleep (63%) and safety in terms of finding a safe place to sleep (58%) were the second most difficult needs to satisfy. . . . There was a strong consensus . . . that shelters were unhealthy, dangerous, stressful." Dockett, *Street Homeless People in the District of Columbia: Characteristics and Service Needs,* pp. viii, ix. When one realizes that many homeless persons—mostly men—often choose street life over shelter life, one begins to get a sense of just how "unhealthy, dangerous, stressful" some shelters can be.

[5]The chapter-by-chapter discussion of these needs is not meant to imply a hierarchy.

Having to get up at 5:30 A.M. and be out of the shelter by 7:00 was a major hardship of shelter life. It was not simply the fact of having to get up and out, but rather that the women had to do this every day of the week, every day of the year (Thanksgiving and Christmas Day excepted), no matter what the weather or how they felt. On any given morning, as the women drifted onto the street, one might see two or three ailing women—this one with a fever or cough or headache, that one with a limp or stomach ache or other ailment—pick up their bags and walk silently into the weather.

The women especially missed Saturday and Sunday mornings, which looked just like Tuesday and Wednesday mornings. The occasional opportunity to stay in bed an extra hour or two was desperately missed. Not being able to sleep in, ever, especially on a weekend, was seen by many as a major deprivation that unfairly set them apart from the rest of the world. At 7:15, on a Sunday morning in the park, several women were looking for benches that offered some protection from the wind. The streets were empty of cars and people and the rest of the world seemed to be asleep. The women talked about how nice it would be to sleep in just one morning, just for the hell of it, or because you don't feel well, and how nice it would be to have a place—not even your own place, just *a* place—where you could go and lie down for a while without having anyone else around telling you to do this or do that.

One bitterly cold Sunday morning Betty announced she was going to the mayor's office the next day to tell him what it was like to live in a shelter and to ask him to order the county-funded shelters to allow people to remain there on Sundays, sleeping, resting, doing their nails or hair, watching TV, or whatever. "Everyone is entitled to a day of rest," she said. "Even homeless women." The women within carshot nodded agreement.

Some of the working women took motel rooms on weekends once or twice a month. Jane regularly disappeared on weekends. "She went to a motel for the weekend so she could sleep in," Judy explained to one of the women who asked about her. Samantha, who was working regularly, used the shelter for eating, washing, and socializing, but when the lights went out on Friday and Saturday nights, she left the shelter to sleep in a car so she could sleep late Saturday and Sunday mornings.

When Vicki learned she would be able to move into her own place in 10 days or so, she talked about her shelter experience as if it were already in the past. The hardest part of living in a shelter, she said, was having to get up every morning, no matter how you felt. The next worse thing was having to go out on the street and kill time—really kill time—until the shelter re-opened in the evening.

· · ·

Along with perennial fatigue, boredom was one of the great trials of homelessness. Killing time was not a major problem for everyone but it was high on most women's lists of hardships.[*] Betty could have been speaking for most of them when she talked about the problem. On a social visit to the state psychiatric hospital where, four years earlier, she had been an inpatient in an alcoholic program, Betty sought out a nurse named Lou. They embraced and Lou asked Betty what she was doing these days. Betty said she was living in a shelter. Lou said that was a shame, and asked Betty how she spent her time.

"I walk the streets," said Betty. "Twelve hours and 15 minutes a day, every day, I walk the streets. Is that what I got sober for? To walk the streets?" Betty went on to say that she sits on a lot of park benches looking for someone to talk to. Many times there is no one, so she talks to the birds. She and the birds have done a lot of talking in her day, she said.

---

[*] DIRECTOR: *This world is a place for productive people. The idea of killing time, day after day, was an alien concept to the vigorous, enthusiastic staff. The Refuge volunteers would regularly suggest a plan of action which in a rational world would begin to solve a woman's problems. These solutions were offered with little understanding of the complexity of these women's lives.*

Months later, Betty repeated much of this at her SSI (Supplemental Security Income) hearing. She told the hearing officer about being homeless and sleeping in the night shelter. He asked what her biggest problem was, and Betty said it was staying on the street for 12 hours and 15 minutes every day. She told him about the public library and park benches and the birds. Staying awake with nothing to do was a special problem, she added. You are not permitted to sleep in the library, she said, and she didn't dare fall asleep on a park bench for fear that someone would steal her bags or that a policeman would arrest her for vagrancy.

Some of the women with jobs also had trouble killing time. Like the others, Grace had to leave the shelter by 7:00 A.M. but she couldn't report to work much before 9:00, and her job was less than a 10-minute drive away. "Have you ever tried to kill two hours in the morning, every morning, with nowhere to go and nothing to do?" she asked. "I have some tapes I can listen to in the car—some Christmas carols and some Bible readings. But two hours? Every day?"

For Sara, leaving the shelter in the morning was by far the worst time of day. That was when being homeless hit her the hardest. You can't decide what to do because it doesn't matter what you do. You're not needed anywhere, not wanted anywhere, and not expected anywhere. Nobody cares what you do.

"I can't go on, walking the streets all day and coming here at night," announced Elsie one evening. "It's not my style. It's just not my style." Some women were better than others at finding relief in a book or TV program or jigsaw puzzle at the day shelter, or in conversation with others, but relief was typically short-lived. Sleeping may also have been tried as a remedy. In the parks, the lobbies of public buildings, and the day shelters, the women did a lot of sleeping. Some of this may have been because they did not sleep well at night, or because of medication, or depression perhaps, but some of it was also a way of killing time, a way of getting through the nothing-to-do present until it was time to do something—go to the soup kitchen, show up for a clinic appointment, or return to the night shelter.

Other kinds of behavior were also aimed at killing time or making it more bearable. Many of the women, for example, regularly appeared at the night shelter or the day shelter or the soup kitchen long before they opened, even when there were no lines to give advantage to early arrivals. It was as if the rush to get to the next "event" was a way of moving from a do-nothing to a do-something state.

For much the same reasons, the women might talk about and plan for an appointment with a doctor or a caseworker that was still several days away. In part, this may have been simply a matter of paying attention to what was most important to them at the moment, but this early anticipation may have also served to bring the event prematurely into present time, thereby giving the otherwise boring and undifferentiated present some sort of focus and direction.

Sometimes the women also made what looked like a deliberate effort to take apart a group of tasks and stretch them out over several days. At any given time, for example, a woman might need to make an appointment with a caseworker, visit a clinic, see a housing office representative, go to the unemployment office, or attend to some personal business. Any two of these tasks could normally be done in a day, one in the morning and one in the afternoon, and three in one day was not always out of the question.

Having a task to do, however, was a precious resource that gave point and structure to the day when it had to be done. To do two or three tasks on the same day would be a waste of resources, so the women often seemed to go out of their way to stretch their tasks over several days.[*] Thus, what often seemed

---

[*] KIM: *I think this is overstated. Service providers are spread out all over the county. It can take several bus transfers to reach Point B. Bus stop waits and waits in line add up to many hours. Filling out applications everywhere adds up to more. Particularly when dealing with Social Services, a great deal of time is wasted on the way to brick walls and dead ends.*

to be procrastination or laziness or exasperating inefficiency to those looking in from the outside may well have been, from the women's point of view, an attempt to distribute structure and meaning over as many days as possible.[6]

• • •

It is all too easy to think of homeless people as having few or no possessions ("How could a homeless person have anything of value?" sneered Kim), but one of the major and most talked-about problems was storage—how to keep one's clothing, essential documents, and other belongings secure and accessible. The preservation and protection of belongings could be a major consumer of one's time, energy, and resources. A principal difficulty was the fact that most emergency shelters had only limited space for individual storage—often space for only two bags or two small cardboard boxes.[*] And it was not uncommon to find shelters where one could not store anything at all.[7] Even where limited storage space was available, many women were reluctant to use it because there was no guarantee that their belongings would be intact when they returned. Stealing was believed to be common: "You've got to expect these things in shelters" was heard from staff and women alike. The end result was that many homeless women who would have left their

---

[6]Elderly persons who live alone sometimes resort to much the same strategy of make-work, a sort of remembering to forget. In the morning, a woman goes to the supermarket and buys, say, a carton of milk and a loaf of bread. Later the same morning, she says, "Oh, I forgot to get eggs," and returns to the store. Still later, "I forgot to get potatoes," or "I forgot to go to the post office," and so on through the day, thereby filling it up with things to do.

[*]DIRECTOR: *Without question, dealing with the "stuff" of these women was a great source of consternation. There was absolutely no room for the women's personal belongings. There was also an underlying concern that the belongings were a health hazard: some bags were filled with old food and insects.*

[7]I helped June to move to Mount Carmel, a women's shelter in downtown D.C., and one of the most preferred shelters in the city. She moved in with seven bags, boxes, and suitcases. The sister in charge explained, almost apologetically, that June would be allowed to store only two such items in the

belongings behind had they had a safe place to store them were forced to take most of their belongings with them. Some wore them in layers. Others carried them. They had become, in short, bag ladies.[8]

During a discussion of Luther Place, one of the best-run shelters in downtown Washington, one of the women said Luther Place was OK but she didn't like the women there—they were all bag ladies. One of the other women objected that the women at Luther Place were no different from women in other shelters. They were bag ladies, she said, because Luther Place had no storage space.

With some important exceptions, how much "stuff" one had was inversely proportional to the length of time one had been homeless. The longer a woman had been homeless, the more likely it was that she had had to jettison belongings, often stripping down to just what she could carry. For most women, this stripping-down process was a painful exercise in triage. Much of what they carried around in bags, boxes, or suitcases was clothing. Sometimes there was an emergency food ration. Along with toilet articles, some cosmetics, maybe a can opener, a bottle of aspirin or Tylenol or a prescription drug, almost everyone carried a birth certificate, pocket-size ID, varieties of legal documents or official papers, and perhaps some rent receipts or W-2's.

More important, however, were the other, more personal things. Often there were snapshots or framed photographs of children or other family members, personal letters, a color picture of Jesus, a Bible, and other religious and inspirational reading material. There may also have been a teddy bear or a

---

shelter. June went through her things. She threw some of them out and stored the remainder at the Catholic church she used to attend.

[8]Of course, not all bag ladies were forced into that status. Some women were or had become bag ladies for less obviously rational reasons, but they were a minority. If affordable, accessible, and secure storage space were available, surely many bag ladies would disappear.

bronzed baby shoe, a swizzle stick perhaps, or a matchbook cover, and some objects that looked like nothing more than a rag, a bone, a hank of hair, but which were, in fact, tokens of some treasured secret.

Given the contents of their bags, boxes, and suitcases, it is not surprising that the women were fiercely protective and possessive of them, sometimes to the patronizing amusement of outsiders. The importance of clothing and toiletries is self-evident. Moreover, the women had to carry proof of their social existence with them. Without a home address, telephone number, or job as testimony to their existence, they needed their birth certificates and other documents to prove that they existed as legal persons with rights to assert and claims to make on society.

Many of the personal things—the letters, the religious materials, the photographs, and the mementos of people, relationships, and experiences—looked back to earlier, presumably happier times. In effect, the women carried their life histories with them. To lose one's stuff, or to have to jettison some of it, was to lose connections to one's past if not the past itself. Thus, for women who had only the one or two slender boxes they may have been allowed to store in the shelter, along with what they may have carried with them, their more personal belongings tended to be strongly oriented toward the past.[9]

Many other women, however, mainly recent arrivals to homelessness or those with a car or other resources, often had far more belongings than they could carry or store in the shelters. These belongings were typically stored in their cars, public storage warehouses, a church basement, a fellow Alcoholics Anonymous member's garage, or even a garage or attic in the house of a friend or relative.

---

[9]In this discussion of storage, I have attempted to exclude hoarders—those women who hold on to things because they cannot let go of them. It is useful to keep in mind, however, that the storage problems of the occasional hoarder, even if self-inflicted, are as great or greater than everyone else's.

Most of the time, these nonportable possessions looked forward, not backward. They were things that were being saved for the future rather than remembrances of things past. Here, in the automobiles and the public and private storage spaces, the women kept not only clothing but pots and pans and linens and silverware, lamps and chairs, hat boxes and electric typewriters, and sometimes rugs and other heavy, major household furnishings as well. Sara regularly visited her storage unit to fondle her carefully wrapped crystal and linens. "That sustains her," said Samantha.

Clearly, the main value of these furnishings lay not in sentiment but in the hope, if not the prospect, that they would all be needed tomorrow or next week or next month when the woman would once again set up housekeeping in her own place. So long as she continued to own pots and pans and linens and things, she could remain, in her own mind at least, a temporarily dispossessed homemaker whose return to homemaking was imminent. For the woman who had to give up these furnishings, however, the prospect of returning to homemaking receded into uncertainty and she was plunged deeper into the reality of homelessness.

Past and future, then, and even one's self, were embedded in one's belongings. When Louise could no longer pay for storage and lost her belongings to auction, she was surprised at her own reaction to the loss. Her belongings had been so much a part of her, she said, that now that she's lost them, she's not sure who she is.[10]

Great sacrifices were made to store belongings, and the everpresent threat of losing them was a major source of anxiety and stress. The smallest and cheapest spaces in public storage warehouses were 5'×5' and rented for $37.50 to $42.50 a

---

[10] "To lose a home or the sum of one's belongings is to lose evidence as to who one is and where one belongs in this world." Kai T. Erikson, *Everything in Its Path: Destruction of Community in the Buffalo Creek Flood,* p. 177. See the section "The Furniture of Self" in this beautiful book for additional insights into the meanings embedded in one's house and personal possessions.

month, which meant that some of the women on public assistance spent about 25 percent of their income for storage alone. Others spent much more. During her first couple of years of homelessness, while she still had money from her divorce settlement (her share of the proceeds from sale of the house), Louise paid $156 a month to store her household goods. Kim maintained a storage space in her hometown as well as one in the shelter area. Together, these cost her about $90 a month.

For many women, it was much too easy to fall behind in storage payments, and the penalties built up quickly. The "late charge," invoked one day after the monthly due date, was $10. After 10 days, management put their own lock on the storage bin, denying access to the renter until all due monies had been paid. After 30 days, the stored contents were subject to public auction.

Fierce attachment to belongings meant that many women, storing their things on a month-to-month basis and not knowing how long they would have to continue, ended up making monthly storage payments that totaled many times the original or replacement cost of what was stored. Shirley's experience was a case in point. Shirley had been behind in her storage payments for several months but had managed to stave off the loss of her things to public auction each month by last-minute fund-raising heroics. Eventually, however, she missed another deadline. Suspecting that the auction hammer had come down on the contents of her locker, Shirley and I drove to the storage facility. Yes, the auction had been held, the manager told her, but her stuff was still recoverable because no one had seen fit to bid even $5 for the contents of her $42.50-per-month locker. Shirley was dismayed. This news was probably worse than learning that someone had bought them. "The footlocker alone is worth $50," she protested. "And the chair. Isn't that a nice chair?"

To lighten the financial burden, two or even three women sometimes shared a space, but in a 5'×5' area, the only way to accommodate additional items was to pile them ever higher. This made for a variety of storage and retrieval problems requiring a strenuous and time-consuming reorganization for each use, especially if—as when June and Peggy doubled up— big or fragile items were involved (a sofa up on end, an old, heavy IBM Selectric typewriter, several lamps, a rug, books, dishes, and more).

So important was secure and adequate storage that women sometimes allowed it to be a determining factor in important life choices. Kim turned down a new job at a much higher salary because her current job allowed her to store her belongings in a locked attic at her place of employment. The higher salary would have more than covered the cost of public storage, but Kim decided the extra money was not worth the loss of convenience and easy access to belongings stored on the job. Elsie planned to prepay six months' storage costs when she thought (incorrectly) that she was getting an $800 income tax refund.

Jeanette stored her household furnishings in her 1974 Datsun B-210 Station wagon. The car broke down and was towed away by police before Jeanette could assemble the money to repair it. Distraught, Jeanette traced the car to the county's Abandoned Auto Lot. We drove there to salvage some of her smaller, more valued possessions. The lot attendant told Jeanette that the next auction would be the following Friday and that she could probably buy back her car (and everything in it) for $25 or so, the going rate for junk autos. Successful bidders, he told her, would have three days in which to remove their purchases from the lot.

But Jeanette's station wagon had three flat tires, a dead battery, dead license plates, and surely a string of invisible problems as well. The cost of repurchasing the car, having it towed off the lot, and making even minimal repairs would be many times the value of the car, but Jeanette was determined to buy it back. Not for transportation, she explained, but as the only way she could retrieve and afford to keep her belongings. For her, the car had become, purely and simply, a storeroom.[11]

. . .

Homelessness and health care don't mix well. In part because of homelessness, the health of homeless women is generally poor. Moreover, for minor health conditions, dozens of remedies routinely available to most people—bed rest, remaining off one's feet, frequent bathing or soaking, using a vaporizer—were typically beyond the reach of homeless women. What would be minor ailments to other people could become major complications to homeless persons. Given this situation, one would expect health care to be seen as a major problem. It was, of course, seen that way by individual women with one or another acute or painful condition, but not, surprisingly, by the women as a whole.

There were many reasons for this. The chief reason was the feeling that if push came to shove, health care would be available. This reassuring assumption was based on the widespread belief that our society would not let them die, as Betty argued it would, "like a piece of shit in the street."[12] For emergency and life-threatening conditions, and even for less serious illnesses, the women knew they could, and did in fact, use the rescue squad and hospital emergency rooms.[13] For conditions they judged to be less than acute, however, the women, including those covered by one or another form of medical assistance, did not routinely seek out health care.

---

[11]Jeanette did, in fact, buy back her car for $25, and she found "a Christian gas station owner" who agreed to tow it to his lot and wait for the money. The car never again moved under its own power, but Jeanette was able to keep her things there until, six weeks later, the minister of the church she attended found a church member who allowed her to store her things in his garage.

[12]Coarse language came naturally to many of the women, especially to Betty and Kim. But there were just as many, Grace and Jeanette among them, who winced at the cursing and vulgarity.

[13]In Kathleen Dockett's study, 98% of the street homeless persons who reported having health problems also reported getting medical care in the previous 12 months; about 50% reported getting this care from hospital emergency rooms. Dockett, *Street Homeless People*, p. v.

This is not to say that the women did not go to clinics and doctors but that, given their ailments, one would have expected them to seek treatment with much greater frequency. Some of the more common ailments included headaches, arthritis, bursitis, allergies, swollen legs, back pain, stomach aches, rashes, shortness of breath, chronic cough, bad colds and sore throats ("If one of us gets sick," sighed Abigail, "all of us get sick"), bad teeth, and a variety of other ills. These were often of an intensity that would normally send most people to seek treatment, but here they were commonly self-treated with aspirin, Tylenol, other over-the-counter medications, or nothing at all. Like athletes, and like poor people generally, most women seemed to take aches and pains for granted; they came with the territory.[14]

Ailments were not always borne in silence, however. Discussions of symptoms and diagnoses of self or others were commonplace, and there were always a handful of women forever prepared to talk about their symptoms or conditions as the reason they did not work or seek work.

Actual experiences with health care also contributed to this apparent underutilization of services.* Many of the ailments either were chronic, such as arthritis, or were predictable products of homelessness, such as swollen and painful feet. Since

---

[14]In a study of the physical health of homeless persons that included physical examinations of 75 women, women in shelters were found to have an average of 10 physical health problems (a health problem being defined as "a finding ... deemed to be of clinical interest to a primary care physician"). Two-thirds of the women had gynecological problems; more than half of the total homeless sample had missing teeth and more than a third had obvious caries. William R. Breakey and others, "Health and Mental Health Problems of Homeless Men and Women in Baltimore," *Journal of the American Medical Association* 262, no. 10 (September 8, 1989), p. 1354. I suspect that dental problems such as missing teeth are as much a marker of working- and lower-class origins as they are products of homelessness. Kathleen Dockett reports that "the self-perceived need for dental care was greater than for medical care" (*Street Homeless People,* pp. 98, 99).

*GRACE: *I did not make enough money for health care. Most of the time with those programs you had to take your chances getting someone who basically did not know what they were doing. I did not trust those people.*

DIRECTOR: *Without question, the medical system was not ready to cope with homeless patients.*

most of these conditions did not lend themselves to effective treatment other than what was available through self-medication, the women soon learned there was little relief available for these conditions through professional care.

In many cases, the very conditions of homelessness produced poor health care as well as poor health. On the one hand, the women sometimes failed to tell the doctor that they were homeless; on the other hand, even when the doctors knew their patients were homeless, they often failed to appreciate the significance of that fact. When Patty's back pain drove her to the doctor, she neglected to tell him she lived in a shelter that required her to be on the street all day. He prescribed three days of bed rest. When Abigail went to see a doctor for a boil under her left arm, he told her to take four hot baths every day. ("Will you please tell me how I can do that?" she demanded rhetorically of the women around her that night.) Betty's doctor knew she lived in a shelter, but when she went to him for an infected and badly swollen foot, he told her to stay off it and to keep her foot elevated. Betty was beside herself with the impossibility of it all and swore she'd never go to a doctor again.

Obesity, stomach disorders, diabetes, food allergies, cardiovascular irregularities, and other disorders for which diet is integral to treatment made up another class of common health problems that resisted treatment by the very nature of homelessness itself. Typically, in shelters and soup kitchens, one could eat what was served or not eat it; few other choices were available. Low-fat, low-salt, low-cholesterol, low-calorie, and other low-this-or-that dietary injunctions were almost impossible to observe.

In general, then, the treatment of choice was often not available to homeless people because they could not comply with it. When doctors were aware of the limitations imposed by homelessness on the patient's ability to comply, they were obliged to compromise severely on the treatment of choice. The end result was that, in either case, homelessness itself produced seriously flawed health care.

The health situation was more complicated and probably worse for those homeless women with substance abuse or mental health problems. Here, too, the very fact of homelessness seemed to create problems that allowed for no solutions. For example, almost every shelter had a policy of refusing entry to persons with serious and active substance abuse or mental health problems. The rationale for these exclusionary policies—the need to maintain peace and good order and to protect the health and safety of the staff and shelter residents—was unassailable, but the effect was to force those with the greatest need for shelter and health care onto the street where the possibilities for either were remote indeed.[15]

Sometimes the rejecting staff consoled themselves and the persons being rejected by assuring them that, on the street, they would be helped by one or another "outreach" program. But the assumption that persons with alcohol or serious mental health problems can receive effective treatment while living on the street is, at best, wishful thinking.[16] Even if one can overcome the initial problem of locating such persons and persuading them that they need what the program offers, there remains the even more difficult problem of getting these persons to remain in one place long enough to receive continued treatments over

---

[15] There is sometimes little difference between homeless persons in shelters and those who live on the street, partly because they are often the same people who move back and forth. At any given time, however, there are some homeless persons *in extremis,* and these are almost always on the street. It is probable, however, that they do not occur in sufficient numbers to be picked up by most sampling strategies. Kathleen Dockett's study, for example, shows few major differences in the demographic characteristics of her sample of street homeless persons and those of the 1989 D.C. shelter sample studied by N. G. Milburn and J. Booth. Street homeless were more likely to be male, more likely to be single, and more likely to be unemployed. Dockett, *Street Homeless People,* pp. ii, 120, 120a.

[16] "Therapeutic efforts on behalf of the [homeless] mentally ill are all but doomed to failure in the absence of decent housing." Robert M. Hayes (Counsel to the National Coalition for the Homeless), Testimony, U.S. House of Representatives Subcommittee on Housing and Community Development of the Committee on Banking, Finance and Urban Affairs, December 15, 1982.

time. Set against outreach and other intermittent, catch-as-catch-can programs for people on the street is the fact that homelessness in general, and living on the street in particular, are times of great stress, instability, and insecurity. Such conditions are known to aggravate alcohol, drug, and mental health problems and to render their carriers maximally resistant to treatments that are of uncertain effectiveness even under the best of conditions.

The same arguments apply, with only slightly less force, to those with substance abuse and mental health problems who live in shelters. Here, too, these conditions tend to be aggravated by the stress of homelessness and shelter living, and one generally finds a striking lack of interest in seeking treatment. Some women explained that their mental health problems were caused (not merely aggravated) by homelessness and shelter living, and there was nothing to do about them so long as one remained homeless. For these women, the remedy lay in housing rather than treatment.

There were important exceptions, however. At any given time, there were a few women who saw their therapists regularly and who allowed the shelter staff to supervise their medication regimen (remaining in the shelter was sometimes conditional on such supervision). A more important and instructive exception can be found among those women with mental health problems who did not seek out treatment. Many of them fared poorly and often seemed to worsen. But others among them, over time, seemed to become less crazy or depressed, to become stronger and happier and more confident. Why this should have happened is unclear, but it is difficult to avoid the impression that, in some shelters and for some people, shelter living itself was therapeutic. Clearly, there were women who found safety and security in the shelter, and levels of camaraderie and support and love that were not available to them elsewhere.

• • •

The main problem with sex—and this did not seem to be a major problem for most women—was that there was so little of it. Sex as something to talk about, much less something to engage in, was a sometime thing. As a topic of conversation, it ranked well behind work and religion. As an activity, with some important exceptions, especially among the younger women, sex was noteworthy by its absence.[17] Martha said. "It's been nine months since I had a man." Betty said it had been a year and a half for her, that she had been looking for a decent man, "but there's no end to the drought in sight." I suggested that she be more aggressive at her AA meetings or other points of contact. Betty sneered. "Aggressive how? Should I invite them to the shelter for dinner?' Martha laughed and slapped Betty on the back in approval.

Many of the references to sex were of a casual, bantering nature. Cora was fond of talking about her tubal ligation at a time when three of her five children were under five. The doctor assured her he was going to "remove the nursery but leave the playpen intact." When Martha once complained that her teddy bear had been her only bed companion in more than a year, one of the other women said that she wanted something more real than a teddy bear, and another contributed the observation that the gas company says it's better to keep it up all the time than have it go up and down.

The presence of a man often triggered a sort of grade-school humor built on teasing and innuendo. In the absence of a

---

[17]Lesbianism was extremely rare. To my knowledge, there was only a single confirmed instance of it in the three shelters. Many more instances were rumored. Queen volunteered that she had been evicted from a D.C. shelter on the false charge of sexual abuse (there was nothing sexual about it, she said). One woman, naming 14 women, claimed to have identified them as lesbians she had met over a period of three years in the shelters; another said there were more lesbians among homeless women than alcoholics. AIDS, by the way, in the mid 1980s seems not to have been a particular concern of the women, but staff people sometimes expressed concern about their physical proximity to possible carriers. In subsequent years, there was progressively greater concern.

younger male volunteer, the women sometimes settled for me.[*]
Hilda (a self-proclaimed virgin in her mid-50s) often talked
about "trying Elliot out," and DeeDee, to her puzzlement and delight, could always get a laugh out of some of the women by asking me to take her home with me. And when Ruby served the
women hot dogs one night, Abigail complained about the taste
and said they weren't true wieners. "They're as close to wieners
as anything we've got," said Ruby. "No they're not," said Abigail,
"Elliot is," and pleased with her witticism, she looked around to
accept the plaudits of her audience. Only a handful of women
engaged in this juvenilia, but this handful never seemed to tire
of these tiresome jokes.

Occasionally there was a serious discussion about safe and
unsafe periods in the menstrual cycle, or a group of women
might talk about their childhoods and deplore their early ignorance of everything associated with sex and childbirth. Most
women, however, shied away from any explicitly sexual language or subject matter. DeeDee asked Cora, Beverly, and Judy
if the men and women in the TV ads are really having sex when
they are shown in bed. Beverly said no, they are wearing
bathing suits, and it's all play.

"What do men and women really do when they 'make love'?"
asked DeeDee.

At a loss for words, or afraid to use them, Judy deferred to
Beverly. Beverly, laughing, passed the question along to Cora,

---

[*] DIRECTOR: *My instinct is that Elliot was a catalyst for the women's comments
about sex. When one of the evening's volunteers was a man, the behavior of the
women at The Refuge was remarkably different. A few women would not come
into the shelter if a man opened the door to them. It was clear to me that these
women had suffered at the hands of a man. However, a certain number of the
women enjoyed a man's company, flirting some, giving extra energy to their conversations, and more often than not appearing modest before a male volunteer.
In my experience, the women were rarely bawdy in their conversations about
sex. I assumed this was because the shelter was in a church building, and almost
all of the women had a background that in some way held a reverence for a
house of God. Perhaps the women were also more cautious in my presence, for
I was the "Director."*

noting that Cora was a nurse, older, more experienced, and had been married longer. Cora, too, shied away, saying that what goes on behind bedroom doors is private and can't be known.

DeeDee sighed, resigning herself to continued ignorance of what "making love" really meant.

"I wish I had a man," she said.

"Take Elliot," said Beverly.

"He's too tall," said DeeDee, and the rest of us looked in wonderment at one another, unable to imagine what images DeeDee had in mind.

This general aversion to explicitly sexual matters and language, consistent with their working-class backgrounds, made the women tempting targets for some of their less inhibited fellows. Queen was hemming a green and white sheet into still another robe. She answered a couple of questions about her sewing project and then, continuing in the same warm, chatty voice, she said her mother had gotten very angry when she found Queen in bed with her father and threw her out of the house. Shoot, she couldn't see what all the fuss was about. What difference does it make whose husband she has sex with, her mother's or some other woman's?

The women around her looked at one another in shock. Peggy asked Queen if that was her real father or stepfather. "Shoot, how the hell should I know," said Queen. "Real father, stepfather, I don't know. What difference does it make, anyway?" Queen didn't look up from her sewing but she must have sensed the effect she was having, so she went on, tossing off the fact that she had had sex with her son—"no big deal"—and ending with the observation that her mother had always said you can't make any money by sitting on it all the time. In the embarrassed silence that followed, Queen went on sewing, a small smile of satisfaction on her lips.

Kim, too, liked to shock the women with vivid descriptions of her sex life with Patrick. All this was mainly in fun; Kim enjoyed telling the stories and the women, titillated, enjoyed hearing them. Sometimes, however, Kim went too far in extolling the virtues of sex; the women would have preferred to hear about a little more tenderness, a little more romance. Toward the end of one of her monologues about her love life with Patrick, Kim said that all she wanted from life was to marry Patrick and have sex every day, all day long. Lisa, who could have been speaking for almost any of the women, said that Kim was talking about lust, not love. Kim conceded that lust was a part of what she felt, but only a part. There was love, too.

Lisa disagreed. "What if something happened and you couldn't have sex anymore? What if something happened and Patrick didn't want sex anymore? What would you do then?"

"You mean, he couldn't have intercourse?" said Kim.

"Yes."

"Well, there's still lots of things he could do. There's more to sex than straight intercourse."

"No, no," said Lisa. "What if he doesn't want to have sex? Any kind of sex. Would you still love him? Would you still want to be with him?"

Kim seemed not to understand what Lisa was getting at. "Look," she said, dismissing all of Lisa's 'what if's.' "If we couldn't have intercourse, he'd still be my boyfriend. As long as I have this mouth and these hands, I can get him off and he can get me off in the same way."

Lisa shrugged in surrender. "You're still talking about lust," she said.[*]

In all serious discussions, sex was almost always subordinated to concerns with love, romance, and ultimately with self-respect. Betty didn't say she was looking for "a man"; she was careful to specify "a decent man." Marian reported to a local supermarket to begin her new job but was told she would not be needed. Back at the day shelter, Marian said that that sonofabitch Buck, the assistant manager, was behind this, and she's going to put her foot

---

[*]KIM: *Lisa was 100% correct! My relationship with Patrick indeed was lust, not love. This is not a reassessment of feelings on my part, but rather a redefining of terms.*

up his ass the next time she sees him. He's getting back at her for refusing to go to bed with him until they got to know one another better "because I'm not that kind of girl."

Regina struggled mightily with the issue of casual, loveless sex. One day she moved out of the shelter, having accepted a job as housekeeper/companion to an elderly man in which sex was a condition of her employment. As she gathered her belongings together, she talked about the terrible guilt she felt. She had been telling herself that this was a matter of survival, she said, but that hadn't helped much. She talked about how she had come close to God since she became homeless two months ago, and here she was, preparing to do something that she knew was wrong in the eyes of God. I told her not to presume that she knows what God thinks, that maybe He makes allowances for people in her situation. Unconvinced and troubled, Regina left the shelter.

The next evening, clearly relieved and even jaunty, Regina was back at The Refuge. She said she had talked everything over with her new employer and told him she couldn't go through with their agreement. He told her he understood and it was OK, that she could stay until she found another job. He offered her some money if she needed it. Regina said he was a real nice man, a decent man, and she might have learned to love him if given enough time. "But you can't rush nature," she said.

Other women had less benign experiences along the same lines with employers or landlords who wanted to use sex as a medium of exchange. When Ranji found a modest-priced room nearby, she swore she would never return to the shelter. A week later, however, she was back in the shelter when the landlord refused to take the rent in cash. Grace had several similar experiences, and surely there were many others that did not come to my attention.

• • •

In addition to these general problems, there were hundreds of annoyances, some of which could indeed become serious problems, such as not having access to toilets when one needed them, especially on Sunday mornings and holidays when most public buildings and retail establishments were closed. In bad weather, the women were often forced to spend time in eating places where they had to drink a lot more coffee and nibble on a lot more snacks than they wanted or could afford, just for the privilege of being able to sit down out of the rain or cold or heat. Sexual harassment was commonplace, on the street, trying to sleep in one's car, everywhere.[*] And sometimes harassment became assault.[18]

Homelessness also put people at risk for difficulties that almost no one could anticipate, such as the snowy night that 64-year-old Irma found herself excluded from the shelter and went to sleep in a car in a parking lot, only to awaken in the morning to find herself imprisoned in the car by a snow plow that had done its job too well.

These, then—problems around sleeping, fatigue, boredom, killing time, storage, health, sex, along with harassment and dozens of unpredictable difficulties encountered on the street—were some of "the little murders of everyday life" that confronted homeless women.[19]

By themselves, these physical problems of day-to-day living could easily have drained the women of their strength, leaving them overwhelmed and discouraged and unable or unwilling to go on. Perhaps a few did give up at this point, or perhaps they were just resting, waiting to catch their breath, regain some

---

[*]GRACE: *Two times I slept in my car. When I would park, wherever that might be, men would approach my car and knock on the window and ask what I was doing! I could never figure out why that would happen, but I know the Lord must have been watching out for me, because of all the dangers that could have happened. When you are a single woman and alone, it seems the male population think you are up for grabs. Strange mentality!*

[18]In the study by William Breakey and others ("Health and Mental Health Problems"), more than a third of the homeless women reported having been raped.

[19]This beautifully descriptive phrase is from Constance Perin, "A Biology of Meaning and Conduct," pp. 96–97.

strength, and try again later. But most of them pushed on, often in several different directions, seeking out some self-respect and a sense of connectedness to the outside world. The most important such direction was the world of work and jobs.

2

Work and Jobs

"Work is the fundamental condition of human existence," said Karl Marx. In punch-the-clock and briefcase societies no less than in agricultural or hunting and gathering societies, it is the organization of work that makes life in communities possible. Individual life as well as social life is closely tied to work. In wage labor societies, and perhaps in every other as well, much of an individual's identity is tied to his or her job. To be engaged in a task that the community says is useful is the principal way one earns a living and becomes a valued member of that community. For most of us, then, jobs are a principal source of both independence and connectedness to others. It should come as no surprise that, in the work force or out, work and jobs are important themes in the lives of homeless women.[*]

*DIRECTOR: *Honestly, I felt that the women's looking for work, wanting work, and needing work was one of the most ordinary things about them. In a different environment, they [would be] no different from my own circle of friends.*

There are women who want to work and do, and women who want to work and do not. There are women who cannot work and others who should not work and still others who do not want to work. Some work regularly, some intermittently; some work part-time, some full-time; and there are even those who work two jobs. At any given moment, there is a lot of job-searching, job-losing, job-changing, and job avoidance. Within months or even weeks, these may all appear in the same person. Values and behavior around jobs and work are awash in ambivalence, contradiction, and paradox.

Underlying this apparently capricious behavior, however, one sees over time a steady and serious concern with work. When homeless women speak about themselves in relation to work, they almost always identify themselves as working, as looking for work, or as one who would work if she could. They often characterize other women as wanting to work (good) or not wanting to work (bad).[*] The most talked-about value of work has to do with its presumed relationship to homelessness. "A job is the way out of homelessness," the women often tell one another, just as they are told by service providers, social workers, volunteers, casual passers-by on the street, and everyone else they meet. At any given moment, perhaps half the women are working or looking for work, and even those who cannot work often go through the motions of looking for a job.

For homeless people, the road to looking for, finding, and keeping a job is strewn with obstacles. Having no telephone where a prospective employer or employment agency can reach you during working hours is, by itself, enough to discourage some women from looking for anything at all other than the most menial walk-in-off-the-street job. Reciprocally, having no telephone is often reason enough to discourage prospective employers and

---

[*] DIRECTOR: *The older women who lived at the shelter were anxious or angry when the younger women in their 20s were languishing without jobs. It was as if they understood their own joblessness, but felt there were fewer excuses for young and healthy women. Their loss of self-esteem was clear to me when Kathy said, "Why are you here with us? You could have a job. You could be somebody."*

agencies from wanting to hire you. It is not simply that communication is difficult, but rather that the person who confesses to having no telephone of one's own, or even access to one, is suspect. From the employer or agency point of view, such a person is probably a bad risk. He or she might even be homeless.

The process is almost routine. A homeless woman registers with an employment agency. Since there is no way for them to call her when a job comes up, she calls them—three, four times a day. By the third day, they usually tell her, in the best tradition of employers, agencies, and casting directors, "Don't call us, we'll call you." If she confesses there's no way to reach her, they lose interest.

The telephone problem has been somewhat alleviated since 1985 when the day shelter opened. Here the women are allowed to make and receive calls on the staff phone. To make a call, you give the number to a staff member to dial. And the call—not unreasonably since there is only one phone—has to be related to job, housing, health, or a personal matter of some urgency. But the day shelter is open only from 2:00 to 6:30, and not all the women go to the day shelter. Moreover, to give the shelter telephone number as one's own is, in effect, to announce that one is homeless: staff at the day shelter answer the phone with "Mainline Church Day Shelter for Women."

Shirley protested that she could never get a job so long as shelter staff answered the phone that way. "Everybody knows that homeless women are prostitutes or alcoholics coming off a toot," she said, and suggested that staff answer the phone with a simple "Hello." Staff refused to change the procedure. They were under orders from the shelter board of directors, they said.

Several women reported losing jobs or the opportunity to get them when their homelessness became known. Carolyn sneered, "An employment clerk marked my application 'No suitable jobs available' because 'We don't refer bag-carrying applicants to interviews.'" Kim had been working as a receptionist in a doctor's office for several weeks when the doctor learned she was living in a shelter and fired her. "If I had known you lived in a shelter," Kim said the doctor told her, "I would never have hired you. Shelters are places of disease." "No," said Kim. "Doctors' offices are places of disease."[*]

. . .

Most job applications ask at least for name, address, telephone number, Social Security number, last job, and one or two references. An arrest record can cause problems. Kim returned to the shelter one evening barely able to contain herself. Earlier that day she had filled out an application form at an employment agency, admitting to having been arrested once for assault and battery, another time for disturbing the peace. The agency told her they could not process her application because of her police record. Kim was shocked at the agency's squeamishness. "How can you get to be 32 years old without ever getting arrested?" she asked, appealing to the audience around her with upturned palms. "I don't even *know* anyone over 20 who's never been arrested." And everyone laughed, as Kim surely intended them to.

The woman who somehow surmounts these initial difficulties may then get a job as a stock clerk, a cashier, or a counter worker in a fast food place. But for all these jobs, as well as for more menial ones such as pulling trash, being a messenger, or photocopying, one must make a minimally decent and unremarkable appearance—be clean, neat, and free of body odor. For most women living in shelters this may require a special effort, but it is not a particularly onerous task because most

---

[*]GRACE: *Those of us who worked had to keep "our secret" [homelessness]. I had been dismissed from a job because my co-workers found out I lived in a shelter. This happened at several different temporary jobs. Many people wondered why my clothing was hung in the back of my car and assumed that I was moving all the time. At one agency, when I told them I lived in a shelter, jobs were no longer made available to me, although I had worked for this same agency for the past nine years when living in my townhouse as a "normal" person.*

women's shelters have showers, a washing machine and dryer, and an iron and ironing board.[1]

ᴵThe bare minimum of presentability will not do, however, for those women seeking to get or keep a job as a receptionist or other office worker, or as a salesperson in a department store. To meet this higher standard while living out of bags and boxes calls for an extraordinary level of discipline, organization, and physical effort.

Nevertheless, some women do manage to get and keep jobs that require a good appearance. Grace is one of them, but she has the advantage of being able to use her automobile as a clothes closet.[2] She hangs her blouses, jackets, and skirts on a crossbar. Underwear and accessories are piled neatly in a tattered suitcase on the front seat. Each item is tagged and coded so that she can pull out a matching outfit with relative ease. Elsie, too, uses her car in this way, but tags and coding notwithstanding, entropy soon takes over. What was order quickly becomes disorder, and full-scale reorganization is required with disheartening frequency.

[1] For homeless women living on the street or in automobiles, however, even this level of presentability requires enormous effort and ingenuity. Of course, the more classic bag ladies in shelters or on the street would, almost by definition, fail to meet this minimum standard, but they are less likely to be in the job market.

For men and women in some of the worst shelters, looking minimally presentable is beyond their reach. Here is a partial description of the Pierce and Blair shelters for men run by the D.C. government: "[Both shelters] are . . . infested with roaches, mice, rats, lice and scabies . . . overcrowded. . . . Blankets were washed on only one occasion [in a six-month period]. . . . There is a cold water hose but only on occasion are the men provided with soap. The men are not provided with towels . . . urine water spreading onto the floor where the men are sitting. . . . The men frequently sit in . . . contaminated water. The stench of urine pervades both shelters. Many men refuse to use the bathrooms." Sister Veronica Daniels. *Affidavit (V) in Support of Plaintiffs' Memorandum . . . ,* pp. 2–3.

[2] Public (rented) storage bins were also used occasionally as closets and dressing rooms, but they were usually too distant and inaccessible to be of much practical use on a daily basis. Some women, Louise among them, even tried sleeping in their storage lockers, but eventually they were discovered and evicted.

Beryl is a handsome black woman in her 40s. She has no car
and lives entirely within the resource limitations of the shelter,
yet she works as a full-time saleswoman at the Woodward and
Lothrop department store in Crystal Lake Mall and also has a
part-time job in a specialty shop. Like the other women, Beryl
is awakened every morning at 5:30. She gets up from her cot,
lines up to wash, pulls some clothing from a bag or box, maybe
irons something quickly, has some coffee, perhaps also toast or
cold cereal on the run, does some things with a curling iron, lip-
stick, and eye makeup, and in an hour or less she is ready to
meet with discriminating co-workers, a boss, and a public.
Whatever she wears, she looks almost elegant when she leaves
the shelter, often in an earth-colored woolen skirt and coordi-
nated blouse and scarf, her hair, nails, and makeup impeccable.
The transformation is nothing short of magic.

Beryl and Grace are exceptional but by no means unique. There
are others who also manage to look like middle-class career
women. But the exceptionality of Beryl and Grace and a handful
of others must be emphasized. Not only do they have the clothes
(Grace makes her own), but they also have the planning and organizing skills that are everywhere scarce, especially among a
largely impoverished and sometimes demoralized population.

Keeping a job could be as difficult as finding one. Keeping a job
might mean having to suppress an awareness of one's real-life situation. Gwen struggled against that awareness. Once, when she
had to go to her salesclerk job the next day, she was trying very
hard not to be discouraged and not to worry about the fact that
The Refuge would close the next week.[3] "You've got to have a
clear head on a job," she said. "If your mind is on your troubles,
you can't do your job. Customers want you to pay attention to
them, and that's what your boss wants you to do, too."[*]

---

[3]To staff people and others, Gwen's apparent lack of concern about the imminent closing of The Refuge was further evidence of something wrong with
the women "up here," further evidence that they couldn't deal with reality.

[*]GRACE: *The most serious reason for homeless people not working has to do
with the fact that the mind will not function the way you want it to. You can't think*

Having found jobs, the women often left them. It is difficult to know whether their explanations were reasons or excuses, mainly because the explanations were usually plausible. Inadequate or costly transportation to a job was sometimes cited as a deterrent to taking or keeping a job. When Abigail asked for more hours at the County Donut Shop (located in a light industrial area), they offered her very early morning and late night hours, which she had to refuse because there was no public transportation between the donut shop and the shelter at those times. Carol had to refuse a similar counter job on weekends for the same reason. When Kim was fired as the doctor's receptionist in downtown Washington, she wasn't too upset: public transportation was costing her two hours and $5.50 a day.

Difficult or expensive access to certain jobs did not always prevent women from taking and keeping them. Even lousy jobs were important. When Vicki finally landed a (menial) job in another county, she complained bitterly that she seemed to be spending her life riding buses or waiting for them in lousy weather, but after four months she was still on the same job. The women thought Jennifer was dumb or crazy for taking an office cleaning job in D.C., spending most of her life and most of her earnings on buses and subways, but Jennifer had her reasons.[4]

It is also likely that the limits of public transportation directed women toward lower-status, lower-paying jobs, since these tend to be the jobs best served by public transportation.

---

through the questions and problems that come up in a job. . . . You cannot think clearly, cannot hold an intelligent conversation, your mind wanders, you have difficulty following directions, difficulty remembering, and an attitude of despair, depression, and eventually bitterness sets in. These [homeless women] are not lazy people, but products of abuse in the broad sense of the word.

[4] Jennifer is in her early 30s. She is very quiet, very shy, and very slow, but those around her who are interested and patient with her are rewarded with straight and thoughtful talk. In the spring of 1986, Jennifer worked for a print shop and cut her hand. The boss fired her when she filed a workmen's compensation claim. Jennifer had a small car given her by her parents, and she used it in her next job with the Fast Buck Delivery Service. One evening she returned to the shelter disconsolate. "What's the matter?" "I totaled my car." "What did you hit?" "The Jefferson Hotel." A week later she found the office

Those sleek, stand-alone buildings around the Washington Beltway, for example—so rich a source of better-paying office and clerical jobs—were far less accessible by public transportation than were lower-paying jobs in fast food and retail establishments stretched out along main arteries in the downtown areas.

Typically, better-paying jobs with big firms required new employees to wait as long as a month or more to get a first check. Grace worked out of a temporaries agency and got many receptionist, switchboard, and secretarial jobs at places such as IBM, Raytheon, and other IBM clones around the Beltway.[5] One such place was looking for people to do telephone surveys for $4.75 an hour. When Grace told Kim, Kim applied, and was immediately offered a job, which she rejected when she learned that her first paycheck would be more than a month in coming.[6] Kim was living on the edge. Her debts—mainly her monthly storage bills—would not wait, she said, and she continued with her $3.75-an-hour job as a cashier at Bradlee's.[7]

---

cleaning job—the kind of job, she explained, where she needed neither a car nor a bicycle.

Incidentally, whenever a woman used her car on a job—such as a messenger or delivery service—she was not hired as an employee but as a self-employed contractor. In this way, the employer was free of any liability and free, too, of paying for insurance, Social Security, or any other usual employee benefits.

[5]But not *for* IBM *or* any of the others. Increasingly, corporations and governments contract out their need for janitors, typists, clerks, secretaries, and even higher-level personnel. These workers are employed by labor contractors, not by the corporations or governments where they do their work. These temporary and technically self-employed workers have no benefits and are subject to immediate dismissal. It sometimes seems that we are on our way to becoming a nation of part-time workers and self-employed or independent contractors—workers but not regular employees—without benefits, health coverage, or job security. See also p. 65, n. 13.

[6]The women themselves were often one another's best source for jobs. They told each other about jobs and often worked together. At one point, a Dart Drug Store employed five women living in the shelters.

[7]In late October, Kim walked in off the street and was hired at Bradlee's (a discount department store chain) for the holiday season. After Christmas, she was invited to stay on as a permanent employee. In February, she was named Cashier of the Month.

A variation of this delay-in-pay is what threw Jane into her present spell of homelessness. While working for the Two Hearts Dating Service in nearby Barryville as a telephone solicitor, she was living in an apartment in Tolltown, paying $400 a month rent; but she could not make the utility payments and had to do without heat, light, and refrigeration. When her automobile insurance lapsed, she was afraid to do all that driving and quit the job. It was a mistake taking it in the first place, she said. It was all straight commission, and on that kind of job, you fall too far behind before you can start producing enough to live on. She swears she would never take another straight commission job selling an unfamiliar product or service.

• • •

Only infrequently do the women admit to leaving a job because it was too difficult. Suzy quit her McDonald's job because she was assigned the drive-in window station. Counter work is OK, she said, because slack periods allow you to recover from the mealtime rushes. But the drive-in window! Run, run, run! No stopping! She just couldn't do it, so she quit. No, she didn't ask to go back to the counter. She just quit.

Sherry started out behind the counter at Roy Rogers. She couldn't move as fast as they wanted her to, so they transferred her to mopping floors in the eating area. She worked hard at this, but some patrons complained that her mop hit their shoes and she was reprimanded. She tried again, with the same results. It was impossible, she said. There was just no way to mop the floor while people were there and stay out of their way, so she quit.

Many of the women who quit jobs because they were "too hard" were involved in housework or personal care of some sort. Many of these women, in fact, place themselves somewhere along a continuum that ranges from housecleaning or maid at the low end, through housekeeper, live-in housekeeper, companion, nurse's aid, practical nurse, all the way to registered nurse. Cora is, indeed, an RN; Martha, an LPN. Rose was a live-in housekeeper for 18 years, Carlotta for four or five, Sheila for two, and Regina intermittently for several years.

Work as a domestic is sometimes too difficult to sustain, however, even for women who are good at it. Shortly after Grace arrived at the shelter, a staff member recommended her to an acquaintance for a housekeeping job that involved taking care of a (six months) pregnant woman, her husband, and three children, six years, four years, and fifteen months old.

Grace started work on Monday. By Tuesday evening she talked about trying to stick it out until Friday so she could get at least a full week's paycheck. She was finding the work harder in one day than a whole week of office work, she said, and the pay was working out to be less than $3.50 an hour. On Friday evening she announced that this had been her last day. She had done more than 20 loads of wash during the week, and had starched and ironed God knows how many shirts. And much like most domestic work situations, it was always, "Can you do this too, or a little of that? It won't take you long!" And everything always took longer and was more exhausting than you expected. But the worst thing about the job was being watched by the woman she was supposed to be caring for and by the mother-in-law as well, who had come down from Baltimore to make certain that "the new maid" didn't steal anything or rest too often. No, she hadn't told them she would not be coming back. She'd probably call tomorrow.[8]

---

[8] Because this job came through a personal recommendation by a staff person, Grace felt a special obligation to let them know she was quitting. After all, she said, the woman *was* very pregnant, and there *were* three little children. But she really hated making calls like that and would I call them for her? Tell them she got sick or found a better job or something? After a second heartrending appeal, I called the house and reported Grace's non-return. The man who answered was angry and said he wanted to hear this from Grace herself. (He never did.) The following week he called the staff person who had recommended her to say that Grace was "magnificent," extraordinarily productive and efficient at both housekeeping and childcare and they would "do anything to get her back." Grace wasn't impressed.

Betty got a job as companion to an elderly woman in a wheel-chair. She quit after three days, saying the work was too hard and the woman too unreasonable and demanding.

Live-in jobs as housekeepers or companions, however, are special jobs. They are special because they are both the high-est- and the lowest-paying jobs within reach of many of the women. They are especially high-risk jobs because the live-in housekeeper is thrown into such close and constant contact with her employers or charges that she has to please them at a very personal level as well as in terms of objective job perfor-mance. Most important, live-in jobs are special because they can lead directly into or out of homelessness. To get such a job is to get a place to live. To lose such a job is to lose one's place to live. That was the path into homelessness taken by Shirley, Rose, Sheila, Carlotta, and Regina. And that was the path out of homelessness for all of them (with the possible exception of Shirley) and for June as well.

Shirley lost her job as "a residential nurse" taking care of an old sick man when the man's daughter, against Shirley's and the doctor's advice, put her father in a nursing home. Rose lost her job as a live-in housekeeper after seven years with the same family when she "took a few tastes(drinks) too many and let my mouth run a little bit." They gave her until 10 o'clock the next morning to move herself and her things out of the house.

After a long career as a bank teller interspersed with periods of physical and mental illness, Sheila got a job as a live-in house-keeper/companion to an elderly, mentally ill, occasionally vio-lent woman. Sheila and her charge lived on the top floor of a "very nice" house in Takoma Park, Maryland. Sheila shopped, cooked, and kept house for the two of them. The woman's chil-dren and grandchildren lived on the two lower floors. Sheila was very pleased with her living and working conditions. She had a beautiful bedroom and a private bath. Every day, from 1:00 to 4:00, she and the woman watched soap operas on ABC, never changing the channel. Sheila even learned to use a few

words of Serbian to help the woman understand what was going on.

Sheila's wages increased from $5 a month during the first
year to $10 a month by the end of the second. When the family
decided to move to Detroit, Sheila was given two weeks' notice
and no severance pay. She arrived at The Refuge with a suitcase, several plastic bags, and $3.70 in her purse.

When Louise and Martha expressed shock and disbelief at
Sheila's wages, she assured them that many of the houses in
that area had live-in housekeepers/companions for elderly persons and that $5 to $10 a month was the going rate. The other
housekeepers were foreigners, she said. Most were Spanish-
speaking women from South America.[9]

After a few months in the shelter, Sheila gave up looking for
bank teller jobs (she had 27 years' experience) and looked for
another live-in job. After a personal interview, she was offered
a job caring for an old woman, wheelchair-bound, who was
about to leave the hospital. Sheila told the woman's daughter
that she wanted at least $25 and preferably $50 a month. Friday
night the daughter called the shelter. Her mother was coming
out of the hospital tomorrow. Could Sheila start to work this
weekend? For $125 a month? Sheila was radiant all evening. She
said she would need some ballast to keep from floating away.

The next evening, I drove Sheila and her suitcase and plastic
bags to an old frame house in an old neighborhood in
Alexandria, Virginia. The house was large and elegant. We put
Sheila's belongings in the hall and I talked with the daughter as
Sheila got acquainted with her new charge. They took an instant

---

[9] These workers were almost certainly illegal aliens, and Sheila didn't seem
to know (or mind) that the wages were largely determined by the fears and
desperation of the workers rather than by the market value of their labor. It
is also likely, however, that if the wage scale were much higher than room and
board and $10 a month, these same families, no matter how great their need,
could not have afforded Sheila's services. Takoma Park is not a particularly
affluent community.

liking to one another. The daughter beamed as her mother and Sheila chatted away.[10]

The better-paying live-in jobs often come with strings attached. Carlotta's experiences over a two-year period have often been tangled in these strings. Carlotta came to the shelter (several times) by way of live-in jobs and left the shelter (several times) by the same route. On one occasion, she moved out of the shelter on Tuesday and moved back in on Friday. She quit the job because it was too hard for her, she said, too hard for any one person. She was expected to do cleaning, laundry, and cooking with an eight-month-old infant on her hip. "Didn't they tell you they had a child?" I asked. "Yes, but I didn't know it was an infant."[11]

Later that month Carlotta found another live-in job ($150 a week) with a working couple and their three young sons, ages nine, seven, and five. I drove Carlotta and her belongings to her new job. To her surprise and mine, it was a two-bedroom apartment. The woman escorted us to the living room and motioned to Carlotta to put her belongings on the floor next to the sleep-sofa, which was to be Carlotta's. To her credit, the woman showed no surprise when Carlotta picked up her things and said she didn't think this arrangement would work out. "I told my husband this wouldn't work," the woman said, mainly to herself.

On still another live-in job, which Carlotta kept for a few weeks, she was not permitted to remain in the house on her day and a half off—Saturday afternoon to Monday morning. She had

---

[10]That was in March 1985, the last time I saw or heard about Sheila.

[11]Carlotta tried to get the job back a few days later, but she had already been replaced. Living on the street and in the shelter is very hard, she explained, and the employment agencies for live-in help wanted $100 every 15 days for six months if one got a placement through them. Carlotta put her own ad in the local county newspaper ($16 for four lines for five days), and a foreign couple offered her $50 a week plus room and board, but Carlotta turned them down. "I'm worth the going rate," she said, "and that's $150 a week" (January 1986).

to roam the streets on the weekend and sleep in the shelter on Saturday and Sunday nights. And on still another job, Carlotta felt she just could not keep up with the incessant demands made on her. When she told her employer she was quitting, the woman threatened to call the police if Carlotta didn't show up for work in the morning. Carlotta was bewildered and scared. "What does she mean? Can she really force me to work? Does she mean she will charge me with stealing or something?"[12]

Regina came to the shelter when she lost her job as a live-in housekeeper. A misunderstanding with her employer over the amount of money she spent for groceries for the two of them quickly escalated out of control, and Regina's things were put on the street by the sheriff's deputies.

Regina almost made it out of the shelter a few weeks later when she was offered $300 a week to take care of an old, sick man with a urinary catheter and other tubes elsewhere, all of which he was constantly trying to pull out. Regina would have had to be on duty 24 hours a day, six days a week. The women in the shelter cautioned Regina that she'd "earn every penny." Apprehensive of the responsibility and the confinement, Regina took the job but lost it on the first day when the man had to be hospitalized. The man's daughter told Regina that she could resume the job when her father left the hospital, but Regina thought this job wasn't right for her just then. It was too isolated, too confining, too lonely. Maybe she'd be better off with a regular day job in a drugstore or something.

Shortly before Christmas Regina took a full-time job at People's Drug Store. She was mainly a stock clerk, but she said she wanted to be a pharmacist's assistant and she was assured she could quickly work her way up to that position. But New

---

[12]Carlotta was small and dark and spoke with a heavy Spanish (Colombian) accent. My guess is that her employer assumed she was an illegal alien and was threatening to report her to the authorities as a way to force her to remain on the job. I suggested that she mail the woman her house key and forget the whole thing.

Year's Eve, Regina was laid off, along with three other recently hired employees.

"Is it anything personal?" she said she asked the manager, and he said no, it was just that business was slow and the four of them were just not needed. Then why, she asked, did he have a part-time help wanted sign in the window? "He shrugged his shoulders and walked away."[13]

Perhaps because most women were committed to defining themselves as working or looking for work, they did not talk easily or often about reasons for not looking for a job or not keeping one. Sometimes the reasons were more or less self-evident. Sometimes I had to guess at them.

At a very general level of unexamined beliefs, most women accepted the proposition that a job is the way out of homelessness. But when they confronted their own concrete situations, they knew this was not true for most of them. At best, it was only a small and partial truth. It may have been true, for example, for those few women like Lisa, smart and competent, who aced a standardized test and got a good job with the Post Office, or Grace and a few others, who could command jobs paying $7 or more an hour. And it was true, too, for those few who got live-in jobs at any wage. Night work, which usually came with premium pay and might have been easier to get than day jobs, was ruled out because the women had no place to sleep during the day.

For most homeless women, then, jobs by themselves were not a way out of homelessness, even if one discounted the large number of women who were too old, too sick, or otherwise too

---

[13] Regina was in tears at what she took to be another personal failure. I tried to explain to her that part-time and temporary help was a lot cheaper for an employer than permanent, full-time employees, but Regina was sure the blame lay with her. That same week, the Reagan administration urged federal agencies to hire more temporary workers. Temporaries receive no benefits, no credit for length of service, and no eligibility for pensions. They have none of the usual job protection and may be laid off at any time. See Spencer Rich, "Federal Offices Urged to Hire Temporaries," *Washington Post*, January 3, 1985, p. A3.

disabled to work.* There were many working women who earned anywhere from $3.50 an hour to $5 or even $6 an hour. These women, often poorly educated, in desperate want, living under pressures that strained their judgment and even sanity, would have found it almost impossible to become self-sufficient on such wages even if they possessed extraordinary money management skills, which most of them did not. In the Washington, D.C., metropolitan area, in the mid-1980s, efficiencies and one-bedroom apartments started at $450 or $500 a month (with $1,000—security deposit and one month's rent— required up front); a room in someone else's two-bedroom apartment (with few or no kitchen privileges) cost $350 (if you could find someone who would take you in); fare for a one-way ride on the subway during rush hour (which was defined to include seven hours of the day) ran from $.80 to $2.40; coffee was $.60 at Roy Rogers and a pack of cigarettes $1.50 at 7-Eleven.

Gwen's situation was typical. "I try to support myself. I work hard and I want to pay rent, but how can I pay $100 a week when I earn $4 an hour [as a salesclerk at McCrory's 5&10]?"[14] The result was that most women worked at jobs that paid so poorly

---

*KIM: *But the #1 reason why a job is not the way out of homelessness is discrimination in housing. We may have the money to rent an apartment, but the "minimum income requirement" is out of reach for many of us. Apartment management companies require an established positive credit history and recent rental references that homeless persons, due to circumstances and situation, very often do not have. Rental policy restricting the number of persons per apartment directly prevents poverty-level wage earners from obtaining housing.*

GRACE: *A job does not get you out of being homeless. I worked every day for 11 months, missing only one day out of all my temporary jobs. I used a lot of money on the public phones trying to stay in contact with my other four agencies. I made just enough to get by and continue to repair my 12-year-old car. I worked to feed my car. That darn thing kept breaking down. All my money went to keep that thing running. A car was my survival. I was living in this "prison." The only way I could escape was to drive my car. I would have died without it. I drove to the place [townhouse she used to live in] that meant the most to me. Finally, my ex-husband let me see my children, the youngest two. I took them to the movies, I went to synagogue and church. But mostly, I went to work.*

[14]Kim reached $3.90 as a cashier at Bradlee's. Lisa received $3.50 for the same job at the same place. That's what County Donuts paid, too. Luana received $4.11 an hour for working as a maid at a nearby nursing home. Beverly

that, without some kind of assistance, one could work at them for 20 years and still remain homeless. This did not prevent the women from looking for work or keeping their jobs, but it often served to take the heart out of work-life, to render the job search somewhat less diligent than it might otherwise have been, and to render attachment to one's job as something less than fierce and tenacious.*

Another deterrent to job seeking was the fact that, in strict economic terms, low-pay jobs were not clearly superior to public assistance, which itself was nothing to write home about. To the woman on public assistance, for example, the cost of taking a job could be substantial, even if the cash wage was as much or even more than the cash payout of public assistance.

To leave public assistance usually means to forfeit food stamps and medical assistance as well. Permanent full-time jobs at a fast food place or in retailing or other entry-level positions typically offer health coverage only after a probationary period of anywhere from two to six months, but such coverage is prohibitively expensive and most employees decline it. Typically, there are no fringe benefits for part-time or temporary workers. Kelly Girls and other temporary workers hired out of employment agencies are, in fact, employees of the agencies rather than of the firms to which they are assigned. And here, too, health coverage is optional, very expensive, and routinely declined.

---

received $3.35 (minimum wage) for bussing dishes at Horn and Horn. Abigail received $3.70 as a file clerk for a collection agency in D.C. Better-paying office jobs were not usually available to most of the women.

*DIRECTOR: *Women who had jobs when they came to us, or who were just recently unemployed, were the most successful in being re-employed and leaving The Refuge permanently. . . . It is my observation that mental illness or fragile mental health interfered with the ability of most of the women to get a job and to keep a job. In the shelter journal, volunteers were quick to register their anger or disbelief when a woman who had obtained a job would work for two or three days, and then simply decide not to go back. To the question of why, the response was often, "I have to visit a friend this morning," or "I have an appointment this morning."*

If one cashes out the dollar value of public assistance and its associated benefits—especially health care—and compares the total with the net return of an entry-level job, it is surprising that so many women who were probably eligible for assistance chose jobs instead. Indeed, it was not unknown for a woman to quit a job that offered no health coverage when she knew she was about to incur medical expenses. Thus, Kim was working as a GS-3 Temporary for the federal government when she decided the time was right for elective surgery. With an eye toward getting medical assistance from Social Services—not available so long as she was employed or unemployed voluntarily—Kim set about getting herself fired.

Other times, the women's reasons for not taking jobs or keeping them could only be guessed at, especially if they involved things like fear of failure, embarrassment, or other risks to one's self-image. Much of what appeared to be nonrational job behavior could be traced to a subtle but powerful social class hierarchy and class consciousness that permeates the universe of work.[15]

Consider this exchange. Ranji was talking about her problems in getting public assistance and casually mentioned that Giant Foods was her last employer. Brenda was obviously impressed. "You worked for Giant?" she asked, and Ranji said yes, for three months.

Why was Brenda impressed? What was so special about working in a supermarket? Events surrounding the closing of a discount department store chain suggest an answer. In 1988,

---

[15]It is difficult for middle-class observers to imagine the reluctance, if not the terror, of some lower- or working-class persons as they contemplate entering a middle-class work setting. And when class combines with race, as in the case of many minority ghetto youths, reluctances and fears are multiplied, sometimes to an almost paralyzing intensity. "When an opportunity like . . . a better job opens up that will erase some disability felt before, society seems suddenly to make itself invisible, leaving the individual to grapple with class change as though his personal strength must suffice for all he faces." Richard Sennett and Jonathan Cobb, *The Hidden Injuries of Class*, p. 183. Many parts of Sennett and Cobb's book deal directly and insightfully with some of the issues suggested here.

Bradlee's announced the closing of 33 of its department stores, nine of which were in the Washington metropolitan area; several hundred employees were to be let go. In most respects, Bradlee's was much like K mart and Zayre's, but unlike them, it was unionized. Giant Foods, Safeway, and Woodward and Lothrop (a department store chain with an image of a middle-class clientele) were also organized by the same union. All three of these firms needed trained cashiers, stock clerks, and other workers, and asked the union to help them recruit new hires from among the Bradlee's employees.

To everyone's astonishment, most Bradlee's employees declined the offer, despite starting salaries of $5.75 an hour at Giant and Safeway (far above their current wage levels), with increases to $10.65 an hour after 24 months. From their discussions with Bradlee's employees, union officials concluded that the employees feared that the work at Giant and Safeway might be too hard, too fast-paced, and too high-pressured. As for Woodward and Lothrop—well, maybe Bradlee's employees felt the same way about Woodies, too.[16]

However tempting it might be to cite these refusals as evidence that some people really do not want to work hard (sometimes true), or that some people do not want to "better themselves" (sometimes true), or that some people are irresponsible and downright lazy (also, perhaps, sometimes true), these characteristics are surely not the principal dynamic at work here. The cashiers at Bradlee's were already working just as hard under the pressure of impatient customers lined up at each checkout counter as the checkers at Giant and Safeway, and probably harder and under more pressure than most Woodward and Lothrop employees.

But at Giant and Safeway, where the pay is much higher, your fellow employees are likely to be better educated than you, the Bradlee's cashier, and they're likely to be smarter, better spo-

---

[16] Interview with Ermaun L. Joe, Director, Central Virginia Division, United Food and Commercial Workers Union Local 400, District of Columbia, Maryland, and Virginia.

ken, and better dressed, and less likely to be foreign-born or black or other minority, and your supervisor would probably expect you to perform at their level, which you surely can't do. Moreover, the customers would be not only working people like yourself but middle-class and even rich people who can make you feel like dirt without even meaning to.

Surely, social class considerations such as these played a large part in the Bradlee's employees' decisions to turn down the Giant/Safeway/Woodward and Lothrop job offers. In the same way and for the same reasons, they probably also explain why Brenda was so impressed by Ranji's having worked for Giant. Fear of not measuring up, fear of embarrassment, fear of being snubbed or disdained by one's social betters—these are always and everywhere at work, and especially among those at the bottom.*

Some of the women were particularly vulnerable to such feelings. Crushing work experiences had deprived them of their self-confidence, and they feared the threats that further job exposure would pose. It is for this reason, I believe, that a few of the women made job hunting a somewhat casual and desultory enterprise. For these few, the danger in looking seriously for a job was that they might find one.

One job strategy that was more talked about than pursued was to get trained for higher-paying jobs. Michelle knew that any job she qualified for would not lift her out of homelessness. That is why she was taking a course in computer programming three nights a week and working at any job she could get during the day.[17] And that is why Elsie turned down a cashier's job at a car wash in favor of a year-long live-in training program in

---

*KIM: *I do not believe that the distance we feel when dealing with customers/co-workers of a higher social class is (necessarily) a matter of intimidation. More likely, it is a matter of us just not being able to relate to them.*

[17] She said she was doing well in her course work and enjoying it. Her one disappointment was learning that computer programmers don't actually work with computers. Michelle's tuition was paid for through the Federal Student Loan Program.

typing, word-processing, and hospital record-keeping at the state's Vocational Rehabilitation Center. Martha, who was usually in control of her alcoholism and depression, had serious neck and back problems and guessed she would not be able to continue much longer as an LPN, but she was confident that she could work her way out of homelessness. "I'll be OK with office retraining," she said.

This strategy had its problems, however. Not many homeless women had the educational background, the talent, the ambition, or the self-discipline necessary to train for the kind of jobs that might lead to self-sufficiency. Or so it appeared. Perhaps many of the women had these things but lacked only—only!—the opportunity. Crucially, they lacked the economic and social supports for such a sustained undertaking.

For those who were eligible, another major strategy was to work at a low-paying job and wait (one year? two years? longer?) for housing assistance to come through.[18] Most housing assistance programs required that the recipient pay about one-third of her gross income for rent, with the program picking up the balance. Even a low-paying job or public assistance, when coupled with a housing subsidy, could enable the women to move out of the shelter and into independent living. Indeed, the housing subsidy was the principal avenue of escape from homelessness.

Another strategy was to work more than one job. A few women attempted this, and even fewer were successful. Jane always knew she would need two jobs, but it took her some time to find two that could go together. She finally made it out of the shelter when she put an evening-and-weekend job as telephone solicitor together with a full-time day job as a clerk with an insurance company. Grace combined a $7.50-an-hour data entry job with an evening-and-weekend job as a model-home hostess in a new housing development. Kim combined a weekend donut shop job with whatever full-time job she could find.

---

[18]See Appendix D, "Social Service Programs."

A variation of the two-jobs strategy was to substitute welfare for one of the jobs—that is, to become a "welfare cheater" by receiving income from a job while also receiving public assistance. That was the only way out of homelessness that Martha could see for herself when she first went on public assistance. She thought she could get a place to live by tripling up with two other women, which would leave her with $30 from her monthly assistance check of $180. By moonlighting on weekends as a practical nurse, she guessed she could get by. Martha said she couldn't give up her public assistance because she needed the medical assistance that went with it. Her pain-killing prescription drugs cost $16 a week and the doctor had told her she'd almost certainly need surgery for her disc problem.

Cheating on welfare, however, can be dangerous. It can lead into homelessness as well as out of it. So did it for Bessie, who was drawing a welfare check while working as a monitor/aide on a school bus. Her deception discovered, she was removed from the welfare rolls and quickly found herself jobless and homeless, without food stamps and without medical assistance. Other women on public assistance who also held jobs were smarter than Bessie. They took their jobs in the relatively safe "irregular economy"—small businesses and personal services where payment is "off the books."

Even if one could not work one's way out of homelessness, there were other reasons for working. One was that "Jobs are for money." Many women took hard, low-paying jobs simply because it was better to have money than not to have it, even if one must remain homeless. Terry spoke eloquently on the subject. "How do you like your job?" she was asked.

"I love every penny of it," she said. Another time, however, while she was actually on the job in a local discount drug store, she was careful to discriminate between the idea of work as a generalized good and its particularization in a cashier's job as a specific evil. "I hate my job," she said, "but I love working. And I love the money."

Elsie, too, put a high value on the money-producing potential of a job. On her first day of workfare, Elsie was assigned to assist a regular county employee. Together, they cleaned the 18 toilets in the local high school. With ammonia, soap, a toilet mop, and a floor mop, they did it all between 7:30 A.M. and noon. After lunch, they washed down the tables and floors of the cafeteria, then moved on to other rooms for more cleaning until they finished their work at 4:30.

Elsie's workmate liked Elsie and her work. She herself was going into the hospital, she said, and a replacement would be needed for a month or so. She would recommend Elsie as her replacement if Elsie were willing. The job paid $9 an hour. "I'd clean toilets day and night, seven days a week, for $9 an hour," said Elsie, but she heard no more about it.

Like Terry and many others, then, Elsie would sometimes have you believe that a job is only or mainly for money. Other times, however, the importance of working, or simply having a job, was so taken for granted that a woman might forget, for the moment, why she wanted or needed a job. Once, when Elsie applied for a job as a cashier in a hardware store, she returned to the shelter at night to report that the interview had gone well. The work hours were not good, she said, but that was not so important.

"How much does it pay?" Grace asked.

Elsie clapped her hands to her temples. "I forgot to ask!" she said. "I completely forgot to ask!"

It is possible that Elsie forgot to ask because most jobs pay pretty much the same thing—somewhere between $3.50 and $4.50 or $4.75 an hour. Had this been the reason, however, Elsie would not have been so surprised at her own forgetfulness. Certainly she didn't "forget to ask" for lack of caring about the job. On Sunday, her pastor invited the members of the congregation to go on a three-day fast if they wanted a special favor from God. In vain, Elsie fasted. She wanted that job "soooo bad."

When Hilda moved into a subsidized apartment, she got a part-time job in a cafeteria. She wasn't working for the money,

she said. After rent, Social Security, and taxes, she was left with
$45 a month for food, clothing, and everything else. The real
value of the job, she said, was that it allowed her to build up a
work history.

The importance of having a job is sometimes measured in
pleasure and pain. Sometimes one wants or keeps a job for the
sheer pleasure of working, without bothering to analyze it any
further. One evening in the shelter, the women had just finished
dinner when Kathleen stretched her arms toward the ceiling
and threw back her head. "I feel great!" she announced to the
world, and explained that this was her second day on a new job
and the doctor had also cut her anxiety-reducing medication.
She went on to compare her current feelings with those of the
previous week, when she was awakened in the middle of the
night by a terrible stomach pain. "What's the matter with me?"
she wondered, and then she realized that she was jobless and
that was why she had this pain in the pit of her stomach.

Job pain can work both ways. Jane recalls her first job in
Washington in the 1950s. She was working as an analyst at the
National Security Agency, and during all the months she worked
there she suffered from migraine headaches. It was not until
many years later that Jane came to realize that she had never had
such headaches before or after, and that it must have been the
job itself that caused the headaches. Now, however, she works
mainly as a telephone solicitor and there are no migraines.

When Jane broke her arm, she had to keep it in a cast and
sling and it still hurt quite a bit. The doctor suggested she not
go to work for a day or two, but Jane thought it would be better to go to work and lose herself in her telephone solicitation
job than to walk the streets all day and feel the pain.

Martha was sometimes called to work as the only night nurse
for a D.C. government-operated ward of mentally ill persons.
She returned to the shelter feeling miserable because she was
"spread so thin" she couldn't be of any real help to any of her
patients. "I leave those jobs feeling like there was a cross on my
soul" (for failing her patients and God).

Kim gave up her office job with a construction company to deal with a love affair that was crumbling all around her. She was so despondent that she tried to kill herself with a handgun, but the gun misfired. Weeks passed and she could not bring herself to look for a job, she said, because her pain was too great and because she was so absorbed in her own situation that she couldn't perform on a job anyway. But then she saw an advertisement for the job she used to have with an animal rights group. Kim applied for the job because, she said, this was the only job she could handle right now—a job in which she would be confronted by the suffering of animals all over the world, a suffering much greater than her own. "I can drench myself in their pain and suffering," she said, and this would help her put her own suffering in some perspective.

Not everyone, of course, was enthusiastic about working, and at times some women found it difficult to find any positive value in a job. Pam worked only because it was better than the alternative, and only grudgingly conceded that "working is better than walking around."

Betty was only modestly more enthusiastic, but Betty had reasons. She said that if she was turned down for SSI again, she'd take a live-in job somewhere, anywhere. Sure, the doctor told her she shouldn't work, but she'd rather die working than stay here in the shelter over another summer and die of boredom and the stress of being homeless. Betty often presented herself as the passive subject of a tug-of-war between go-to-work and don't-go-to-work forces. She herself wanted to work, she insisted, and that's what the Department of Social Services and shelter staff were pushing her to do, under threat of withdrawing all assistance. But her doctor told her that she must not work.

At the day shelter, after she had just been turned down for the second time for SSI, Betty went stage front and proclaimed her dilemma for everyone there. "Society says, 'You must work.' My medical doctor says, 'You must not work.' Let's get together, OK?"

Like Betty, some women are too old, too sick, or too crazy to work, and again like Betty, most of them are working-class or lower-class women who have no special job skills other than housework, if that.* Even most of the nonworking women, however, strove mightily to identify themselves as being in the work force and seeking work, laying claim to being housekeepers or nurse's aides or companions or practical nurses. It was as if, to them, these jobs were simply occupational labels for the domestic skills that most of them learned as daughters or wives or mothers. Thus, almost anyone could lay plausible claim to be looking for such jobs—plausible to the listener and, more important, perhaps, even convincing to the claimant as well.

Brenda and Dorothy were talking about jobs. Dorothy says she has recently applied for two restaurant jobs but didn't get either of them. Brenda asks Dorothy if she can do housework. Dorothy laughs. Who hasn't done housework?" she says. Brenda, with great seriousness, assures Dorothy that she, too can do housework. Of course you can, Dorothy agrees reassuringly, and Brenda, as if to prove her point, adds that she has worked as a nurse's aide in a couple of nursing homes in the area, and as a dietitian's assistant, too, in a nursing home kitchen.[19]

Even those who were not working or looking for work sometimes traced their failure to the very importance of work in their lives. Judy had just turned down a job at County Donuts. "I can't take the stress of working," she explained.

"Maybe not the donut shop, but how about another data entry job like the one you had last fall? I thought you enjoyed that."

"I did. But when they fired me, they destroyed me."

A woman's determination to see herself as a worker and to present herself as a worker was not always self-serving and may

---

*KIM: *This chapter could leave the reader with the false impression that homeless women are less job-skilled than the general population. Plenty of people are of this opinion, including people in charge of the money.*

[19]She did, in fact, get such jobs, but she couldn't hold them. She says her biggest problem was that she did not move fast enough to please her bosses.

even have worked to her severe disadvantage. Louise had just been dropped from the workfare rolls (GPA-E—General Public Assistance, Employable) as unemployable after failing at several workfare assignments because of her various compulsions and anxieties. She went back to taking voluminous notes on the want ads in several papers but somehow was never able to follow up on any of the leads she read or heard about. A staff person at the shelter suggested she apply for ordinary welfare (GPA—General Public Assistance), noting that the $200 a month would take care of her storage bills and leave her with some spending money.

Louise was livid at the suggestion. "I'm not eligible for public assistance," she said. "I'm employable. I've worked before and I can work now. Can't you understand that?"

Nor would she agree to check her eligibility for public assistance with Social Services or allow anyone else to check with her caseworker on her behalf. In her head, her heart, her bones, she was a worker and wanted nothing to do with welfare.

One doesn't have to be crazy to want to dissociate oneself from public assistance. Vicki isn't crazy. Vicki has a withered arm but a clear eye. "I don't want that welfare bullshit. I want a real job. At Navy, I liked the work and the people, and they liked me."

Because of her disability, Vicki has never been able to realize herself fully as the self-sufficient worker she desperately wants to be. "I've never gotten a job on my own, through an interview. Personnel people all seem to be cheerleader types, and they hire cheerleader types. If you're aggressive and verbal, you get the job even if you don't have the experience or a good job history. But I'm like a turtle: it takes me a long time to come out. . . . I got my CETA (Comprehensive Employment and Training Act) job because there were 10 of us, equally qualified, and the personnel officer said she'd break the tie by hiring the one who'd been unemployed the longest. That was me . . . I worked at the Naval Medical Hospital for two summers as a GS-2. That was through their program for the handicapped."

Another time, over lunch at Big Boy's, Vicki took aim at the Department of Vocational Rehabilitation. "DVR is shit. They don't need to train people to make allowances for handicaps and they shouldn't pay so much attention to disabilities. That's not the issue. The issue is, can I do the job and do it on time, and can I get along with the people I work with? Will I blow up if someone calls me a cripple or will I go on and do the job?"[20]

And when Connie told Vicki about a live-in job (room and board, no pay), Vicki was offended by the implication she couldn't do better. "I can do a real job," she told Connie, "and I'm going to get a real job." Indeed, whenever Vicki talked about work and jobs, which was often, anything like supported work or workfare, anything other than "a real job," was, to her, "bullshit."[*]

● ● ●

The energy the homeless women put into working and looking for work is in part a measure of their determination to leave the streets, in part a measure of the (limited) economic rewards of work, and in part a measure of the noneconomic rewards of work. The women value work over and above its economic rewards for much the same reasons that other people do—because it is through work that we engage the world and become a part of it, and through work that we lay claim to membership in the larger community and, in getting paid for our work, have that membership confirmed by others. For most people, including Vicki and Elsie and others, this social value of work is experienced, at the individual level, as a principal source of independence and self-respect.

---

[20] Once, in a discussion of disabilities, I told Vicki I thought there was more prejudice against persons with mental problems than those with physical problems. Vicki conceded the point but noted that, unlike physically handicapped persons, those who are mentally ill can hide their problems. "Adolph Hitler could have gotten a million jobs in this country, but I can't even get one."

[*] KIM: *Money is poured into job training programs, job-seeking workshops, interviewing/resume-writing seminars. Whatever these programs are they are not about results or solutions. They point their fingers at the homeless. They do not address the vital issue of discrimination. In its extreme manifestation, discrimination threatens the homeless person with institutionalization or incarceration.*

In looking at the homeless women, however, I suspect that work also has a more primitive, pre-social value that is most clearly seen (or sensed) in some of the deeply troubled women in the shelter. As one watches them go through the motions of looking for work, one senses an extraordinary urgency and intensity that cannot be accounted for by traditional social and psychological values of work. Louise defiantly proclaims her employability as she struggles with the terrible demons of obsession and fear that render her unemployable. And Dorothy continues to go job hunting, even as the ever-changing bus destination and street signs prevent her from getting where she is trying to go. There are others, too, who cannot work but continue, mindlessly, instinctively, to go through the motions of looking for jobs.

Theirs is certainly not a struggle for the economic rewards of work, nor even for the social or psychological rewards. Their needs are pre-social, elemental. They know they are in deep trouble, in danger of losing their sanity and their humanity, and they are struggling to hold on. It is as if the Louises and Dorothys believe with Freud that "work is man's principal tie to reality," and they feel that tie slipping away.

In summary, at the heart of the contradictions and ambivalences that characterize the women's approach to the world of work is a simple fact: with some notable exceptions, the jobs they can get do not pay enough to enable them to support themselves. On one hand, the women desperately want and need the money, the independence, and the self-respect that most of us have come to expect from a job. On the other hand, to get a job and keep it, the women must run an obstacle course at the end of which is a low-pay, low-status job that offers little more than they have without it.

In this situation, the women—perfectly socialized to the values of work—continue to value work for what they know their jobs cannot provide. Hence the ambivalence, the starts and stops, and the periodic surrenders to a workless shelter life.

3

Family

D inner was over and four women stayed at the table to talk.
The topic of conversation bounced around and, as often
happened, came to rest on the subject of homelessness.

"I'm not homeless," protested Abigail. "I'm familyless."

That simple assertion bore eloquent witness to the important and complex connection between family relationships and
homelessness.[1] Homeless women had not always been homeless and familyless women had not always been familyless. Like
everyone else, they were born into families or family-like net-
works of human relationships. On the street and in the shelters,
one meets many homeless women who had been kept afloat by

---

[1] "Family" was conceived narrowly. For the never-married women, "family"
usually meant family of orientation—the families they were born into, their
parents and siblings. For women with children, "family" included family of
procreation—their husbands and children. Perhaps predictably, mothers and
sisters were more likely to be sources of support than fathers and brothers.
There seemed not much to choose between sons and daughters. Nieces (but
not nephews, uncles, or aunts) occasionally came to a homeless woman's assistance.

family members until, for one reason or another, the family had to let go. For most women, living with relatives or receiving significant financial or other support from them was the last stage in their descent into homelessness.[2]

Shelters and streets are littered with the bits and pieces of broken families. Some of the women are desperately trying to rebuild family relationships, some are just as desperately trying to run away from them, and others are struggling to hold on to what they have.[*] This complex pattern is further complicated by the fact that a family relationship is not a single strand but a collection of many, and each strand can itself be complex and slippery in its own right.

Family relationships ranged from no family or no contact at all to regular and intense contacts. At the low end were some of the older women who had been familyless a long time and were more or less accepting of this condition. For them, family was not an issue, one way or the other; at best, it was simply something other women talked about a lot. Phyllis, for example, was

---

[2] Peter Rossi reports that "the time elapsed since last being employed is much longer than the time homeless." From this, he properly infers that while they were unemployed, even for years at a time, the now-homeless persons "managed to stay in homes mainly through the generosity of family and perhaps friends." *Down and Out in America: The Origins of Homelessness,* pp. 115–16.

This is an ongoing process and many people continue to avoid homelessness through the support of family members. Of course, we do not know how many such almost-homeless or about-to-be-homeless there are, but it is reasonable to suppose that they far outnumber the "real" homeless. It is estimated, for example, that in the District of Columbia, one resident in five and one-third of all children live in a doubled-up household. In Chicago, it is estimated (1989) that 50,000 to 100,000 additional tenants are living illegally in 40,000 public housing units. Karin Ringheim, *At Risk of Homelessness: The Roles of Income and Rent,* p. 9. For New York City, it has been estimated that the doubled-up families in public housing outnumbered the officially homeless by 20 to 1. Kim Hopper, "The Ordeal of Shelter: Continuities and Discontinuities in the Public Response to Homelessness," *Notre Dame Journal of Law, Ethics, and Public Policy* vol. 4, no. 2 (1989), p. 317.

[*] DIRECTOR: *Fractured families were the most difficult issue that volunteers had to handle. That The Refuge residents, staff, and volunteers became a new family was truly wondrous.*

doesn't
sound
like it.

72 and had never married. Her only brother had been killed in World War II and her mother died in 1965. Since 1955, Phyllis had lived alone. If she had more distant relatives, they were not a part of her remembered life, and Phyllis was never heard to associate having no family with homelessness.

Maude, at 61, said she had no family, no, no family at all. She hadn't had a family in 40 years, not since she disowned the family she was born into. "You're my family," she said, making a circle with her arms to embrace everyone in the day shelter. "All you people here, you're my family. My family is whoever I happen to be with, if they're congenial."[3]

Louise was also familyless, but she didn't live easily with this knowledge; family issues were central to her causal analysis of her own and others' homelessness. Like Abigail, Louise, too, defined homelessness in terms of family. Divorced for more than five years, Louise had no living blood relatives that she knew or remembered. For her, to have a family was to have a home, and if one couldn't go there, it was one's own fault. On this reasoning, Louise often insisted she was the only person at the shelter who was homeless. In fact, she said, she had been in seven shelters over the last five years and, with the possible exception of Phyllis, she had never met a truly homeless person other than herself.

"How about Betty?"

"Betty has relatives. She has a daughter."

"But her daughter won't let her live with them."

"That's her own fault," said Louise. "She would have had a home if she'd acted differently. Like Judy. Judy isn't homeless. She just can't get along with her mother."

While Abigail defined her problem as being familyless rather than homeless, and Louise defined true homelessness as having no family, Iris took the more conventional view that she was

---

[3] The observation that "the extent of disaffiliation varies directly with age" is roughly accurate for this particular group of women. Howard M. Bahr and Gerald R. Garrett, *Disaffiliation among Urban Women*, p. 1.

homeless because she had no family to prevent her from sliding into it, or, being there, to help her climb out of it.[*] Iris's sick and senile mother lived in Chicago, and Iris had just come from there herself. Iris said she wouldn't be in this fix of having to live in shelters—"it's temporary, of course"—if she had a brother or sister like most people do. But she didn't have a single relative besides her sick mother.

Clearly, Iris was wrong because many of the homeless women did, in fact, have brothers and sisters "like most people do."[4] But Iris was also right, given the obvious fact that many people are kept from dropping into homelessness because of the support given them by family members. As general propositions, it is difficult to choose among Abigail's, Louise's, and Iris's analyses of the relationship between family and homelessness. For any given homeless woman, any one of these propositions—or any combination of them—might apply.

Grace was at the opposite extreme. While Phyllis, Maude, and Louise had no family at all, Grace had parents, a husband, children, and siblings, and remained in more or less regular and sometimes intense contact with them during 11 months of homelessness. In the fall of 1984, the police forcibly removed Grace (in handcuffs) from her townhouse for refusing to comply with a court order that awarded her husband temporary custody (four years) of their two teenage children, the house, and their two automobiles.[5] After a day in jail and a hearing,

---

[*] KIM: *Money is the only difference between someone with no home and who is staying in a motel, or even renting a room at the Y, and someone living on the street or in a shelter. In the same way, indeed, those people who are without a home of their own, but who have a family they can crash with, are spared the stigma of "homelessness."*

[4] Elsie had a married brother in a neighboring county. He did not, perhaps could not, help her financially, but he did not have to do much to please Elsie. When she returned from a one-month evaluation at the State Rehabilitation Center, someone asked if she wanted dinner. Elsie said no, she had eaten at her brother's house and added, beaming, that her brother had told her she ab-so-lute-ly had to have dinner with them before she returned to the shelter.

[5] The basis for this decision seems to have been Grace's refusal to appear at the hearings where custody of her children and house were to be decided.

Grace was released on her own recognizance. She was penniless and homeless. She had a married brother who lived in the Washington area but "he did not want to get involved."

Grace went to Pennsylvania to live with her sister and her family. There she slept on a cot in the basement and tried to stay out of everyone's way, but things didn't work out. Her sister, a nurse, wanted someone to do the cleaning, the laundry, and the ironing. After four months, Grace returned to the Washington area and was referred to The Refuge. That was December 1984.

There was an edge to Grace's voice as she remembered those events. She was quiet for a moment; then she began again and this time the edge was gone. She said her sister probably felt guilty about not being able to help her, to really help her. That's often the way with well-intentioned people, she said. They feel guilty and their guilt makes them do strange things.

In most cases, I have only the homeless woman's perspective on facts, events, and motivations. Surely we would get a different story—or many different stories—from the other family members. There are some elements here, however, that all would probably agree on: Grace probably did sleep on a cot in the basement; she probably did try, unsuccessfully, to stay out of everyone's way; and her sister probably did ask her to help with the housework.

Taken together, these probabilities point to a near certainty: this was not a middle-class, even moderately affluent household; at best, it was a crowded, working-class household, with no spare bedroom and no spare anything else. It is probable

---

Courts and judges can't take your children away from you, she insisted. Only God can do that. And courts can't keep you from living in your own house. Not in this country. Grace believes that she was a victim of a conspiracy. Her husband, she observed bitterly, was the successful man about town, active in community and church affairs, an important part of the old boy network, while she stayed home and raised five children and kept house and made no friends except for a few other housewives who were just as powerless as herself. Foolishly, she trusted her husband's lawyer, who insisted he was the family lawyer and could represent her as well as her husband. What chance could she have had? she asks. A powerless and unknown woman against her husband and his buddies, the lawyer and the judge.

that the sister's family could ill afford the loss of space, the loss of privacy, and the increased work and expense that Grace's presence entailed.

The cost of Grace's presence to a middle-class household would be far less, and such a household could far better afford what costs there were. Given higher income and educational levels, the middle-class family is also perhaps better able to make effective use of public and private helping resources in the community. Thus, it is easier for a middle-class household to take in a needy family member, and easier to allow the person to remain. Clearly, homeless women are primarily from working-class and lower-class families, and the limited resources of their families are a major factor in the class character of homelessness.

Another difficulty is raised by Grace's insistence that her husband was mentally ill ("Sick! Sick! Sick!") and that he won the house and custody of the children because he was part of the small-town "old boy network" that included the lawyer and the judge. For present purposes, whether this was true or not is less important than the fact that it could have been true.

It is usually too easy to assume that the homeless woman has been rejected by husband, parent, or other family members because she is crazy, incompetent, dependent, hateful, or otherwise too difficult to live with. Some of the homeless women I knew may have been those things, but most were not. In some cases, it was the husband, the parent, or other family member who was crazy, unreasonable, greedy, violent, or otherwise impossible to live with. But raw power determined who would leave and who would stay, not competence or stability. For obvious reasons, poor women have less power and fewer personal and social resources than their more affluent middle-class counterparts, and this fact too contributes to the class character of homeless women.

. . .

Standing out by themselves, apart from all the others, were Natalie, her husband Biff, and their children, known collectively as "The Family." They deserve special attention because no "explanations" of homelessness seemed to explain them. In contrast to Abigail's lament about being "familyless," members of "The Family" had each other. Natalie and her family seemed to have made a permanent adjustment to homelessness. She and Biff were still in their 30s. They had married as teenagers and they and their three teenage children measured their homelessness in years. Natalie stayed in one or another women's shelter; Biff and their 17-year-old son Rick stayed in a nearby shelter for homeless men. Babs, 14, and Biff Jr., 16, were in foster care placements out of state. When the courts returned them to their family, Babs joined Natalie in the shelter and Junior joined Biff and Rick. The family was known throughout the county, but most agencies had long since thrown up their hands in frustration and discouragement. The family had been in and out of subsidized housing, on and off of welfare.

Biff and Rick and Junior met Natalie and Babs every morning and they spent their days together, going to Social Services, this or that soup kitchen, the library, the park, trying to get something, anything, from someone, anyone, and listening to Biff talk about what they would do when Biff (usually wearing his dirty neck brace) won his damage suit against the transit system and they all became millionaires. Some of the young homeless women hung out with them, partly because Rick and Junior were exceptionally handsome young men, partly because Natalie was a sympathetic motherly type, and partly because they were indeed a colorful group and often fun to be with, especially when beer or pot were available.

At night, Biff, Rick, and Junior escorted Natalie and Babs to the women's shelter. There they agreed on where to meet the next morning, everyone kissed everyone goodnight, and the men marched off to the men's shelter, about 20 minutes away.

Biff drank a lot, and Natalie and Rick spent much of their time running away from the beatings he was trying to give them.[6] Sometimes Natalie worked as a waitress, but Biff and Rick would insist on visiting her on the job and the jobs seldom lasted beyond a week or two. Sometimes Natalie would be hospitalized after trying to kill herself, and Biff and Rick would make the visitors lounge—and after hours, the hospital grounds—their home.[7] Once, for a period of months, the family lived in an abandoned bus. Another time, they set up housekeeping in a parking garage.

· · ·

Nowhere in the spectrum of family relationships was the struggle to mend, maintain, or restore these connections more intense than in relationships between mother and child.[*] The most casual mention of children was often sufficient to bring out several wallets and photographs, which were then passed around for mutual admiration. With some minor exceptions, the women almost never derogated their children as they often did their husbands, parents, or other family members.

Often, relationships with children were the only or principal family contacts. The most obvious and regular mother-child

---

[6] One day, when I had had my fill of Biff and his grandiose remembrance of things past and even grander vision of the future, I asked Natalie why she let him fill the kids' heads with all that bullshit. "He doesn't like to be contradicted," she said, and pressed her fist against her jaw.

[7] Biff explained Natalie's most recent suicide attempt: The family had gone to Social Services and was given an emergency check just for the asking, then and there, with no fuss, no bother. Natalie went into shock and overdosed on pills in the ladies' room.

[*] KIM: *The most tragic case I witnessed was Marjorie's newborn son taken from her in the hospital and given over to a foster family. Marjorie was told she had to get her own place in order to have her baby back. She did so in short order, but the foster family had become attached to the little boy and petitioned to adopt him. The social workers tried to intimidate Marjorie, tried to make her feel guilty by telling her how much the foster family could "offer" her son, and when that didn't stop Marjorie from fighting for her child, they even threatened to institutionalize her. The system has ruined her life, and it has torn a child from a mother who loves him more than anything else in this world.*

relationships were those in which both mother and (grown) daughter were in the shelter together.[8] As one might guess, these situations were not commonplace, and only exceptionally did they seem to involve ordinary people in temporarily straitened circumstances.

Ciserine, her mother, and her daughter—35, 55, and 18, respectively—seemed to be ordinary people. They had lived together since the daughter was born. They lost their rented house when it was sold out from under them with almost no notice and they moved into the shelter. The three of them were inseparable, spending their early days in the shelter waiting for county approval of their request for housing assistance. When that came through, they spent their days looking for a two- or three-bedroom apartment and a landlord who would accept black tenants with a housing voucher from the county.

In the shelter, they ate together and slept next to one another and did one another's hair. On Christmas Day they oohed and ahhed at the presents they received from the shelter and from one another. On Valentine's Day, they gave one another cards and gifts. They delighted in one another's company, but they also welcomed the conversation and fellowship of the other women. Ciserine was the principal spokeswoman for the family. She and her daughter were vivacious and were well liked by the other women, but the three of them were so close that they seemed to relate to the other women as a single entity.

One of the most intense relationships was between Leona and her daughter Rima. Their relationship was not at all obvious in the way of Ciserine and her family, but so real was it that one could almost touch Leona's struggle to hold on to Rima as she gradually slipped away into her own private world. Rima was desperately in need of help but Leona, however great her love, could not give it to her.

---

[8]The Refuge and Bridge House did not accept anyone under 18. New Beginnings, with a capacity of only nine women, did occasionally accept a mother with small children.

Leona was 64. Innocent, delicately beautiful Rima was 24 but looked more like 14 or 15. Both Leona and Rima were very small and both were shy, even timid. They kept pretty much to themselves, both in the shelter and out, but both were easily approachable and responsive to others' overtures. Gradually, however, as the weeks and months wore on, Rima withdrew into herself and began to spend her days alone. It was like witnessing the progressive destructiveness of homelessness in real time, in real life.

Puzzled and scared, Leona watched helplessly from a distance as Rima began hearing voices and acting in ever stranger ways in obedience to the daily commands she was receiving from God ("Do not take any showers, Do not step on any lines, Do not . . ."). From day to day, Leona and Rima talked less and less to one another, and one day they stopped talking altogether.[9]

As Rima deteriorated, Leona and the shelter staff became alarmed. Leona had the telephone numbers of her two older, married daughters. One lived in a town about 20 miles away, the other on a farm in New Jersey, with her own family and her father, Leona's husband. After many three-way telephone calls, it was decided that Rima would live on the farm with her sister, father, and sister's family, and she would also get therapy.

The night before her New Jersey sister was to pick her up, Leona helped Rima pack her things. After dinner, about eight o'clock, Rima lay down on her cot, eyes closed. Leona crouched on the floor beside her, silently stroking her hair. At ten o'clock the lights were turned off, but Leona seemed not to notice.

Other mother-child relationships were conducted at a distance but were nonetheless intense. Several young women in their 20s, most of them bright and competent and most of them black, had one or more children living with their mothers or

---

[9] One evening Leona asked me to engage Rima in conversation and try to learn where she had gotten $100. I learned that an anonymous volunteer had slipped the money into Rima's lunch bag.

other relatives in the Washington metropolitan area. Their determination to remain mothers pulled them into a close working relationship with whatever family members were caring for their children. Most of these women were never-married, divorced, or separated, and were working and saving with the aim of getting a place to live and taking back their children. A few were trying to do this entirely on their own efforts, but most were waiting to come to the top of the list for housing assistance.

The women saw their children regularly and continued to take some financial and parental responsibility for them, though they may have been two or more hours away by bus and subway. Sometimes, the women themselves or a relative might bring the children to the shelter for a brief visit. Lisa typified this group of women, as when she took a day off from work because she had to pick up her 10-year-old daughter at her mother's house in Southeast D.C. and take her to the hospital for some tests. In her attachment to her daughter, Lisa saw herself following in her mother's footsteps. In a discussion with other women about mothers, Lisa talked about how hard it had been for her own mother to "turn loose" her children. Laughing, she recalled the first time she moved out on her own. "I told her goodbye," she said, "and before I was settled in my own place, my mother was there too."

Ties to children were almost the sole concern for those married women whose families were in the process of breaking up. Together with their homeless husbands, the women struggled mightily to keep their families together. These women were more likely to be new to their situation, more likely to be in a state of crisis, more likely to be in a women's shelter as a last resort and only until they worked out a next step, often a matter of days. The children, meanwhile, were in the care of one or another family member.

Ronald drops his wife, Stella, off at the shelter. She is tall, thin, dark, and speaks with that roundness of speech that seems to characterize many deaf or hard-of-hearing people.

Ronald stays at the overflow shelter for men. Their two children live with his sister in New Carrolton. It's been two weeks since they've seen their children and Stella despairs of the likelihood they will ever be together again. But she and Ronald keep working, keep hoping...

Priscilla is 28 and married. Her two children live with her mother in Alexandria, Virginia. Her husband stays at the Bethesda Shelter for Men. He got a job last week as a stock clerk for Toys R Us in Upton. Priscilla works at McDonald's. She and her husband are "living for the day" when they can be together with their children in their own place.

Sometimes, women fight alone. Dressed in jeans and a leather jacket, Yvette looked much too young to have two daughters aged 16 and 12. Yvette spent her first night in the shelter in the smoking area, smoking and sobbing. A staff person asked if she wanted anything. "No," she said, "I just miss my kids."

Yvette and Tommy, her husband of eight years, had been divorced but got together again in Fort Lauderdale. They came to the Washington area and moved in with his sister in Wheaton, Maryland. Yvette found a job in Virginia. But Tommy left her again, and Yvette didn't get along with her sister-in-law, so she moved out, too, and that's when she came to the shelter. She returned to Wheaton from Virginia every day after work to visit her children. Yvette sustained this expensive and lengthy interstate trip from work to children to shelter for about a week. Then she left, presumably because she had made other and better arrangements.

Grown children often gave emotional support to their homeless mothers but never, to my knowledge, any significant financial or other material support, at least not while their mothers were homeless. Nevertheless, these children played powerful parts in their mothers' emotional lives, although it is not clear that the relationships were always reciprocal. Kathleen had two grown daughters, both in their 20s. One lived in Baltimore, the other in a very nice apartment development only a couple of

miles from the shelter. On Saturdays, Kathleen would sometimes meet her local daughter for lunch. Then they might go
shopping or to the daughter's apartment where Kathleen would
luxuriate in the tub for most of the afternoon, shampooing her
shoulder-length platinum hair "three times." Kathleen took
great pleasure from these easy Saturday afternoons with her
daughter. At those times, she said, the two of them were more
like sisters or good friends than mother and daughter.

Kathleen was late for the surprise birthday gala of punch and
hot dogs arranged for her at No Name shelter because her
daughter had taken her out to dinner for her birthday. And
when Kathleen was suddenly hospitalized for "a depressive
episode," it was her daughter who came to the shelter to report
what had happened to Kathleen and to take her belongings to
her. Months later, out of the hospital and settled in a halfway
house, Kathleen talked proudly about her daughters. "They're
both rooting for me," she said. "I couldn't make it without their
support."[10]

Kathleen appeared to be very grateful for very little. Both
daughters seemed in a position to do a lot more than root for
her. Kathleen herself had been a devoted mother and looked
back on the days of driving the children to school, to the pedi-
atrician, to dancing class, or to a shopping mall as the happiest
days of her life.

In my car one day, Kathleen was reminiscing about her own
childhood and her foster parents. "You know," she said, "my

---

[10]Kathleen had been ready for discharge less than two weeks after entering the hospital, but the doctor would not release her to return to a shelter.
With no place to live, she remained in the hospital for four months until a vacancy opened up in a halfway house.

An aside: While Kathleen was in the hospital, she told me she had just been
elected president of her ward. I congratulated her. She raised her arm in a Nazi
salute. "President of a ward for the insane today! Tomorrow, the world!" I
laughed with her and looked for a Pollyanna-like comment. It's always nice to
be thought well of by one's associates, whatever the setting, I said. (My God,
did I really say that?) She conceded that she was pleased, sort of, but noted
she was elected only because she had no enemies.

sister and I, we were never really adopted. We were 'wards of the state.' I never really knew what that meant. Sounds like something out of a Gothic novel. Imagine belonging to 'the state'! What the hell is that? How can you belong to something so big and vague? Can you come home to the state? Can it hold you and make you feel safe?" And she laughed dryly at the futility of trying to anthropomorphize the state into a living, loving parent.[11]

Regina's son was an engineering student at a university about a four-hour bus ride from the shelter. He was raised mainly by his father, but he and Regina exchanged Christmas and birthday cards. When Regina first came to the shelter and it was her turn to talk about her children, she proudly explained that her son always complained that he could never come to visit her because she never had a place of her own—always a live-in housemaid or companion in someone else's home. From now on, things would be different. When she got settled in with her next job and her own place, she'd have him visit her and they'd write to one another, too.

At Thanksgiving, Regina received an invitation from her son to come to the school and have Thanksgiving dinner with him. "I had a lovely time," she reported on her return. In June 1987, she received a formal invitation to her son's graduation. An accompanying letter from her son noted that his father and his fiancée were going to be there, that it was going to be a hectic day, and why didn't she come down a day or two after graduation when the two of them could have more time together? Regina was touched by his thoughtfulness and shared the letter with everyone who would look at it.

---

[11] Very early in Kathleen's attempt to put her life history on tape, she said her second foster mother used to tell her and her sister that they were responsible for the death of their parents (killed in an automobile accident when the sisters were both under three years old). She said it took her a long time to realize she was not responsible for her parents' death in any way at all. Before she could finish talking about her childhood, she broke down sobbing, and we called off the taping.

Hester would have been much better off had she had a more distant relationship with her son and cared less about him. Hester was born and raised in Montana. She was a sweet-looking, round-faced, gray-haired women in her mid-60s. She and Agnes were having a long talk about cabbages and kings. When the subject turned to family, Hester went to her locker and returned with a large, unmounted color photograph of her nine-year-old towheaded grandson. The child lived in Montana with his mother, Hester's daughter-in-law, who kept Hester posted on his achievements and sent her pictures. Hester's son Dwight, the boy's father, was a sometime auto mechanic who lived in the Adams-Morgan section of D.C. He and his friends "do drugs and that's their whole life."

"How old is he?" asked Agnes.

"He's 29," said Hester. "They're all 29. Twenty-eight or 29. And by the time they're 32, they're dead or in jail or they're straightened out." Hester continued with a tone of resignation. She had been trying to get Dwight into a drug treatment program, but he said he'd tried that and was not ready to try again. Because of the drugs, she said, they couldn't live together, and she even had to stop visiting him at his apartment because she was afraid of his friends who were always lying around.

Grace tried to be a mother-at-a-distance, and maintained an almost daily connection with her 15-year-old son Andrew, being careful not to let him know she was living in a shelter. She had four daughters in addition to Andrew. The three older daughters had grown away from Grace and her rigid, fundamentalist code of behavior, and two of them had married out of the area. Although Grace still carried pictures of them, she had only indirect communication with them through the two younger children still at home. Grace was living in the shelter when the third daughter got married. Grace was not invited to the wedding. The daughter had moved in with her fiancé before her marriage and Grace made no attempt to mask her disapproval. Grace did not know why she was not invited to the wedding.

GRACE's heart was with Andrew and daughter Eunice who were still "living in my house." She telephoned them often and often offered to take them to a Sunday lunch and an afternoon movie. Midweek, Grace frequently called the house when Andrew came home from school and before his father got home, and she and Andrew would have long talks on the telephone. Eunice, who was approaching graduation from high school, had long been dating and drinking and Grace felt a growing estrangement between them. Neither Andrew nor Eunice nor any other members of her family knew that Grace was homeless and living in a shelter.[*]

One of the most striking aspects of family relationships was the fact that very distant relationships or the ghosts of former relationships were often as active and salient in the emotional lives of the women as their real-life counterparts might have been. In this sense, even those women who claimed no family relationships might have been deeply involved with one or another family member. These family "ghosts" appeared most prominently in relationships between mother and child.

Eva, in her 50s, had two grown sons, a fact she mentioned somewhat casually one evening. Over the next several months, she never mentioned them again, and I wondered whether she thought about them as she walked the streets during the day or before she fell asleep at night. Did she miss them? Worry about them? Or was it "out of sight, out of mind"? The answer came unexpectedly months later when some volunteers organized an "arts" evening. Eva was one of six women who agreed to participate. She offered to read a poem she had written for her eldest son, whom she hadn't seen in six years. She wrote it for him on his last (32nd) birthday. Eva took a pile of $3'' \times 5''$ cards from her purse, cleared her throat, and read aloud a long, nonrhyming poem about the sun and moon and Indian names for the constellations.

---

[*] GRACE: *Sometimes God has a plan for your life, something you need to learn. I did not know that my spiritual education would include my five children who had to live in pain also. I thought the lessons were for me to learn and change, but I found out that it included the children as well. That was not by my choice.*

All of us applauded and asked for more. Eva offered to read another poem she had just written for her younger son, who lived in Chattanooga, Tennessee. "He's homeless," she added, by way of introduction. "He has a job, but he's homeless." She shuffled her cards and read again.

> Moonlight, starlight, candlelight—
> Wish I had a home.
> I'd like an electric lamp at night
> Even go all the way to Rome.
>
> I'd travel almost anywhere
> If someone thought I ought;
> For I'm a man who likes to share
> And I would like a closet for the clothes
> I bought.
>
> I'm just a guy who wants a bed
> A quiet evening once or twice;
> Give me a fluffy pillow for my head
> Oh! Wouldn't that be nice![12]

Surely Eva's sons—out of sight for years—were an important part of her emotional life, and just as surely, she received aid and comfort from thinking about them.

It is less certain that Queen was comforted by thoughts about her dead son, but he occupied an important part of her mental life as a homeless woman. Queen said she had been married three times. The men she married claimed to be men, she said, but they were just children wanting a momma who would take care of them. Queen seemed to have taken these failed marriages in stride. Much more difficult to handle was the death— the suicide—of her 28-year-old son. She almost always carried a book with her, *How to Deal with the Death of a Child.*

I pointed to the book. "Do you have to deal with that?" I asked her, soon after we first met.

"Oh, yes," she said. "I miss my son. They say he killed himself."

---

[12]Copied from Eva's 3″ × 5″ cards. Line length and punctuation as in original.

"How old was he?"

"Twenty-eight," she said. "I don't know, but that's what they tell me, he's 28. My mother doesn't believe in reincarnation, but who knows how old anybody really is?"

Queen was almost always open and outgoing, often sitting in a chair next to her cot, doing her nails or sewing on a sheet as she chatted casually with the women around her, effortlessly dominating the conversation. But once in a while a storm would gather in Queen's face and she would sew ferociously, oblivious to everything except her own thoughts. One could only wonder what these thoughts might be.

• • •

The women's relationships with their parents were dramatically less benign than those with their children. Relationships with parents tended to be bad or nonexistent. Some of the most intense ongoing relationships with parents were those of women who had been officially labeled retarded or learning disabled and were recipients of SSI (Supplemental Security Income), probably because their presumed dependence and vulnerability evoked a special parental concern, even if this was not always evident to the child. Sometimes, however, it seemed as if, from the perspective of the women, the only issue between themselves and their parents had to do with money and power. What often appeared to an observer as evidence of parental concerns or fears was sometimes seen by the homeless "child" as a malicious attempt at control or outright greed.

Ginger, who was 24 and retarded, was pretty and looked younger than her years. Her father came to the day shelter several times, usually leaving some money for her. At least once he called the night shelter just to make sure she was all right. When Ginger telephoned him one day and ended the call with deep sobs, he came the same afternoon, during the workday, and met with her at the day shelter.

Almost weekly, however, Ginger announced that she was going to sue his ass for her $400 monthly SSI payment. On one such
occasion, I said it looked to me as if he loved her very much. If
he loved me, she said, would he let me live on the street? Her father, suspicious of her boyfriend and not wanting to trust Ginger
with the $400 in a lump sum, chose to dole it out in smaller
amounts. Ginger was especially angered at the thought that her
father might be spending some of her money on his wife. Ginger
thought her stepmother was OK, even liked her, but she felt her
father had betrayed her dead mother and herself by remarrying.

Bonnie was also retarded and in her mid-20s. She claimed to
hate her father, mainly because he hated her, she said. Her SSI
check, which went to her father, was for her living expenses, she
explained, but he kept the money even though he had kicked her
out of the house. When Bonnie complained to Social Services,
her father told the authorities that Bonnie was in and out of the
house, that he gave her whatever money was coming to her, that
she was his daughter and he loved her, that his home was her
home and she was welcome to come and stay.

Bonnie sneered as she recounted this one evening at the soup
kitchen, while friends of hers cheered her on and filled in the
gaps. This was early in Bonnie's self-declared emancipation. As
she settled into shelter living over the next two years, her relationship with her father was defined almost entirely by their tug-
of-war over money.

For 22-year-old Judy, the SSI issue worked the other way
around. Judy was in regular, sometimes weekly, contact with
her parents, who lived in an adjacent county, about 20 miles
away.[13] Judy, too, had a running battle with her parents, not

---

[13] Their brick bungalow was in a neat, working-class neighborhood. Tables
in the center of the small living room and dining room were given over to the
display of a variety of Amway products. Amway sales and organizational
charts shared the wall space with family pictures—many of them of a young
man in army uniform—and a copy of the United States Constitution and other
patriotic memorabilia. Miniature U.S. and Israeli flags were prominent.

over money but over her refusal to be more of the daughter they wanted her to be. Her parents would sometimes meet her in the parking lot when she left the shelter in the morning. They might then drive to a cafeteria to eat and talk or—to Judy's annoyance—simply sit in the car. The talk was almost always the same, said Judy. They wanted her to come home, but always with conditions—that she agree to give up Abigail and other shelter associates, that she lose 100 pounds, that she look for a job or work alongside her salesman father, accompanying him on his rounds, and that she give up her (imagined) love affair with Kent, a rock/gospel singer.

For Judy, any one of these conditions was unacceptable (although she would very much have liked to weigh 100 or even 150 pounds less), so her parents persisted with their pleading and cajoling, and Judy persisted with her naysaying. Sometimes her father would become exasperated and say he did not want to see her again until she had a job and a place to live. Sometimes Judy's mother would report hearing about a job opportunity that sounded "just perfect" for Judy. Once her mother found an ad for a school bus aide and, on the spot, Judy was forced to develop a disabling condition that prevented her from applying for the job.

Sometimes Judy moved to the attack, denouncing her father for conspiring with her therapist and telling the therapist what to say to her. One evening Judy charged into the shelter, fit to be tied, she said, because she had just discovered that her most recent psychiatric evaluation would probably have qualified her for SSI, but her father had withheld the results from her in the hope she would get a job instead.

On at least two occasions Judy's father brought food for the women in the shelter, and he sometimes drove Judy to or from the hospital emergency room for one or another of her ailments. When one of Elsie's Amway friends backed out of an agreement to come to the shelter and give the women a demonstration on cosmetics and personal grooming, Judy asked her father if he could give them the same demonstration, and he agreed to do so. (The event was canceled by shelter management, however.)

Clearly, Judy's parents were deeply concerned about her. For her part, Judy denied that her parents really cared about her, sometimes claiming that they were only her adoptive parents anyway, and sometimes claiming that her father—"he's not my real father, of course"—had sexually abused her or had wanted to. But as with her imagined love affair with Kent, it was difficult to shake the feeling that, even as she spoke, she herself did not believe what she was saying.[14]

Beverly was also in her early 20s and learning disabled. She and Judy remembered one another from the special school they had attended as children. Beverly was very pretty and had a soft lisp that somehow added to her appeal. She had a warm and easy relationship with her father, a tall, thin, distinguished-looking man in his late 40s. Her parents had long been divorced and her father, who worked for a supermarket, lived alone in a garden apartment development about a 20-minute bus ride from the shelter. Beverly had a key to his efficiency apartment and used it freely. When she was job hunting, she often spent the day there, making telephone calls and arranging job interviews while her father was at work. In bad weather and on very cold days, Beverly would go there to stay warm and comfortable and watch TV. Sometimes she remained there until her father returned from work and they would have dinner together before she left for the shelter.

There was a quiet confidence about Beverly, perhaps because she knew Daddy was always nearby and ready to help in any way he could. When Beverly told her father that Suzy, one of the women in the shelter, needed a winter coat, he bought Beverly a new coat so she could give her present one to Suzy.

---

[14]Subsequently, when she had long been out of the shelter, Judy conceded that her parents were her real parents, that they loved her, and that her assertions about sexual abuse and Kent were imagined. See Appendix A.

And when Beverly announced that she had gotten a part-time evening job bussing dishes at a downtown cafeteria and was to report to work tomorrow, Kathleen asked her how she would get there. Oh, she said, waving the question aside, she would meet her father and he would drive her there. He always drove her to anything new, she said—a new school, a new job, anything like that.

In stark contrast was Beverly's relationship with her mother. She hated her mother for "snatching" Beverly's baby at birth to raise as her own. Her mother also got a permanent injunction forbidding her to come near the house or the child, now four years old.

As one might expect, some of the strongest feelings and worst relationships with parents were experienced by those younger women who traced their situations to being forced out of the house by one or both parents or who had chosen homelessness and shelter life over intolerable conditions at home. [*]

Delores knew why she had to live in a shelter. It was because of her "lying, thieving, conniving parents," and she had nothing at all to do with them. But bad feelings were just as likely to result in a bad relationship as in no relationship at all. Nineteen-year-old Cheryl announced she had just come back from Philadelphia.

"Why Philadelphia?" asked Bonnie.

"Because that's where the sonofabitch lives."

"What sonofabitch?"

"My father. He always kicks me out when he gets boozed up. I went up there to get the money he owes me."

"Did you work for him?"

"No. He owes me my child support payments."

---

[*] GRACE: *One thing that did strike me as I began to make friends with the homeless women—all their backgrounds pointed to some form of abuse in their lives as children. Does an abused child grow up to be an abused adult? Does that pattern stay hidden in the secret places of the mind, where as an adult, we seek out unforeseen abusive partners, telling ourselves we deserve this kind of treatment because we were bad children and deserved to be punished for the rest of our lives? Can God really heal the minds of abused adults?*

Ranji needed to get her green card and some other things from her parents' home, about a 30-minute bus ride from the shelter. She had left there about a month before, mainly because her parents, recent immigrants from Pakistan, insisted on treating her like a child, she said, even though she was 26. Ranji asked me to call the house and ask her father if she could come home and pick up her things. I called, and the father, in an apologetic tone, said he didn't know, that Ranji would have to speak to her mother about coming to the house. I gave Ranji the message. "Forget it," she said.

In some instances, it appeared that the parents wished their daughters well, may even have been willing to help them on request (if they didn't make a habit of it), but preferred that they remain at a distance, refusing to allow the daughter to enter the parental home, even for a drink of water. It was as if allowing this now-grown, on-her-own woman into the house would make her a child-daughter again, and make them her parents, with all the responsibilities such a relationship entails. Or more simply, perhaps this was just the parents' way of saying, "You go your way, we'll go ours."

Sophia was 27. Darkly beautiful and obviously bright, she was homeless and addicted to drugs and alcohol. Two weeks ago she had been beaten senseless in the Adams-Morgan section of D.C. but had no recollection of who had done this or why. Discharged from the hospital, she called her mother, who said she could come to the house—but not *in* the house—to pick up a canvas carryall and some other things she had stored there. Sophia said she cared deeply about her parents and they cared about her, but they just wouldn't let her in the house.[15]

So was it with Wanda, not yet 20 years old. Wanda had just given her newborn baby up for adoption and was going to leave the Washington area to live with a friend in South Carolina. Her

---

[15]Sophia says both her parents are alcoholic. Her father, a successful businessman, comes home at five and starts drinking "until he's wasted." Her mother goes on periodic binges. Their parental advice to her and her sister was always: "Don't drink. Don't do drugs." Her sister is married and straight.

mother had promised her $150 toward the bus fare. June went
with Wanda to pick up the money. When they rang the bell,
Wanda's mother came out and they all sat in the mother's new
car in front of the house. Wanda's mother talked at length about
her recent vacation travels.

The day was hot and humid. Wanda asked if she could have
a drink of water. The mother went into the air-conditioned
house and returned with a pitcher of ice water. After another
few minutes of casual conversation, she gave Wanda the money
and Wanda and June left. At the day shelter, June was almost
tongue-tied with anger as she recounted the story, shocked that
this woman, this "mother," would give her daughter $150 to
leave the area but would not let her into the house, not even for
a drink of water.

On at least one occasion, parental rejection led directly to
tragedy. Bland, skinny, pimply-faced Velma had been badly
beaten by her pimp near the downtown D.C. shelter where she
had been staying. When she was released from the hospital, the
police brought her to The Refuge, presumably for her own protection. At The Refuge, she was "adopted" as a daughter into
Natalie's family, but after a couple of months she and Natalie
had a falling-out over Velma's relationship with Natalie's son
Rick. Velma had nowhere to turn. She called her parents in
Texas. Through her tears, she told several of us what happened.
She asked if she could come home. No, you can't come home,
her father told her. Not now, not ever.

Velma left the shelter. It was rumored she had returned to her
pimp. Less than a month later, the *Washington Post* reported
that Velma had been found dead in an alley. She had been
beaten to death. She was 25 years old.

Donna was more fortunate. However reluctantly, her mother
was prepared to open her door when Donna turned to her as a
last resort. Donna had become homeless after being evicted
from a halfway house for the mentally ill. She was in her mid-20s
and did not or could not hide the hate she seemed to feel for

everyone around her. Donna was periodically evicted from one or the other shelter, usually for violence or threats. Evicted, she would disappear for days or weeks, then suddenly turn up again.

One evening she was again evicted from No Name shelter. She must have gone to her mother's home that night because the next morning her mother called the shelter and demanded to know what right the shelter had to evict her daughter! (The irony was not lost on the shelter staff nor on the homeless women.) That evening, mother and daughter came to the shelter to pick up Donna's things. Wordlessly, they loaded a suitcase and a plastic bag into the back of an old car and drove off.

DeeDee's mother was long dead but she remained, as she had been in life, DeeDee's most constant companion. Almost anything served to remind DeeDee of her mother as comforter and mentor. One morning I drove DeeDee and Louise to a Metro station (they were not together). In the car DeeDee was still ruminating about last night's dinner table discussion at the shelter. She launched into a speech that she was to give many times in one form or another:

"These young people today, they talk about love but they don't know what love is. They've never had the love I've had. My mother really loved me. She saw to it that I always had a clean place to live, and she took care of me all the time and explained things to me. She really loved me, but my life has been shit since she died."

"When was that?"

"Fifteen years ago."

"How about your father?"

"That hateful old fart? [Pause] My brother, he's a hateful old fart, too, just like my father. . . . My father blamed my mother for the way I was."

"You mean, for the way she raised you?"

"No! For the way I was when I was born!"[16]

---

[16]Dwarf-like and retarded. See page 18.

Of course, not all relationships between homeless women and their parents were such intense or passionate affairs. At least, every woman did not go around announcing that she loved or hated her mother or father. Sometimes, however, the striking absence of affect or a studied indifference to the death of a parent was itself suspect, and sometimes understatements or denials seemed to proclaim their own falseness.

Grace almost never mentioned her father except on the day she learned of his death, and then it was only to say to Kim and some others, almost in passing, that her father had died the other day. About a month later, she said she was going to Pennsylvania to visit her mother, who was living in a subsidized project for the elderly. She hadn't seen her mother since her father died, she said, as if all this were an onerous obligation. That she made the trip at all is perhaps more significant than that she did so reluctantly.

It was also difficult to accept Betty's expressed feelings about her mother at face value. One afternoon at the day shelter, Betty received a telephone call from her sister saying that their mother was in the hospital, in a coma. Betty turned away from the telephone to ask the world at large, "What the hell do they want me to do?" She said her sister never called her when any decisions were to be made or for anything else. Her sister always knew what was best or right and didn't need any help from anyone, thank you, so what the hell were they calling her for now? She had no money to get to the hospital, and anyway she didn't even know how to get there.

I offered to drive her there the next day, Sunday, and we agreed to meet at the gazebo in the square in the morning. But the next day was gray and cold, and Betty said she wasn't feeling well and could we put it off till Monday? That afternoon, at the day shelter, Betty's sister called again to say their mother had died. No date had been set for the funeral because there was to be an autopsy. Betty was upset to learn about the autopsy and took several minutes to denounce it, without once saying anything directly about the fact that her mother had just died. Over the next several days there was no further word about the funeral. Betty let it all pass in silence.

• • •

Ongoing husband–wife relationships were highly variable. Most marital relationships were in the past. Many of the homeless them had nothing to do with their former husbands.* There were exceptions. A few had impersonal, intermittent connections to their ex-husbands. Bridget, in her late 50s, had been divorced 14 years earlier. The courts awarded her $300 a month alimony, but her divorce settlement made no provisions for cost-of-living increases and she had long been unable to get by on the $300. She had been trying to get her husband to increase the alimony without success.[17]

Some women, like Winnie, came or were brought to the shelter to escape further beatings from their husbands.[18] Some, like Dulcie, came because their husbands abandoned them. In an oft-told tale, Dulcie blamed her homelessness on that goddamn husband of hers who had just left her after 29 years of marriage. She said he was a real momma's boy before they were married,

---

*GRACE: *There is little I can say here about homeless women as wives. I lived an abused life as a married woman. I nearly lost my mind. To remember is to relive all the pain.*

[17] Bridget was severely diabetic, incontinent, and too fat to get into her cot or out of it without assistance. She had to be diapered with Pampers each evening, but these could not contain her urine output, which left the insides of her legs burned raw and puddles on the floor. Clearly, she needed more help than The Refuge could give her. A week or so later, Rachel called Adult Protective Services and they took Bridget into their care.

[18] Winnie had been sent to The Refuge from a D.C. shelter to get her away from her abusive, drug-addicted husband. They had been married nine years, and both had been addicts, but Winnie had now been drug-free two years, she said. She could have quit long ago but he wouldn't let her quit. He used to beat the shit out of her and frequently threw her out of their apartment, forcing her to live in the basement storage room with their young sons. Winnie was hospitalized several times, sometimes for the beatings, sometimes for the depression that went along with the beatings and everything else.

with no friends and no family to speak of. Then he met Dulcie and her family, and when he saw how close they were, he wanted to be part of that closeness himself. So he and Dulcie married and had two children, but his mother never really let go of him nor he of her. When his father died, his mother, newly alone, reached out to recall her son and that sonofabitch left Dulcie to go crawling back to Momma at the age of 54! Fifty-four![19]

Della, who was "almost 30," also blamed her husband for her homeless state because he forced her to choose between a lifetime in jail and being homeless. They had been married almost three years when they had a fight and he ordered her out of the house. She thought about getting a kitchen knife and letting him stay there forever. If she had not kept her head, she said, it would have taken four cemeteries to hold all the pieces of his body.

With those and a few other exceptions, talk about husbands and marital relationships tended to be more general than talk about children or parents, perhaps because these severed ties were painful or no longer relevant to their lives, "water under the bridge" or "spilt milk." But general comments or casual observations about husbands or marriage were commonplace. These tended to be wry and derisive and to evoke responses in kind, as in "My husband was a chronic alcoholic," "Tell me about it," or "Men have it easier than women," or "If it wasn't for a man, I wouldn't be here," or "I was married for *fif*teen, *too* long, *god*damn years," or "Women go around looking for a man they can depend on, but they stopped making men like that 50 years ago."

At any given time, however, a handful of women were always engaged in a steady, ongoing struggle to stay together with their

---

[19] After he left, Dulcie lived with some neighbors until she used up her welcome because of her terrible single-minded anger (according to a staff volunteer who knew the neighbors). For the same reason, she periodically exhausted her welcome at all the local shelters, too, and slept in her red station wagon when no shelter would have her.

husbands. Like the Priscillas and Stellas and their husbands and children, they are more accurately seen as homeless families or homeless couples than as homeless individuals. Sylvia, a black woman in her middle 20s, was one of them. During her months at The Refuge, her husband stayed at the men's shelter. Both worked during the day and spent their evenings together, sometimes taking a motel room on weekends.

Millie was in her late 20s. She and her husband were saving their money to return to her hometown on the west coast. Her husband, who worked as a carpet installer, picked Millie up after work and they spent their evenings together. At night, he dropped her off at the shelter before returning to the Karpet King parking lot, where he parked his 1974 Dodge Dart and went to sleep for the night.

Other homeless couples were more clearly drifting, more clearly lacking the wherewithal to change their situation or even the desire to do so. There were Mavis and Buster, sleeping alternately in their car or their respective shelters, using the car mainly to drive from shelter to soup kitchen to shelter, and forever cadging gas money for their ancient Cadillac, which may have gotten six miles to the gallon. Mavis was in her 30s and Buster, who looked like an alcoholic, was probably 10 years older. Mavis usually wore jeans and a black leather jacket studded with metal stars and bars. She also whined a lot.

Mavis's mother lived in a neighboring town but wouldn't let her near the house if Buster was with her. Mavis and Buster seemed accepting of shelters and soup kitchens as a way of life. Neither of them was noticeably bright and they seemed to have no plans or even aspirations for a different future.[20]

Then there were competent Melissa and incompetent John, both in their late 20s. They had been married a little more than

---

[20] If they had such plans, I would not have known it. I saw them at the soup kitchen and the shelters over a period of years. We were friendly, said "hi" and whatever else needed to be said, but I never got to know either of them well.

a year and Melissa was very pregnant. Melissa slept at The Refuge and John slept in their jalopy in the church parking lot, using blankets Melissa brought him from the shelter.

"The only way for me and John to make it," said Melissa, "is to hold on tight to one another." So they held on tight to one another and spent all their waking hours together, but to no avail. When Melissa was about to deliver her baby, they went to Pennsylvania, fearing (correctly) that local authorities would not let them keep the baby because they were homeless. Shortly after the baby was born (his middle name was Elliot), the state of Pennsylvania took the baby (for "failure to thrive," explained Melissa), and Melissa and John went their separate ways.

Gloria was a black woman in her middle 30s. She had a clerical job in Cleveland, and when the opportunity came for a promotion with transfer to the Washington area, she took it with the reluctant blessing of her (much older) husband. After two months in Washington, the girlfriend with whom she shared an apartment moved out to get married. Gloria, unable to find a suitable roommate and unable to carry the apartment on her own despite financial assistance from her husband, moved to the shelter. Her husband wanted her to come home and that was what she wanted too. She was expecting a retransfer back to her old job to come through by the time The Refuge closed at the end of the month.

Denise's relationship with her husband was more complex—very brief stays at "home" (a week or less) alternating with much longer periods of hospitalization and homelessness. Denise was in her early 30s, tall, thin, blonde, sometimes pretty, often depressed. She kept very much to herself, slept a lot, and almost always appeared to be heavily medicated. Denise had been in and out of the state mental hospital, spending most of her "out" time in shelters. But once a month or so, usually after she received her SSI check, her husband allowed her to bring some money for their child and remain in the house for a few days.

Sometimes one catches only a glimpse of a husband-wife relationship, but it may be enough to help one imagine what the relationship may have been like over time. In some such cases, one may even be seeing women in the process if not the very moment of becoming homeless.

Annabel has been in and out of mental hospitals. She is a short, chunky white woman, about 40, and wears exceptionally thick glasses. She says she is a manic depressive and has been in the hospital 10 times, each time for a month or so. She and her husband—"He'll be here soon"—are in the process of getting a divorce. They decided on that last week, and that's when he brought her here to the shelter. They love one another, she said, but he's a workaholic and she is "sort of in his way."

Later this evening, her husband comes to the shelter. He looks like Annabel. He takes some money out of his pocket and counts it. "Twelve dollars," he says. "Here's six. Will that hold you until I get paid?" Annabel says it will and thanks him. They kiss goodbye, hands at their sides, each bent forward slightly so their protruding lips might touch. As her husband leaves the shelter, Annabel bites her lip and waves goodbye to his back.

It was late at night and bitter cold. Two policemen brought Vivian to The Refuge. She was drunk and had just been evicted from the "transitional housing" where she had been staying with her husband. She was a tall, well-dressed woman in her early 40s, and she carried an expensive-looking suitcase. As she settled in, she was horrified to learn that she would have to leave the shelter at 7:00 A.M., to be "on the street" with the other homeless women.

In the morning, Vivian was allowed to telephone her husband. "Don, get your ass over here and get me out of this place," she said. Then, incredulously, "You don't really expect me to go out on the street, do you?"

Don must have said something about having to go to work because Vivian then demanded to know if his job was more important than his wife. There was a long pause as she listened to his response. Suddenly, her whole body sagged and all fight was gone. She was stunned and scared. A staff person gave her $2. Betty offered to show her the cafeteria and the library. Bewildered, she allowed Betty to lead her down the stairs and onto the street.

• • •

Despite the great range and variety of family relationships, some things are clear. Homeless women are mainly from working-class and lower-class families that can no longer support them or from families whose members can no longer live together as husband and wife or parent and child. The weakest one (wife, mother, daughter) gets pushed out.

Many homeless women maintain significant contacts with family members ("family" here almost always means first-degree relatives—parents, children, siblings—and sometimes husbands). Overall, however, it appears that family relationships are almost as likely to be sources of pain and rejection as pleasure and support. (Dorothy had two grown children in Delaware and a brother in Michigan. "Delaware wants me to go to Michigan and Michigan wants me to go to Delaware.") Sometimes there is little overt affect: the family member is simply an occasional emergency resource.

Because the families of homeless women are generally poor and not in a position to offer significant and regular material assistance, the most consequential relationships are those built on emotional support. It is mainly the mothers among homeless women who fight most fiercely to maintain their family connections, especially the younger women with young children. Against impossible odds, many of them attempt to function as mothers-at-a-distance and sometimes as wives as well, working for the day when they can close the gap.

In sharp contrast, relationships with parents are often unsatisfying, even destructive, and here the younger women fight to break away. Anger and resentment appear to be the basic stuff of these relationships; power, control, and sometimes money are the major issues.

With some important exceptions, relationships with husbands are only memories, usually unpleasant ones and not, perhaps, any longer of great significance.

Finally, in the family relationships of homeless women, there is certainly more than meets the eye. Sometimes, even if the women never or seldom see some of their kin, alive or dead, they still derive emotional support from their remembered relationships with them. Sometimes a working relationship is present, just under the surface, but neither party will invoke it and give it life so long as the woman is homeless. Jeanette, for example, had several relatives who, she felt, would have been happy to take her in or otherwise assist her out of homelessness. But Jeanette was embarrassed by her situation and could not bring herself to impose on them, not even to let them know she was homeless lest they press her to accept assistance. Shirley found it too difficult and too painful to petition her children for assistance, not after she had spent years teaching them the importance of being self-reliant and independent. (However, she did once ask an obliging niece for help—money to pay for her storage locker—and got it.)

For different reasons but with the same outcome, Sara avoided her family. She could have gone back to her mother in New York or her maternal aunt in D.C. at any time, she said, but she was determined to show them she could make it on her own. When Jeanette and Sara got places of their own, they were once again free to take their places as family members.[21]

[21] Hopper and co-authors report a variation of this non-use of available resources that I never detected: putting social network resources in the bank, so to speak. "The reservoir of material aid contained in one's social network [is] less an asset than . . . a strategic good to be deployed in what may be complex and delicately titrated ways . . . Thus, what is observed as an immediate 'lack' of housing may on occasion be an artifact of a decision to reserve a privileged resource for later use." Kim Hopper, Ezra Susser, and Susan Conover, "Economies of Makeshift: Deindustrialization and Homelessness in New York City," *Urban Anthropology* 14, no. 1–3 (1985), p. 215.

Conversely, there are certain families that contribute importantly to making women homeless, and having done so, the families then want nothing to do with them precisely because they
are homeless.[22] Later, if the women escape from homelessness,
they are surprised to find that they are no longer pariahs and
at least some family members are prepared to restore relations.[23] Grace was not only surprised at the invitation to rejoin
part of her family, she was angry as well. "I was the same person when I was homeless," she said. "I haven't changed. It's only
my situation that's changed. I have my own place and possessions now. That's the only difference.[24]

Clearly, Grace's experience is by no means unusual; just as
some women are homeless because their families can no longer
support them, other women have little or no family support because they are homeless. Some of the families break off relationships with the women because they are ashamed of them,
because they can no longer support them, or because they feel
guilty for failing to do so. The result is that homelessness can
cause the loss of family support as well as be caused by it.

Crucially, in either case, this estrangement may be a sometime thing. If the homeless woman, by whatever means,
manages to get a place of her own, both parties are once again
free to mend or restore the earlier connection. Many poor and
working-class families would probably be willing to provide
monetary assistance and emotional support after the fact of
homelessness just as they were before the fact. They just can't
do it all by themselves.

Who is there to share this burden? Private sector volunteers?
The social service agencies?

---

[22] One night in the smoking area, Eleanor complained that "a lot of homeless people don't know how to accept responsibility." "Neither do their relatives," said Louise.

[23] See Appendix A for the restoration of several family relationships once
the women (Betty, Grace, Sara, and others) were no longer homeless.

[24] But that is a major difference. Family members were probably not only
embarrassed by Grace's homelessness but afraid she would make too great a
demand on them.

4

The Servers and the Served

S ome shelters are terrible places, some are not so terrible, and some are as nice as one can reasonably expect a shelter to be. Location, size, facilities, amenities, and layout all contribute to the quality of life and personality of any given shelter, but these can easily be overridden by the people who staff the shelter and the philosophy that defines their jobs and shapes their relationship to their homeless clients.

Irrespective of staff and shelter philosophy, however, and even under the best of circumstances, there is a coarseness, a rudeness, even a brutishness to life in shelters and on the street. This brutishness has its roots in the conditions of homelessness, but sometimes it appears to have rubbed off onto some of the homeless persons themselves, and sometimes people seem to have brought this brutishness with them. Whatever its source, this appearance of brutishness serves as a marker of social class and contributes importantly to the widespread presumption of a readiness to violence among the homeless.

Fear of violence, however, is only one of many salient features of homelessness produced by the differences in class, status, and power between homeless people and the people designated to serve them. The servers may be physically afraid of the homeless person, who may fear, in turn, that the server will withhold essential goods and services; the server may express contempt or disgust for the homeless person, and the homeless may be afraid of becoming an object of contempt or disgust. Between servers and the served there is often patronization and obsequiousness and much else, including, sometimes, respect, compassion, and even love. Whatever the content of the relationship, however, its structure is essentially vertical, strongly conditioned by the differences in social class, power, and status.

Fear in all its forms stands out. It seems to take the shape of a giant circle of mutuality: the shelter staff and other providers are afraid of the homeless and the homeless are afraid of the staff; the citizen on the street, the merchant, the householder, and whole communities fear the homeless, and the homeless fear the non-homeless citizens. And to complete the circle, the homeless are afraid of the homeless. Thus, everyone is afraid of the homeless, including the homeless themselves, and what is so terrible and intractable about this situation is that everyone is right to be afraid.

The effects of fear are profound.[1] No one can remain fearful all the time, but one senses an almost ever-present anxiety or tension among homeless persons and those around them, as if a referee has cautioned each one, "Protect yourself at all times." So is it in all the ghettos of our society, our inner cities as well as shelters and soup kitchens and other cul-de-sacs that poor people have been pushed into. In many such places, the state—through failure of strength or will—has retreated from its con-

---

[1] "Fear and anxiety are as significant in ordering human affairs as are sex and subsistence." Constance Perin, "A Biology of Meaning and Conduct," p. 97.

tractual obligation to protect its citizens and secure their lives and property. It is not Hobbes's state-of-nature war of every person against every other, but there is no mistaking the fear and the relative dearth of trust and civility that set the public worlds of the dependent poor apart from others.

. . .

Wherever one turns, one sees evidence of the ways fear and mistrust routinely pervert the operation of institutions designed to help homeless persons. In the soup kitchen, unable to locate a shelter vacancy, I offer $3 to a big, powerful-looking man of 50 or so to go to CCNV (Community for Creative Non-Violence) in downtown D.C.

"Keep your money," he said. "I'm safer on the street." He went on to say that there are a 1,000 people a night at the CCNV shelter, but only 500 of them are homeless; the other 500 are there to prey on the homeless.[2] He pointed to the mud on his shoes. "If I go down there like this, with mud on my shoes, I'll get mugged."

"What's the connection?"

"If you've got mud on your shoes," he said, "they'll think you've done a day's work." (That is, you have a laborer's day's pay in your pocket.)

. . .

The building that housed The Refuge on the top floor contained classrooms on the floors below. Parents of the children who attended nursery and day programs in these classrooms protested the presence of the shelter, saying they were afraid for the physical safety and mental well-being of their children. The fact that the women had to be out of the building and the immediate area by 7:00 A.M. and could not return before 7:00 P.M.

---

[2]"[CCNV] is a place fit for vermin and trash." Mitch Snyder, founder and director of CCNV, quoted in Dorothy Wickenden, "Abandoned Americans," *New Republic*, March 18, 1985, p. 19. This comment was made before the renovation of the CCNV shelter and before it came under its present management after Snyder's suicide in the summer of 1990.

was not sufficient to allay their fears, and parents threatened to pull their children out of school. Despite the threatened loss of much-needed income, the church refused to close the shelter and some 20 percent of the children were pulled out of the school.

• • •

Sometimes, reasonable community fears of the homeless clash with the equally reasonable needs of the homeless to produce a bizarre outcome. In 1984, the federal government agreed to turn over to Montgomery County, Maryland, an underutilized Walter Reed hospital research facility for use as an emergency shelter for homeless men. Neighborhood residents resisted fiercely. After several months of negotiation, a compromise was reached. The community would accept the shelter so long as the men would not be permitted to walk in the neighborhood. And so it was: in the evening, a bus collected the men at a soup kitchen about four miles away and drove the men to the shelter. At 7:00 in the morning, it collected the men at the shelter and drove them back to the town center.[3]

• • •

In general, there appears to be more fear of violence than is warranted by the actual violence. But in a world where violence is a fact of life, it is difficult to say how fearful one ought to be. Women are somewhat less fearful of violence than men.[4] Nevertheless, the fear of violence was sometimes an overriding concern among the homeless women and those who dealt with them.

I had not seen Marjorie for a couple of months when I met her on the street. I asked her where she was staying and she pointed

---

[3]Now that is "bussing." And if, for any reason, one of the men decided to leave the shelter in the middle of the night, the agreement called for shelter staff to pay for a taxicab for this purpose. Thus, in addition to the bussing, men were sometimes taxied in and taxied out of the shelter, thereby leaving the neighborhood unstained.

[4]Although homeless men appear to be most fearful of other homeless men, beatings by shelter "security" workers or staff are by no means unknown. The fear of such abuse is often sufficient to keep men from going to particular shelters, however great their need.

to a nearby building still under construction. "Why aren't you in a shelter?" I asked. "Why aren't you in The Refuge?" She said she had had an argument with Maxine and Maxine threatened to kill her, so she left.

"Don't let Maxine push you out," I said. "You go back there and tell the staff what happened and demand protection."

Marjorie smiled wryly. "Sure," she said, "and maybe they'll kick her out for threatening me. Then she'd really kill me. Thanks, but no thanks. I'll stay where I am."[5]

Queen, who had been in St. Elizabeth's (D.C.'s mental hospital), in shelters, and on the street, also preferred the street on occasion. There are a lot of crazy people in shelters and on the street, she said. The street is safer because you can run away from crazy people on the street.

Fearful of violence, many shelter providers use elaborate "intake" mechanisms—three-, four-, or five-page questionnaires, face-to-face interviews—to screen out potential "troublemakers." Many shelters also keep card files on each client, recording dates of attendance and behavior history. Others seem to use unnecessarily long questionnaires salted with irrelevant questions to test for docility of the would-be shelter occupant.[6] Blacklisting is common.

---

[5]Some women forced to leave a shelter for one reason or another may move on to a shelter in downtown D.C. or another city. Others seek out one of the two other shelters in the area. Failing to gain entry in either of them, they may, like Marjorie, nevertheless choose to remain in the area, even if this means living on the street. Many women waited out two-day, three-day, or even week-long shelter suspensions on nearby streets. Phyllis and Louise spent months there. These are the women for whom this area always was or had become their home territory. Here is where their roots were, however shallow they may have been.

[6]At one of the men's shelters, in addition to asking fairly standard demographic questions, the staff also asked first-timers their mother's maiden name and place of birth, and many other questions whose relevance to the request for a place to sleep for the night was not immediately apparent. I asked the staff person why he needed all this information. Was it for research purposes? He said he didn't know, he just knew he had orders to get it. He thought maybe it was to see if the guy was going to be cooperative or give them a hard time.

Given the conditions of shelter life, there was less violence in the women's shelters than one might have expected. The occasional incident, however, was sufficient to generate a level of fear that often colored the dealings between staff and women. As a group, shelter staff, paid and volunteer, were more fearful of violence than the homeless women themselves. Connie, for example, was a paid staff person in her 40s, conscientious, with some professional training and on the job for more than a year. Connie said she wasn't sure she was doing a good job with the women, and she was fearful that the pressure and stress would build as the weather worsened.

"Are you afraid of the women?" I asked.

"Yes," she said. "Sometimes I can't go to sleep at night because I'm afraid that one of them will attack me."

Although the staff were somewhat reassured by their power and authority, that same power was itself, perhaps, a source of their uneasiness and fear. Whether volunteer or paid, it was the staff who made and enforced the rules. All legitimate power was in their hands, sanctioned by the threat of eviction or arrest. In a confrontation that went by the rules, the staff were the certain winners. The women—powerless in law and fact—had no appeal regardless of how arbitrary or unjust the decision might appear to be.[*] The frustration and helplessness produced by such an unequal relationship would seem to encourage an occasional outburst of violence. In any event, at staff meetings, it was not uncommon to hear people confess that they were afraid to enforce the rules if it meant a direct, one-on-one confrontation with one of the women.

· · ·

---

[*] DIRECTOR: *There were few rules at The Refuge, but it was the expectation of the management that those few rules would be followed. A basic parenting concept, be fair and be consistent, was employed with the intention of creating a safe and secure environment. The few rules that existed were a promise that everyone, staff and guest alike, would be safe. No one would become prey. Just fair rules, applied fairly; the issue of having power and not having power never entered the mind of The Refuge management.*

The staff, then, were often fearful because the possibilities of violence were very real, because the logic of the women's powerlessness seemed to allow for it, and because the staff shared the assumption that homeless people are inclined toward violence because they are lower class and because some of them are mentally ill.[7] In fact, the women were almost never violent with staff, although there was occasional verbal abuse and an even more occasional raised fist. No doubt the impulse to strike back for what was perceived as unfair or undeserved treatment was inhibited by the power of staff to order peremptory suspension or eviction from the shelter.

Indeed, some of the more fearful, less competent staff were extraordinarily quick to suspend or evict the women. Virginia refused to move her storage box? Call the police to evict her. ("Elliot, would you stay here until the police come? I'm afraid of Virginia.") Elsie, in an argument with Patty, throws Patty's blouse on the floor and refuses to pick it up? One week's suspension. Terry is locked out for the night because she went out onto the porch for a smoke, thereby violating the rule that once in the shelter, one may not leave and return the same night. For the same reason, Grace and Elsie are denied permission to go down to the parking lot to start their cars and charge their weak batteries.[*] Jane (4'10", delicate), arrives with the

---

[7] In addition, some of the black women seemed to inspire greater fear among both black and white staff because they were black. In part, this fear probably reflects the powerful association most of us make between being black and being lower class, and in part it reflects the related and probably derivative belief that blacks are more violent than others. For the record, however, I did not hear anyone discuss this issue head on, with the possible exception of one black woman who objected to another woman's readiness for violence as "that nigger (excuse the expression) showing her nature."

[*] GRACE: *What I got from him [the volunteer who refused her permission to charge her battery] was an attitude of dominance over these women. It made him feel good to be lord over all these ladies. He had a great time walking around the room looking important. I had to get that car towed the next day. It cost me a good portion of my week's salary. . . . When you live in a shelter, other people control your life. They tell you when you may come in and when you must go out. They tell you when you can take your shower and when you can wash your clothing. Control, control.*

smell of alcohol on her breath (not against the rules) and tries to push through the door after she's refused entry? Out for a week. Louise complains about Phyllis's snoring, wants her bed moved, the discussion escalates, Louise is ordered to leave, refuses, and the police arrive to charge her with trespassing and take her out in handcuffs. The week before, Kim "jumped all over Louise" and is evicted permanently ("We can't have violence here, can we?") *

What is so striking about these particular incidents is the way some of the staff leaped to suspension/eviction as the proximate rather than the ultimate sanction. Here, too, fear played a decisive role. Because staff were often afraid to engage the women one-on-one on the issue at hand, there was little room for negotiation or compromise, or for graduated penalties that attempted to fit the punishment to the crime.

The rate of suspensions/evictions was dramatically lower at The Refuge than at Bridge House—perhaps in a ratio of 1:3 or even 1:5. Since the women served by the two shelters were much alike and sometimes identical, often shuttling back and forth, the difference probably lay in the shelters rather than in the women.[8]

The greatest difference between the two shelters flowed from the way they defined their roles with respect to the homeless women. The rules at The Refuge were few and mainly limited to what one must not do—carry a weapon, use abusive language, bring drugs or alcohol into the shelter, and so on. There was nothing that one must do. Everything not forbidden was allowed, thereby maximizing personal freedom. The women were allowed to be themselves. The Refuge let Betty be Betty.

---

* GRACE: *I was appalled that many situations were handled in such a chaotic manner. I remember another blond young girl who was put out in the middle of the night. We found out later that she had been raped while walking down a dark road to find another shelter.* [E.L.'s note: After this event, expulsions after dark did not take effect until the following evening.]

[8] In April 1985, when The Refuge closed for the season, 12 women transferred from The Refuge to Bridge House, which did not yet have a permanent home, nor indeed a name. In the month of March, two of these women experienced suspensions at The Refuge. In April, the same group of women experienced 11 suspensions at Bridge House.

At orientations for volunteers, Rachel, director of The Refuge, repeatedly emphasized that the staff are not professionals. "We are not therapists or job counselors or social workers of any kind. We are not here to change the women. We are here to offer them a safe, warm place to sleep at night."[9]

At Bridge House, in contrast, the staff saw themselves as professionals whose job it was to change the women, to help them out of homelessness. They took detailed personal histories, held regular weekly meetings where the women were expected to talk out their problems, developed individual goals for the women in the form of personal contracts (in accordance with the prevailing theories of behavior modification), and held individual evaluation/compliance meetings with the women as needed. For the homeless clients, remaining in the shelter was more or less conditional on fulfilling the terms of one's contract.

Inevitably, this determination to force people to behave differently (for their own good) created many opportunities for conflict, most of them generated by pressure from the top to bring about change and counterpressure from the women on the bottom. This ideology of forced change required an authoritarianism that the staff, by training, experience, or personal need, were all too ready to deliver. The goal was to force change on Betty, here and now. To let Betty be Betty, to be herself, to do things on her own schedule, was to be complicitous in her dependency and failure.

There were, of course, sometimes similar impulses on the part of volunteers at The Refuge. But there the desire to change people, or the need to exercise power over others, was inhibited rather than encouraged by the prevailing laissez-faire philosophy.

• • •

Some volunteers had always been uncomfortable with letting the women "get away with murder." They argued that a periodic

---

[9]In fact, they offered much more: hot dinners, ready-made cereal breakfasts, take-out bag lunches, toiletries, sanitary napkins, underwear, nightwear, sometimes outer clothing, and always companionship.

show of force on general principles, like calling the police to evict Kim or Queen or Maxine—it didn't matter much which one—would "work a miracle" on everyone else. "It's important to stop this stuff [in this case, calling a staff member a "mother-fucker"] before it spreads."

Until the winter of 1989–90, this approach was clearly a minority viewpoint. As the numbers of women seeking shelter grew, however, the daily population at The Refuge climbed steadily to more than 30. The more crowded the shelter, of course, the more likely the flare-ups; problems among the women were commonly around issues of space and resources rather than more directly personal issues. Inevitably, then, the increase in population put an enormous strain on the facilities and threw the women into dangerously close proximity; their cots, for example, were now only inches apart. People increasingly bumped into one another physically and psychologically, and there was a noticeable increase in snarling, intimidation, and fear.

At a staff meeting in January 1990, the consensus seemed to be that this increase in hostility was a consequence of the overly permissive philosophy that had prevailed at The Refuge since its inception. Some staff people also thought that the growing proportion of black women was a major factor. The volunteers talked increasingly about the need to take back control of the shelter from the clients. "The inmates are running the asylum," said one. "We've got to come down hard, with both feet—the slightest infraction and 'You're out!'"

Others agreed and threatened to quit if there was not a general crackdown that made The Refuge, once again, a safe place for women and volunteers. They talked at first about the need to enforce the rules, but as they got into the spirit of the meeting, they talked about changing them: not making food available except at mealtime ("and no substitutions!"); not allowing the women to come inside before the official 7:00 P.M. opening, irrespective of the weather; denying entry to anyone arriving after 10:00 P.M. or with alcohol on her breath; and so on, with the tone sometimes more suggestive of vindictiveness than a search for effective control. Eventually, there was a voice of protest. "You all say you'll quit if we don't do those things. Well, I'll quit if we do. These are fragile women. They think—I think— we are here to foster their dignity. [If we adopt the proposed measures] we might as well be a psych unit with beepers and black boxes to monitor them."

This passionate speech turned the tide. It was agreed that something had to be done, that many women and staff persons no longer felt safe, but that stricter enforcement of the current rules—especially the injunction against verbal abuse—would probably restore the sense of safety and well-being that almost everyone had enjoyed until recently.

Among some of the staff, fear of "disrespect"—perhaps as loss of face, or perhaps as leading to loss of control—was the paramount concern. Phyllis, who was in her 70s and had been in the local shelter system for some five years, was widely respected by staff and women alike because of her steady, quiet dignity. At a shelter-wide meeting, the new director of Bridge House who had taken over the month before was trying to explain some of the changes she planned to introduce. Phyllis had a question and raised her hand. The director continued to talk. Phyllis shook her raised hand. When the director continued to ignore her, Phyllis moved her hand closer to the director's face. At that moment, the director evicted her peremptorily and permanently.

When Phyllis told me this the next day, I asked one of the staff about it. "I was there and saw it all," said the staff person. "Phyllis was wrong. She shook her finger in Marvella's face. She disrespected Marvella in front of all the other women."[10]

---

[10] It was February 1989, and bitter cold. Phyllis could no longer manage the steps at The Refuge and New Beginnings was full. For the next several nights, she slept on the stone tile floor in the lobby of the Executive Office Building, along with six or seven other persons. Physical safety was assured by a sympathetic night security officer.

Staff tolerance for verbal abuse and "disrespect" ranged widely, and even those with extraordinary tolerance were sometimes sorely tested, as when a new arrival at Bridge House got into a shouting match with pregnant, white staff member Jean and was ordered to leave the shelter. "You've got as much love in your belly as a son-of-bitchin' dog," she shouted, and advised Jean to get an abortion lest she pollute the whole world with whatever she was carrying if it were allowed to come to term. She then turned to Maria, a young, black staff person. "And I'm fuckin' tired of nigger lawyers, nigger gynecologists, and nigger staff people, too."

Jean and Maria watched her as the woman packed a small suitcase and marched out of the shelter. Several of us, black and white, witnessed the exchange and were embarrassed by it. Maria laughed uneasily and assured everyone that she was used to this and it didn't bother her in the least. It was difficult to accept this assurance at face value.

• • •

Staff came with many different attitudes. Some, both volunteers and paid staff, actively resented homeless people. To them, homeless persons had chosen to be where they were, and were too weak-minded, too lazy or crazy to better themselves. Freeloaders. Undeserving poor.[*]

A commonplace incident at the soup kitchen catches some of the character of this resentment and the casual way it compromises even the most ordinary and impersonal exchange. The night was exceptionally cold and some of the men complained that the soup was not hot. I picked up two bowls and carried them to the kitchen.

"The men say the soup is cold," I said to the woman volunteer who was ladling out the soup.

---

[*] KIM: *"It's your choice" is the all-time #1 favorite line of shelter staff. Over and over and over, we are told this. The shelters refuse to take responsibility for the consequences of rules they inflict upon us. Even Elliot has been guilty on occasion of saying, "It's your choice"—because he heard it so much?*

"I heard them," she said. "They didn't say it was cold. They said it wasn't hot. And it won't get any hotter. It just came off the stove."

I sought out the manager.

"The soup is cold," I said.

He made a face and said he had already been told that and was having it brought back for reheating. The assistant manager overheard us. "I don't know what they're complaining about," he said. "This ain't the Waldorf Astoria, and they're getting it for free."

Similarly, a dedicated volunteer at The Refuge harbored a hard-edged resentment against the same women whom she routinely served in a friendly and conscientious fashion. As she and I worked in the kitchen on one of my volunteer nights, we talked about how, as children, we were served dinner by our mothers on a take-it-or-leave-it basis. One of the women came back to the kitchen and said she really didn't like tonight's tuna casserole, and could she have something else? The pantry was uncharacteristically bare that evening and I gave her some peanut butter, jelly, and crackers. The volunteer shook her head in disapproval and spoke with great earnestness. "Those seven people who were killed last week [the *Challenger* astronauts]—they gave so much to the world, and they died giving more. But these people, they give nothing. All they do is take and take and ask for more."

That a serving of peanut butter and jelly could tap this much resentment is a measure of its depth. But this expression of resentment by a volunteer who was routinely courteous and considerate in her dealings with the women also points up the complexity and ambivalence of people's values and the complexity and ambivalence of their connection with overt behavior. There was not always a perfect match between what people felt, what they said, and what they did. Feelings of resentment and contempt, for example, did not usually play themselves out in simple ways. Some expressed these feelings only when the

women were out of sight, but struggled to suppress them in
their face-to-face dealings with the women.[*]

Others believed that homeless people are generally undeserving freeloaders except for the real-life women they had
come to know personally. For still others, whether or not they
believed the women to be deserving was not relevant to the
quality of service they were prepared to deliver. They had come
to do the work of the Lord, or simply to do good, although this
was not always easy.[11]

The result was that one sometimes saw extraordinary caring
and love on the part of staff. Routinely, there was more kindness, courtesy, and generosity shown to the homeless women

---

[*]KIM: *Usually, their disrespect for us took a more subtle form, but it was not
as well-contained as Elliot, or they themselves, may have thought. At The Refuge,
I ask Alison for a towel for my hair. I see her get it from the dirty clothes basket.
I confront her. "It's not dirty," she protests. "Someone was clean when they dried
themselves off with it." I overhear staff discussing the laundering of [incontinent]
Reba's bed linens; "We don't need to use detergent; we'll just run them through
the rinse cycle."*

GRACE: *Staff people did not treat everyone the same. If you acted like you "had
it together" so to speak, you were treated with a little respect. Not much, just a
little. If you had a job and worked regularly, I thought the attitude of the volunteers seemed more tolerant of you as a person. I always felt volunteers had a superior air about them.*

[11]Staff Note, Log, February 27, 1985:
Received a ration of crap (excuse my language) from Betty about getting
out of bed. As a volunteer, I need it. People turning on lights when they want,
complaining that they have a right to more than we are giving them. These
people need to be reminded this is a privilege and that some volunteers will
grow tired of their unnecessary complaining and the lack of respect that the
guests show toward each other.
We had a *very* difficult time having many "guests" through the night and
this morning complaining that we *owe* them more than a bed, food, shower,
laundry. Well, [my husband and I] work *4* jobs to *try* to provide these things
for our own family and this was more than we can give. Selma, a new girl did
laundry by accident (she is new, didn't know and apologized). End result no
towels done.
Please accept this job as the best we had to offer.

Respectfully,
Yours in Christ
The Varner Family

Author's note: The Varners had two small children, and Mrs. Varner had a
major illness. The family income was supplemented with food stamps.

by both paid staff and volunteers than one would have been led to expect by their privately expressed values.[*]

• • •

When we reverse perspective and look at how the women view the staff, there is a change in the order and content of focal concerns. Because the staff have so much power, the women tend not to see their fear or, seeing it, attribute it to more subtle psychological sources. Vicki, for example, sensed the anxiety and tentativeness in Connie and some of the other staff persons and understood it as fear, but only partly a fear of violence. She explained the nature of this fear to Louise and me. The staff, she said, were afraid that they themselves were not as far from being homeless as they would like to be.

"Staff people and volunteers are scared of us. They think they have a decent life because they are decent people, because they're clean and honest and hardworking. [To them,] homeless women are homeless because they're the opposite—dirty and dishonest and lazy. But most of us don't look like that, are not like that, and that really scares them. It's like a Hitchcock movie. What makes them so scary is that the people in them are so ordinary and look like everybody else."[†]

While the primary concern of staff was fear of violence, that of the women was suspension or eviction from the shelter. At

_____

[*]GRACE: *I did not see that much caring, kindness, or courtesy by paid staff or volunteers, as Elliot reports. I'm not saying it was not there, only the ones doing all the shouting and abusing out-did those who were there in sincerity to help and serve the homeless.*

DIRECTOR: *The volunteers worked at The Refuge for a myriad of reasons. Some worked at The Refuge as a natural extension of their faith; others worked because they were paying back God or society for having too much of everything; while others worked to fill lonely nights or to meet new friends. Our training was basic: treat these women as your overnight guests and be as gentle and honest as humanly possible. The door at The Refuge was opened with a glad heart. Every day offered a new opportunity to give and to receive, and on some days we succeeded.*

[†]KIM: *Until I read this enlightening chapter, it had not even crossed my mind that the staff feared violence from us. But I still believe, as Vicki said, that they felt most threatened by the fact that we are like them.*

Bridge House, suspensions and evictions were an ever-present reality; at The Refuge, they were an ever-present threat, but mainly to the craziest, most disruptive women, and sometimes to the more outspoken, more aggressive women as well. At New Beginnings, which tried to limit a woman's stay to three weeks, the threat was not so much of peremptory discipline as of simply having to go on the street when one's time was up.[12]

Most women at Bridge House "went along with the program." Elsie took it for granted that to live in a shelter was by definition to surrender one's autonomy. "I've never lived in a shelter before," she said. "I've always been my own boss."

On some occasions, going along with the program led to major entertainment. Peggy had just been released from the psychiatric ward of the county hospital where she had been confined for two weeks for trying (not very hard) to kill herself. As soon as she returned to the shelter, her contract was rewritten. The next evening, Peggy ate dinner at The Refuge and told her friends there about the new addition to her contract. "I had to promise not to try to kill myself for the next two weeks," she said. Hilarity ensued, and one of the women wet her pants before she could get to the restroom. Another demanded to know, "Now who's crazy?"

At Bridge House, the staff insisted on describing the shelter operation as "democratic" and "participative": "This is your shelter," and "We need you to tell us how we can make it a better shelter." The director and most of his staff believed what they said, but the women quickly learned not to take those assertions at face value, especially if there was any chance that their participation would be understood as critical or, worse, disrespectful of management.

---

[12]At New Beginnings, it seemed that extensions were given routinely to women who were trying to "improve" themselves but not to women who seemed unconcerned with self-betterment.

KIM: *[The director] ran the shelter with a free hand, displaying blatant favoritism toward selected individuals, giving them preferential treatment and special privileges. This type of flagrant discrimination illustrates why shelters desperately need monitoring and regulation from an outside agency.*

Before a regular Wednesday night all-shelter meeting at Bridge House, Cora asked a staff social worker if she could make some critical comments about the shelter. The social worker said of course, so Cora did. After the meeting, Cora said the social worker called her aside and told her she would be suspended for six days if she complained in public again. At another Wednesday night Bridge House meeting, when Louise's disagreement with the director, Jim, moved toward confrontation, Louise pulled back quickly. Later, she appealed to Grace and Jennifer. "I need a roof over my head," she said. "What could I do?" Grace and Jennifer nodded their understanding.[*]

Jim had called Betty into his office for a private conversation, but their rising voices soon carried through the closed door. Jim charged Betty with being disrespectful and Betty, not one to back down easily in any situation, denied it with equal vehemence. Jim quoted Betty as saying that he "didn't have his act together," and he wasn't going to stand for this kind of talk. Betty said she didn't say it; Jim insisted she did. As Jim grew angrier, Betty's denials grew weaker, and so it went until Betty capitulated. "I'm sorry," she said. Flushed with anger, Jim marched out of the office.

Grace had also been charged with being disrespectful by a staff social worker. She explained that she was having a private conversation with Kim a few minutes ago when the social worker insisted on interrupting them. Grace asked her to wait until she and Kim were through talking—the rules of courtesy apply to everyone equally, she said. She and Kim had rights and didn't forfeit them just because they were in a homeless shelter.

Later, Grace admitted she had better be more careful or she would be told to leave. Gretchen had already told her to get out if she didn't like it here—"Gretchen always says that to the women whenever they stand up to her," she said—and the social worker was not likely to let things rest.

Grace knew whereof she spoke. That same evening, she was called into the office for a private meeting with Jim, Gretchen,

---

[*]KIM: *From time to time, staff would challenge us for control, either inciting us to the point of suspension/eviction or suppressing us through fear of suspension/eviction.*

and the social worker. When I stuck my head in to say goodnight and saw the character of this meeting, I retreated quickly. Grace followed me out, distraught and crying hard. "You should hear the things they're saying to me!" she cried. "And if I try to say something, they threaten me and say I'll have to leave." I mumbled some nonsense in a tone of reassurance. When she regained her composure, she returned to the meeting.

The point is not that the women are right but that the power of staff, nakedly exposed in the threat or reality of suspension or eviction, is more than enough to prevent most of the women from defending themselves and their interests as they see them and feel them. The more intact the woman and the greater her personal integrity and pride, the more stifling and demeaning is her powerlessness. "I've got an interview at a D.C. shelter tomorrow," said Eileen, a bright, brash woman of 50 or so. "If I'm not docile and submissive, if I don't let them push me around, I won't get a damn thing from them."

Not all of the women submit all of the time, and some even go on the offensive. Educated by experience—even overeducated—some women are always ready to be offended by what they see as the gratuitous exercise of power, a suspicion that could, on occasion, transform an innocent if thoughtless comment into an intolerable offense.

Shirley and the others were preparing for bed. "Don't forget to wash up," said Gretchen.

Shirley exploded. "I'm 53 years old!" she shouted. "I have children older than you, and I don't need you to tell me to wash up before going to bed."

Having gotten started, Shirley couldn't stop. She denounced Gretchen and the shelter staff for purposely demeaning the women as part of their effort to control them, and continued along these lines until—perhaps to force them to prove her point—she was expelled for the night.

Shirley must have thought that she was properly protesting still another in a long line of patronizing assaults that diminished her self-respect and proclaimed her powerlessness. For years, frequent real assaults on her self-respect had conditioned her to expect more of them. It is not surprising, then, that on occasion she saw such assaults where perhaps none was intended. But an undertrained and harassed staff had no time for an historical or biographical perspective on the situation. They saw Shirley's outburst as clear evidence of her paranoia. Whatever they thought of her before, they knew now, for a certainty, that Shirley was crazy.

Thus, much of the behavior that the staff characterized as crazy was, from the women's point of view, perfectly reasonable. And sometimes staff behavior that the women saw as power-seeking and self-serving was in fact prompted by benign and generous intentions. For a certainty, Jim cared much more for the women and worked much harder on their behalf than they gave him credit for.

. . .

In sharp contrast to the great power the staff wielded over the women was their final inability to help the women meet their greatest needs.[13] In some instances, it is quite possible that the helping professional's sense of helplessness was no less sharp than the homeless woman's disappointment. Here, for example, is a summary of one woman's account of an interview with a social worker in a downtown D.C. shelter:

> I told the social worker that I was out of work; that I don't need food or used clothing; I don't need job training, job-seeking strategies, or tips on interviewing techniques or how to write a resume; I am registered with the state job service and several employment agencies, and I check the want ads in all the papers every day; I've checked out every place on the official list of resources and I'm not eligible for any of their programs.

"What I need," she concluded, "is cash money to buy me time. I need concrete job leads or actual referrals."

---

[13]When Jim asked for agenda suggestions for the next weekly meeting, Lisa said she wanted to talk about jobs and housing. Jim said there wasn't much point to that because those things were beyond the control of the staff.

The social worker shook her head. "It sounds as if you've already tried about everything."

"What do you, exactly, do? What resources *do* you have?"

The social worker's response, said the woman, was clear testimony to her uselessness: "Sometimes it helps just to *talk* about things . . ."

This same sense of helplessness may lead the would-be help provider to believe, almost in self-defense, that the homeless woman doesn't need her help. Tensions mounted as the deadline for the closing of The Refuge drew near. Yolanda was distraught as she enumerated her problems to Marianne, the social worker who had been visiting the day shelter once a week as part of an outreach program. "How am I going to get a place to live when I don't have a job? And I can't find a job because I don't have a place to live. The shelter closes March 31st. Where will I go? What happens to me then?"

There was a long pause. Marianne spoke slowly. "The answer, you'll find, is within *you.*"[*]

• • •

Nobelist and Poet Laureate Joseph Brodsky, when asked by Robert MacNeil why he preferred the United States to the Soviet Union: "The greatest thing a society can do to a citizen is leave him alone."[14] For the great majority of homeless women, the power of staff simply to ask questions about one's life and thoughts, along with the degree to which they exercised that power, was the single most important measure of the quality of a given shelter. Over and over, when the women compared shelters, The Refuge was almost always cited as among the very best. "They don't ask questions." "You have privacy there." "They leave you alone."

---

[*] Kɪᴍ: *I won't ever forget the horror of that moment, at the realization that all the time we'd spent talking to Marianne was wasted, that she didn't have any answer, not even a clue. And that perhaps there was no answer.*

[14]"The MacNeil-Lehrer NewsHour," November 10, 1988.

Indeed, in glaring contrast to the often elaborate screening procedures and intake interviews of most shelters, one could, as a stranger, knock on the door of The Refuge at 2:00 A.M. and have to answer only one question: Do you want something to eat before you go to bed? Similarly, one was typically left alone the next day and the next, for as long as one stayed there.

In large part, this was a function of The Refuge's self-declared amateurism and disavowal of any specific intent to help the women improve themselves by way of counseling, therapy, or other professional services.[15] Unlike the staff at most shelters, the people at The Refuge did not need to know much about the women's life histories or present circumstances in order to provide them with a safe, warm place to sleep and some hot food. Of course, sometimes a curious, concerned, or just plain nosy staff person (or anthropologist) might ask personal questions, but everyone knew that such practices had no institutional force behind them. Some women chose to reveal much about themselves; some chose to reveal nothing whatever. At The Refuge, the women knew it was their choice.[*]

In most respects, Bridge House was more professional, more determined, both by self-definition and county contract, to lift the women out of homelessness. So staff asked a lot of questions. When Bridge House hired an additional full-time social worker, the director introduced her to the women. He said they hadn't pried into the women's lives until now, but with the addition of another social worker to the staff, they were going to need to know much more about their backgrounds and their needs and goals in order to serve them better. Someone pointed out that the staff already had life-history information

[15]Until 1988, The Refuge got little or no support from the state or county and did not, therefore, in the name of accountability, have to administer questionnaires to document (by name, Social Security number, income, source of income, last address, etc.) the number and character of the women it was serving.

[*]DIRECTOR: *Minding our own business was a challenge. How could we tolerate the fact that Janice received Christmas packages at the shelter from her mother? Wasn't there room for Janice on the couch in her mother's house?*

on everybody there. The director shook his head. That information is too superficial for the job we want to do now, he said.

Some of the women rolled their eyes. June wished the staff would lower their sights and give the women some respite from their questions. "There's no privacy at Bridge House," she said. "You have your own room [with two or three others], but you're never left alone with your thoughts, never time to collect your thoughts or plan anything because staff is always probing. They're always asking questions. At The Refuge, everybody is in the same room, but you are left alone if you want to be alone."

In the past year, Denise had stayed in three downtown D.C. shelters before coming to The Refuge. The Refuge was by far the best, she said. "They really leave you alone if you want to be alone. No questions!"

Kathleen concurred. She was "amazed" at The Refuge, she said. "No questions! There's no place like it in the whole D.C. area."

Margaret said she had known a lot of shelters—crossed the country twice, staying in shelters along the way—and The Refuge was one of the best, mainly because they didn't pry and didn't attach conditions to their help. She wanted to keep her private life private, and at The Refuge she could do this.

Of course, it is not only shelter staff who ask questions. The question-and-answer paradigm is everywhere central to the relationship between the appointed guardians of those life-necessity set-asides for the poor and the poor themselves. Whether one is seeking food or food stamps, shelter, medical assistance, or any other form of public assistance, emergency or short-term, one must answer questions.

The questions are often repetitive, and sometimes they are the same questions one answered this morning, yesterday, or the day before. The questions often seem irrelevant to the substance of the transaction and thus appear gratuitously personal and embarrassing. To the petitioner, it is as if the wall of questions that stands between her and life's necessities is a hurdle to be scaled only by those willing to leave their pride and privacy behind them.

To Winnie, the questions were so distant from what she understood as her needs that she suspected they served only the prurient interests of the questioner. She voiced a common complaint about social workers and others who presented themselves as helping professionals. Winnie said she needed help in reapplying for SSI (she had been injured in an auto accident), help in getting to and from job interviews, and help in finding a place to live. But the social worker just wanted to talk, again, about her personal (sex and drug) life before she came to the shelter.

It is difficult to appreciate the intensity of feeling, the bone-deep resentment that many of the women felt at always having to answer questions, often very personal, and often the same ones, over and over again.[*] But having to answer questions was part of the price they paid for being powerless. Even for those women for whom much of ordinary reality had slipped away, the contempt and the resentment and the fear of questioning remained.

Angela and I were having breakfast at the Greezy Spoon and talking about life, liberty, and the pursuit of happiness. For Angela, questions were killers of liberty. "Everybody is always asking those fucking questions. That's all they do is ask questions. God said, 'Don't question me.' He doesn't like questions either. I can't stand those fucking questions. Like the time there was this big anthill and I made my brother come with me and crush the ants."

---

[*]GRACE: *I didn't mind personal questions. As far as I was concerned, my life was an open book. What I did mind was in the course of their asking questions, they then tried to judge me and proceeded to tell me what I did wrong since I now found myself homeless. There was this general consensus, that if you were homeless, you must have caused it to happen. I had paid staff and volunteers tell me what I needed to do, in their opinion, to get myself out of this situation. They told me that I needed to save money! When you are working and making next to nothing, there is no money to save.*

"What's the connection?"

"They make you do things you don't want to do. They force you, against your will, like I made my brother come with me and crush the ants, even though he didn't want to. . . . Like Daniel in the lion's den. Those fuckers in the government, they put him in the lion's den because he wouldn't answer their fuckin' questions. That was a bum rap. Those fuckers busted him for nothing at all. But his guardian angel opened the way out for him, and he just walked out, cool as he could be, leaving those fuckin' lions sitting there, wondering what happened."

At the soup kitchen, a woman I had not seen before sat opposite me. She was white, about 30, and disheveled. She said she had been living on the street since Christmas Day, when the CIA—which had been her longtime employer but was now convinced she was a double agent—ordered the Luther Place shelter in downtown D.C. to evict her. Last week, she said, she was sexually assaulted with a lead pipe in her vagina and another in her rectum.[16] I opened my mouth to commiserate and she raised her hand, palm out. "No, no questions, please. No personal questions. All information about me is classified, so no questions."

We sat there in silence for a moment. Then she said, quietly, "Both of my parents are dead, you know. They were killed by social workers and psychologists who tortured them to death with questions."

This dread of questioning gives rise to a range of problems. First, some questions are legitimate and even necessary. Clinical therapists need to ask personal questions in order to deliver therapy. Other providers may be obliged to ask personal questions for tracking purposes, or for documentation as required by a funding agent, or to tailor services to the needs of individual petitioners. In addition, asking personal questions can be a way for a staff person to demonstrate concern, a way of saying, "I care about you and I want to be your friend."

---

[16]A few years earlier, Washington, D.C. had been shocked by a gang rape/murder committed in this fashion.

Most of the women accept the fact that answering questions is part of the price they pay for needed services, but some women have been so long abused by questions that they have lost the ability to discriminate between those that are legitimate and those that are not. Their hostile or otherwise uncooperative responses to questions—even legitimate or honest ones—can sometimes lead to the loss of a needed service or relationship.

Other women choose not to play the game at all. Last night, Sara reported that Holly had been blacklisted because she never told the same story twice and had forfeited all credibility with shelter staff and other service providers. To the rebuffed service provider or would-be friend, these are simply more instances of people who cannot act in their own self-interest, more instances of behavior unconnected to reality, more instances of craziness among homeless women. There seems to be little awareness that the failure of some women to cooperate may be, at bottom, a prideful refusal to capitulate to what they see as an oppressive system, and therefore a kind of victory for them.

• • •

Given the power of staff and other providers to set the terms under which life-supporting goods and services will be doled out, it is not surprising that the world of shelters and social services takes on, from the homeless women's perspective, an abusive, authoritarian coloration.[17] There is a problem, however, in weighing the women's perceptions of authoritarian abuse against the reality. Enforcement of rules and procedures to ensure a minimum of safety and orderliness, together with the uniformity and depersonalization of group life, inevitably generates a steady current of institutionalized complaining about the institution itself and the people who run it. Even after allowing for this "noise," however, some real and much perceived abuse remains, though one should note that there is great variability among settings and individuals.

---

[17]There is something ironic, a little sad, and surely significant in the fact that most of the frontline persons who have so much power over homeless people are themselves relatively powerless in their dealings with others.

Grace was working one full-time and two part-time jobs when she told me that the social worker at Bridge House had just announced that the Wednesday evening meetings would be mandatory. She said there was no way she could get off her part-time job early enough to attend the meetings, and she was told she'd have to choose between the job and the shelter. I went to the social worker and asked her if the meetings really were mandatory.

"Of course not," she said. "They're only mandatory for Grace and Lisa because they work late. The others have nothing better to do."

Lisa did quit her job, saying she was getting ready to quit anyway. Grace chose to keep her job and to leave the shelter. In tears, she packed her belongings to move into her car. "I can't go on living here," she announced to the women around her. It was not only the mandatory meetings. It was the staff, she explained—their constant threats, their disrespect, their insistence on controlling everyone and everything. The women nodded in sympathy and understanding. "If I had a place to go . . ." said one of the bystanders and the women nodded again.

Shirley complained to the shelter director that "Jailer Jean" made everyone's life miserable by her constant threats to throw people out—"a sword of Damocles over our heads," she said—and that it was impossible to live under those conditions. Jailer Jean and other staff members had made life so oppressive in the shelter, she said, that she and Louise had gone to the county executive's office to register a formal complaint. When they took their complaints to the shelter director, he listened courteously, then referred them to another staff member who would "take care of it."

Other women traced what they experienced as authoritarian abuse to more deliberate policies and motives. At the day shelter one afternoon, some of the women were comparing shelters and one of the downtown shelters came up for evaluation. Sara said she spoke from firsthand knowledge. "They know what they're doing there. That's not a place to get help, that's a place where homeless people get taught a lesson, get discipline. I had to leave there because I didn't think I needed all that discipline. I was getting more than I could stand."

In the park one afternoon, Bernice stretched out on a bench and complained she was bored to death. Judy suggested they all go to the day shelter.

"I can't go there," said Bernice. "You have to go through three locked doors. Three! And then there's someone to write down when you come in and when you go out, and you can't go out for a smoke without someone else going along to unlock all those doors. Ugh! That's Auschwitz!"

It is relatively easy to find real or perceived abuse in the welfare, shelter, and other systems that poor people must engage with. The sources of abuse are many. Sometimes the individuals acting on behalf of these systems have a personal need to be harsh or abusive or are made so by the exigencies of the job or by uncooperative, exasperating clients. Sometimes agencies or systems operate with a philosophy of micro-management or an emphasis on discipline that the women experience as oppressive.

One important source of abuse lies much deeper, in a widespread theory about human behavior that gets expressed in various forms: as public policy, as a theoretical statement about rehabilitation, or simply as "common sense." Whatever the form, it boils down to something like this: We mustn't make things too easy for them (mental patients in state hospitals, welfare clients, homeless people, the dependent poor generally). That just encourages their dependency.[18]

---

[18]This proposition, as applied to shelters and homeless persons, has a long history. Kim Hopper cites "the newly-rediscovered phenomenon of 'shelterization'" and notes its earlier incarnations. "Once in the Progressive Era and again during the Great Depression, the same specter of ... shelter-generated dependency was raised. ... [Critics] railed against municipal lodging houses for habituating men to 'idleness and uncertainty,' rendering them virtually useless should the labor market need them again. ... For all the hand-wringing, however, lasting damage was never documented. In both decades, when the American war machine was cranked up, the ranks of skid row were depleted of all but the elderly and the severely disabled. Shelterized men had apparently no trouble returning to life as soldiers or factory hands." Kim Hopper, "Shelterized Syndrome Theory Has Dangerous Flaw," *New York Times*, June 5, 1990, p. A28.

The problem is not that this proposition is fundamentally wrong; as an abstract proposition, there may be some truth in it. In real life, however, it is difficult to know what is "too easy." Even skillful and well-intentioned attempts to find a balance often go too far toward the hardship end of the scale, thereby violating other and perhaps more important truths about human behavior, such as the law that if you treat a man like a dog, you mustn't be surprised if he barks and tries to bite you.

What makes this proposition about encouraging dependency especially pernicious, however, is that it lends itself so easily to the abuse of poor people. Armed with this theory of behavior, we are freer to deal harshly with them. "For their own good" we may set welfare payments at a level below what is needed to live on or refuse a person a second bowl of soup. "For their own good" it is all right to make them wait in lines for hours, harass them with questions, demand unavailable documentation or otherwise make them jump through hoops for one or another entitlement, treat them discourteously if not with outright contempt, withhold a service or product, "keep them on the move" with limits on the length of stay in a shelter, and so on.[*]

Thus, the fear of "making things too easy" gives respectability to meanness in public policy and legitimizes harshness on the front lines. It not only gives license to those who, for ideological or personal reasons, are predisposed to deal harshly with the dependent poor, but even more important, it contributes to a general downward spiral of concern in which otherwise well-intentioned workers and administrators are encouraged to tolerate or ignore the needless hardships or the system failures that so often attend the day-to-day operations of our support programs. Beginning with the proposition that

---

[*]KIM: *We on the street have long recognized that Social Services operates under the policy of "Don't make it too easy for them." A whole book could be devoted to Social Services horror stories! On "unavailable documentation": A county caseworker told me that before she could process my application I must bring in receipts from all the people I'd panhandled from so she could total my monthly income. But my personal all-time favorite is "Provide proof of no income."*

"you mustn't make things too easy for them," we end up with an array of support systems staffed by administrators, supervisors, and workers who sometimes forget why they are there, and who put organizational needs ahead of the needs of the people they are supposed to serve. Examples abound.

Louise had settled into a comfortable routine at Bridge House and seemed to be increasingly compliant and cooperative. The staff had long pressed her to apply for public assistance, but she had resisted fiercely. Given her obvious improvement, the staff felt that just a little bit more pressure could push her into action. Accordingly, Louise was given an ultimatum: unless you give us written evidence of your having applied for public assistance within 48 hours, you will not be permitted to remain in the shelter.

Louise went to social services to apply for public assistance. They told her she must first go to the state unemployment office (in another town) to get written certification that she was not eligible for unemployment compensation. Louise did as she was told, waited in line, and was rewarded with the certification. She returned to Social Services the next day, signed in, waited to be called, and was told that the social worker assigned to her was out sick, come back tomorrow. She returned the next day and waited in line. When her turn came, she was told her worker was still out sick, come back tomorrow. The next day she came again. Her worker was on vacation, she was told. Come back in three or four days.

Meanwhile, Louise's deadline at Bridge House had come and gone. To help her help herself, Louise was expelled from the shelter. The county police put her up for two nights in a motel, but now she was again on the street where she quickly reverted to her look and demeanor of the year before.

In the park, Louise told me about her recent experiences with Social Services. I called Social Services and was eventually put through to a supervisor. I told her what Louise had told me.

"Is it possible," I asked, "that that's what happened?"

"Oh, yes," she said.

"How come?"

She explained that every social worker carries the same size workload and that they can't transfer clients back and forth among the workers lest the workloads become unbalanced, with some workers being asked to do more than others.

"But Louise is now on the street," I told her.

"I'm sorry for that," she said with feeling, "but it's her own fault. All she had to do was say it's an emergency and I or any other supervisor would have been happy to help her."

• • •

It was the beginning of March. I had made an appointment for Vicki and me to see the man in charge of the Employment of the Handicapped program at the Alcohol, Drug Abuse, and Mental Health Administration. James Wilson was a tall, distinguished-looking man with an air of competence and an impressive social presence. Running the Employment for the Handicapped program was only one of his many duties. He invited us to sit down, and he and Vicki talked about her experience and background for several minutes. Mr. Wilson stood up. He said he thought Vicki would make a fine candidate for the program. Would she like to have her name on the list?

"How long is the list?" asked Vicki.

"There are 65 names in the computer," he said.

"How fast does the list move?" asked Vicki.

Mr. Wilson said he did not know. "No one has been placed yet."

"When did the program start?"

"Last July," he said.

• • •

Beverly filled out an application for medical assistance at Social Services. After several weeks, on July 9, she received a notice that her application had been approved and she was now eligible for 30 days of medical assistance ending July 7. I assured her this was an innocent system error.

Kim filled out an application for medical assistance at Social Services. After several weeks, she received a notice that her application had been approved and she was now eligible for 30 days of medical assistance ending the next day. Somewhat less confidently, I assured her this was an innocent system error.

When it happened a third time with Beverly's reapplication, I called Social Services and reached a supervisor. "Is it possible," I asked, "that people are receiving 30-day authorizations for medical assistance that end before they get the notice?"

"Oh, yes," she said.

"How come?" I said.

"Because we're short-handed," she said.[19]

"What should these people do?"

"They should reapply."

"What's to prevent the same thing from happening again?"

"They'll just have to take their chances," she said.

• • •

The board of directors of the day shelter at Mainline Church Two had contracted with the Bridge House management to staff the day shelter. Some 10–12 homeless women, all of them from The Refuge, New Beginnings, and Bridge House, would come daily, from 2:00 to 6:30, to rest, get warm (cool off), drink coffee and nibble at snack foods, to socialize, and sometimes to stretch out on the floor in front of the television set or in a corner of the lounge and take a nap.

The night staff at Bridge House—some of whom also served as staff at the day shelter—concluded that one reason the women were restless and troublesome at bedtime was that they were able to rest and sleep during the day at the day shelter. The staff therefore instituted and vigorously enforced a new

[19] This explains very little. My guess is that the authorizations are back-dated so that the understaffed workers can appear to be in compliance with the regulation that they respond to every application within 30 days.

rule: No sleeping at the day shelter! And to make certain that no one violated the rule inadvertently, stretching out or closing one's eyes was also strictly forbidden.

In less than a week, the two staff persons at the day shelter outnumbered the homeless women by two. Members of the board of directors began calling around to find out why the women had stopped coming to the shelter. When they learned why, they fired the staff. Soon thereafter, they decided to close the day shelter entirely.[20]

That we tolerate these system malfunctions can be understood in part as the end point of two streams of public thinking about the poor. One is that many poor people are not deserving of public support; the other is fear of giving them too much support and encouraging dependency.[21]

What appear from the outside to be system malfunctions, however, from the inside appear to be perfectly rational processes. Of course agency social workers should have equal workloads, and of course it is the administrator's job to see that they do; of course it takes time, maybe lots of time, to place handicapped workers, and handicapped applicants, if they really want a job, ought to be prepared to wait however long it takes; of course some applicants for medical assistance will receive expired authorizations if we do not have enough workers to process the applications; and why shouldn't homeless women be discouraged from sleeping during the day if allowing

---

[20]My brother-in-law, Stanley Hutt, is a light sleeper and imaginative problem solver. Tormented by birds singing at his bedroom window at the break of dawn, he opened the window and banged pots and pans together the night before, hoping to prevent the birds from sleeping at night so they would sleep late in the morning. This did not work either.

[21]From the perspective of many homeless women, there is no question about the cause of these malfunctions. When Melissa complained about how difficult it was to get something from Social Services, Betty said, "If you've got eyes and any sense at all, you'd know darn well they're doing this deliberately." "There is no way possible that they could be that inefficient by accident," said Kim.

them to do so makes the job of the night shelter staff even more difficult than it needs to be?

For many of the women, these system malfunctions were sufficiently frequent to render the support system unpredictable and reason enough to avoid it. To enter the system is to enter a world of uncertainty, where one may be treated with exquisite compassion one day and contempt the next; a world of hurry-up-and-wait, of double-binds and contradictions, where arbitrary and differential treatment, and myriad rules and regulations, triumph over the very purposes of the system itself.

Fortunately, these malfunctions, however common, are not the rule. Given their mandate, support systems probably function reasonably well, albeit minimally, most of the time. The main problem is that we do not know just what the real mandate is, or perhaps we have not yet decided what it ought to be. Underneath the formal charge to our public welfare system is a latent charge full of ambiguities and contradictions, and we should not be surprised to see them played out in the lives of the dependent poor. Nor should we be surprised that it is not always clear to the poor whose interests the system is designed to serve.[22]

---

[22] I have reread and rewritten this chapter many times, trying to find a right balance in the complex and often contradictory relationship between the women and the providers. I think this version is pretty close; if anything, more could have been said about the genuine caring, the patience, and the goodwill of providers, paid and volunteer, amateur and professional. In an important sense, they, too, especially (poorly) paid shelter workers and agency personnel, are victims of the same ambiguities and tight-fistedness of the same public policies that oppress the homeless women.

PART TWO

Making It:
Body and Soul

5

My Friends, My God, Myself

However hard it was, homelessness was bearable for most women, in part because human beings have an extraordinary capacity for bearing hardship. But homelessness was also bearable because the women had help in bearing it. Not surprisingly, support from people in the community was generally absent, mixed at best, and the women often had to deal with outright hostility from householders, pedestrians, transit riders, shopkeepers, and salespeople. In contrast, police, ministers, security guards, shelter staff, and agency personnel sometimes went out of their way to be helpful.

But this sort of help, however freely given, was small change when measured against the enormous and often existential problems faced by the women. Effortlessly, homelessness generates feelings of loneliness and despair. To deal with loneliness, the women turned to one another for friendship and for confirmation of their own humanity; they turned to God for hope and a sense of self-worth and to give their lives meaning; and they turned to themselves for the strength to keep going, day in and day out, even when, for the moment, their friends and their God failed them.

Not much help at all came from boyfriends and lovers. In general, sex without familiarity, without tenderness, without romance, had little appeal for the women. But sex with those things was difficult to come by, even for those who had lovers.

To look at her—middle-aged, hunched over, a bag in each hand pulling her hard against the ground—one would never guess that next week Peggy would try to kill herself because of unrequited love. In my car, on the way back to the shelter after two weeks in the psychiatric ward of County General Hospital, she explained what had happened. She had been with Charles, her boyfriend of eight years. She asked him to define love. Charles said that love was sitting in a big soft chair with your grandson in your lap, cooing and gurgling.

"No, I mean adult love," Peggy said.

"Married love?" asked Charles.

"Any kind of adult love," Peggy said.

"Whatever it is," said Charles, "you're not what I want in a woman."

So Peggy overdosed herself into unconsciousness and was admitted to County General.

Boyfriends and lovers on the whole were not important sources of either material or emotional support, although exceptions were dramatic and deserve to be noted. The most important exceptions were the handful of cases in which women and their husbands were still trying to cling to their marriages. In these cases, the husband, living in a nearby men's shelter or sometimes in an automobile, was family, friend, occasional lover, and the single most important all-around support for the wife. Husbands who, for whatever reason, did not share the fate of homelessness with their wives were rarely sought out by the women and were almost never helpful.

Ginger and Steven were another exception, perhaps the most spectacular. Steven was 28, bright, and good-looking; he worked as a window washer and lived in a men's shelter.[1] He and Ginger met at a soup kitchen and fell in love, and Steven became fiercely protective of her, as much a father, perhaps, as a lover. In the morning, before going to work, Steven would meet Ginger and arrange with one of her friends to have someone with her throughout the day. Nor would Steven let anyone—not any of the women, not Ginger herself or even her father—refer to her as retarded. "You have a learning disability," he assured her. "You are not retarded."

Ginger basked in the glow of Steven's love. When a full-length mirror was delivered to the shelter, she turned back and forth in front of it, her feet in place and her hands on her hips like a model. "Hey, look at that beautiful chick," she said. "Just look at that beautiful chick."[2]

Ginger and Steven slept mainly in their respective shelters. They slept together only on those few occasions when a friend or acquaintance lent them a room or apartment. Ginger wanted to know why they couldn't take a motel for the weekend more often, like some of the other women, but Steven resisted. Patiently, he reminded Ginger they were saving their money to get married and have a place of their own; going to motels would just stretch out the waiting time.

Like Ginger, several of the younger women in their teens and early 20s had boyfriends, usually from the local community. The boyfriends tended to be male counterparts of the young women—working-class and lower-class youths who lived in

---

[1] One often meets men and women whose appearance, carriage, and obvious competence stand in bewildering contrast to their homelessness. Over time, as one gets to know these persons, the mystery of their homelessness disappears. I did not get to know Steven well enough for that.

[2] The women laughed and some of them shook their heads at Ginger's immodesty. Ginger was 24 and in love. She had a good figure and a pretty face made even prettier by a radiant innocence that sometimes goes along with retardation. (Sorry, Steven.) She was, indeed, "a beautiful chick."

KIM: *Caution: I would not rely too much upon Elliot's description of a particular individual as "pretty" or "beautiful." For the record, the truly beautiful ones included me, Holly, Patty, and Angela.*

shelters or crashed for a week or two, first with this friend, then with that. Occasionally, they were somewhat more stable young men with rooms of their own and steady jobs as supermarket baggers or stock clerks, or laborers in a local lumberyard.

Unlike Ginger's, however, their relationships tended to be short-term liaisons in which neither participant seemed to make a heavy investment. It is difficult to know how much support the young women drew from these short-lived affairs. Certainly there was some sex, some fun, some bragging rights back in the shelter, and perhaps a rise in status. And certainly, for the most part, these affairs made life more bearable, not so much by helping the women deal with their problems as by diverting them from the general grimness of homelessness, while at the same time confirming their femininity and sex appeal.

Unfortunately, the young women sometimes paid a high price for these diversions. Terry got pregnant from her liaison with Natalie's 17-year-old son Rick, who was staying with his father at the men's shelter during this period. Terry had been "adopted" into Natalie's family and called Natalie "Mom," but when Natalie and Rick both denied that Rick was the father, Terry was estranged from the whole family and she and Natalie avoided one another in the shelter and elsewhere. Toward the end of her pregnancy, Terry signed an agreement with Catholic Charities to put her baby up for adoption.[3] When Natalie learned of this, she acknowledged Rick's paternity and begged Terry not to give away her grandchild. Terry refused, and they were still estranged when Terry left the shelter shortly after the baby was born.

Patty's pregnancy was less traumatic. Patty had had a very casual relationship with a delivery truck driver who was based in

---

[3]The agreement called for Catholic Charities and the adoptive parents to pay all hospital and other medical expenses associated with the birth of the child. In the hospital, Terry decided to leave the naming of the baby to the parents-to-be. To the dismay of the nurses, she refused to see the baby for the first three days, afraid, she said, of becoming too attached to the child to carry out her part of the bargain. On day four, Terry relented. The separation and adoption went smoothly.

another city and whose deliveries brought him to the shelter neighborhood only a couple of times a month. Patty seemed to be far less perturbed by her pregnancy than Elsie and the other women around her thought she ought to be. The truck driver was a married man with a family and he had made it clear that Patty and her baby were not among his top priorities.[*] Elsie and her minister helped Patty locate and gain admission to a rural, live-in program for unwed mothers. Like Terry, Patty had agreed to put her baby up for adoption.[4] When she was in her eighth month, two staff persons from the unwed mothers program drove Patty and her belongings to their farm, about 50 miles away.

Ironically, Judy and Abigail, both in their early to middle 20s, may have gotten more support and satisfaction from their make-believe boyfriends than their counterparts did from real ones. Kent and Hugh were real persons, members of the Pente Kostals, a rock/gospel group; it was their status as boyfriends/fiancés that was make-believe. Judy and Abigail had many publicity photographs of the group and all their cassettes, which they were delighted to show and play for anyone who would look or listen. In this *folie à deux,* Judy and Abigail would send (real) letters to their lovers, and their lovers would "reply" in coded messages embedded in the lyrics of every new recording, decipherable only by Judy and Abigail. A personal appearance by the Pente Kostals in a downtown Washington hotel was anticipated with feverish expectancy. Of course, said Judy, after the event, the group's jealous manager would not let its members have personal contact with her and Abigail, but through eye contact, gestures, and hand signals, the young men on stage let them know how they felt and of their plans for the future.[5]

---

[*] KIM: *Rick was not necessarily the father of Terry's baby, although he could have been. And Patty could no way possible pinpoint who her baby's father was!*

[4] Whenever the subject of abortion came up, everyone who spoke—with the exception of Martha—spoke vehemently against it. (Martha had had an abortion.) It is possible that the number and vehemence of the women who spoke against it intimidated those who might have been "pro-choice."

[5] Once, Patty went with Judy and Abigail to see the group perform and, miracle of miracles, Henry, a third member of the group, was smitten by Patty

Judy and Abigail spent hundreds of hours together, planning their futures with Kent and Hugh, deliberating the number of children they would have and where they would live, and each, through commentary and questions, carefully reinforcing their joint fantasy. Given that their lives had no other focus or direction over that two- or three-year period, these fantasies may have stood them in good stead. At the very least, Judy and Abigail seemed to have smoother, more satisfying relationships with their boyfriends than did most of the other young women.[6]

On those very few occasions when some of the older women were able to find or attract boyfriends or lovers, the relationships were much more substantial and profound in their effects.

Peggy was in her 40s. So was Harry, a heavy drinker who lived in the men's shelter. He and Peggy got along well, especially when Harry was sober; drunk, he was prone to beat her. Living in their respective shelters, Peggy and Harry managed to have a reasonably satisfying relationship. After several months, they got married and took a place of their own, where they lived more or less happily for ten months or so until the day Peggy came home to find Harry comfortably stretched out in his favorite living room chair, dead of a heart attack.

(they knew this by his facial expressions and gestures) and she by him, and there it was, *folie à trois!* This lasted until Patty lost interest in Henry, about two months later.

[6]During most of this period, Judy had bad skin and weighed over 300 pounds, making it unlikely she could get a boyfriend any other way. Clearly, an imaginary boyfriend has many advantages over a real one; indeed, the very idea of a make-believe lover is not very far from popular consciousness. Here, for example, are some of the words of "Paper Doll," a popular song at the top of the charts in the 1940s.

> I want to have a paper doll that I can call my own,
> A doll that other fellows cannot steal . . .
> When I come home at night she will be waiting,
> She'll be the truest doll in all the world.
> I'd rather have a paper doll that I can call my own
> Than a fickle-minded real, live girl.

Kim's sex life, to put it in the best possible light, was out of
the ordinary. Kim was in love with Patrick, a 16-year-old Asian
youth whom she had followed to the Washington area when
his family moved there.[7] Patrick—or rather, Kim's love for
Patrick—was the focus of her life. She showered him with gifts
on his birthday. On Valentine's Day, she paid $22 for an ad in the
Washington Post asking Patrick to be her Valentine. Although the
women in the shelter, young and old, black and white, never lost
their disgust for what they saw as Kim's unnatural sexual pro-
clivities, they were almost all enchanted by the uninhibited and
youthful energy that seemed to animate her every word and
movement as she regaled them with thousands of stories, many
of them having to do with Patrick and their love-making. Kim
not only drew strength and support from her affair with Patrick;
her love for him, and their projected future, were at the core of
her life. Homelessness and everything else were remote concerns at best.

With these few exceptions, then, husbands, lovers, and boyfriends were of relatively small importance as sources of assistance and support. Most women had no personal contacts with
men they might have known in the past, and most did not make
new contacts with acceptable men while they were in the shelters. The few who did develop such relationships did so with men
who were in very much the same circumstances as themselves.
It is no surprise then, that these men had so little to give.[*]

• • •

---

[7]Kim was 30 and Patrick was 14 when she first seduced him. "Sick, sick,
sick," said the women at the shelter, and all agreed, those with children and
those without, that they would kill Kim if she were to do something like this
to a child of theirs.

KIM: *Patrick seduced Me.*

[*]DIRECTOR: *We [Refuge staff] saw the men in the women's lives as users. These
men seemed to be "needy," and less strong than the women who yearned for
their male companionship. When a woman became pregnant, the staff, while ex-
pressing concern and urging prenatal care, was genuinely angry that a child had
to be included in the equation.*

By and large, people in the community whose job it was to be helpful did their jobs. Ministers from one or another church tended to be especially helpful.[8] Many of the women came to the shelters by way of referral from a minister or priest, and the women sometimes went to a priest, minister, or rabbi for emergency cash. Churches sometimes allowed women to store their belongings in a rectory or basement, and sometimes a priest, minister, or rabbi would recruit a church member with spare storage room at home. On a few occasions, ministers even solicited their congregants for jobs for particular homeless women.[*]

Police from all three overlapping jurisdictions (state, county, municipal) were typically solicitous and tolerant of the homeless women, helping them locate shelter vacancies, sometimes driving them to shelters in the middle of the night, being patient and gentle when called to assist in evicting a woman from a shelter, or when arranging, with county funds, an emergency placement in a local motel.

Most of the time, women known to be homeless or women who "looked" homeless were barely tolerated in retail establishments and sometimes not even that. Exceptions were important sources of support to the women: individual store managers, salesclerks, and waiters or waitresses sometimes showed them special kindness, including reduced charges, and some did the women the simple but important courtesy of treat-

---

[8]There were exceptions. Rachel, director of The Refuge, called a highly placed clerical official for emergency assistance. "We don't do homeless," she was told.

[*]GRACE: *I never found any minister from any church helpful or sympathetic with the exception of a very helpful rabbi. As a graduate of a Baptist college, I found this an abrasive attitude, for "men of God," so to speak, to ignore people in need. . . . I still had this Christian concept lurking in the back of my brain. I always thought Christians should help each other. That Christian help was not to be found by me. I looked to the Jews and received their love, compassion, understanding, and acceptance. . . . I did not receive any help from police, fire, or rescue. . . . I learned not to ask for help, whether it be from men, who wanted your body, or women who wanted you to worship them for the pennies they threw your way. No, in the world I found hearts of stone. In Ezekiel 36:26, it says, "I will take away the stony heart. . . ." Those people who had hearts of stone needed to ask the Lord to remove that rock from within.*

ing them the same as they treated everyone else. More typical, however, was the local Pancake Heaven which, for a time, required the women to pay for their food before eating it.[9]

The goodwill of security guards, particularly at public buildings, was especially important. These guards controlled access to drinking water, toilets, benches and chairs in lobbies—all routinely important to the women but especially so during weekends, holidays, and non-business hours. For women living on the street or lacking shelter for the night, security guards were often the only hope for a minimally safe night's rest. In the absence of policies to the contrary, security guards—mainly county or city employees—often befriended the women, allowing them to sleep in lobby chairs or stretched out on the floor, or at worst, allowing them to sleep outside, near or against the building, where the women might be watched through the night as the guards made their regular rounds.

Probably for good and proper reasons, security policies with respect to homeless women were not consistent over seasons or even across buildings. In bad weather, for example, when shelters were likely to be filled to overflowing, it was official policy to allow homeless men and women to sleep in the lobbies of county buildings. Sometimes, security policies with respect to homeless persons appeared to change overnight, perhaps because of some complaint, or because some homeless person had created a disturbance. Most security guards, however, some of whom had come to know the women personally, befriended them to the extent that policies permitted.[*]

---

[9] A waitress brought Phyllis her lunch and asked her to pay before eating. Without a word, Phyllis paid for the meal and walked out, leaving the food untouched. To his great credit, when Jim, director of Bridge House, learned of this discriminatory practice, he demanded that it be stopped and it was.

[*] KIM: *I take strong issue with Elliot's portrayal of shopkeepers, and especially police and security personnel, as generally sympathetic. The prevailing attitude from cops and guards was decidedly abusive. "We are not a hotel," Phyllis and I were told, ousted into a frozen-cold night from the local police station. Another time, an officer suggested I hitchhike to D.C. (this, at 2:00 A.M.) where there was shelter space available. Clearly, the system is designed not to lift up, but to force*

As a group, service providers in agencies—however prepared they were to disregard the standard admonition not to
get too involved with clients—had too many cases and too little time to be personally supportive of the women. In one important exception, a hospital social worker agreed to board
Peggy's dog at a local kennel for a month or more, and surely
there were others that never came to my attention.

Shelter staff, on the other hand, were in regular, face-to-face
contact with the women and were a major source of support.[10]
It was the staff who, in effect, offered the women a safe, warm
place to sleep at night, maintained order, and saw to it that they
had food and other essentials. Many staff persons also offered
consolation, encouragement, advice when asked, and a sympathetic ear.*

A kind of tension underlay these supports, however, because
the great power of the staff lay precisely in their ability to
withhold these things as well, beginning with their power to
deny the women entry or to expel them. This unequal power
relationship tended to put a ceiling on the development of

---

*out. The message is: "Go to D.C., go to Baltimore, go to Richmond, somewhere
that isn't here." Go there, and waiting for you is the same message.*

*Once, when Wanda (then eight months pregnant) and I were sleeping in
Courthouse Square, the guards poured gallons of unidentified liquid on us. I
called police. "It's obvious they don't want you here," said the cop, "so leave."
But that is our last precious freedom, freedom to be outdoors on public property.
When I was kicked out of the County Law Library for being homeless, I went to
the Human Relations Commission to file a discrimination case. I was told I
couldn't do so. "There's no place on the form to claim discrimination on the basis of homelessness." The commission's form recognizes Discrimination in
Public Accommodations based on the following: "Race; color; marital status; religious creed; ancestry; national origin; handicap; sex; sexual orientation."
Faggots yes, bag ladies no.*

[10]"Everybody there [at The Refuge] was supportive and, you know, you
could cry and you could talk to those women who were in charge" (Regina,
transcribed from life history taped after she left The Refuge).

*GRACE: Elliot lives in a dream world. He thinks all those staff people and vol-
unteers were around to give love and help. I found some folks sincere in their efforts to help, others it seemed were there to be congratulated for being a volunteer. . . . The way people in authority treated you sometimes, I thought they were
just out to rob me of what little I had left of my self esteem.*

personal relationships, even when the impulse to build them was present. For paid staff, such relationships were also inhibited by the desire to maintain a more or less professional relationship with their "clients." In addition, many of the staff, both paid and volunteer, were separated from the women by the real or imagined abyss of social class.

Despite these obstacles, however, strong, personal helping relationships did occasionally develop between staff and one or another woman. But the material and emotional content of the relationship tended to flow in one direction, giving them all a patron/client coloration.[11]

For the great majority of women, friendships that pre-dated their homelessness might just as well have not existed. Grace said she used to think she had friends all over the county. Now she realizes they were not friends but acquaintances. "If I had friends, would I be living in a shelter?" Elsie telephoned an old Amway friend to ask her to put on a cosmetics demonstration at the shelter. The "friend" turned her down and went on to berate her for being homeless. Elsie, near tears, reported the exchange to Betty and others. The woman said, You're homeless and in the shelter because that's where you want to be. You've thrown away every job you've had because you're lazy and really don't want to work. You're just like all the other women there, and you're a fat slob to boot.

Elsie's response was pitifully defensive. You've always lived in a nice house in the suburbs and never wanted for anything, she said to her critical "friend." You've never been divorced or fired from a job. You've never been unemployed or hungry or homeless so you really don't know anything about me.

For friendships the women could draw on—the mutual support that is exchanged among equals, that builds on both

---

[11]In at least two instances, two of the homeless women—Martha and Sheila—were invited to live with volunteers when The Refuge closed for the season. For Martha, see Appendix A.

giving and taking, on shared life circumstances and perhaps shared fates—the women had to turn to one another.

• • •

Friendships turned on many different axes. Sometimes two women seemed to pair up because they were both black or white, or of the same age, or were perhaps better educated or more refined than the others. But for the most part, race, age, and social class appeared to be low-lying boundaries easily crossed rather than deep structural faults that separated the women cleanly from one another.

There were, of course, individuals on both sides of the color line who merited the label "racist," but they were generally obliged to keep their opinions to themselves. Overt expressions of racist feelings were clearly out of bounds, making racism a primarily private rather than public affair. It was as if everyone, fearful of the destructive potential of racial hostility, had agreed to suppress its public expression as much as possible, thereby enabling those who were prepared to cross the color boundary to do so. The end result was frequent crossings of the color line against a background of simmering racial tension.

Since the great majority of the women came from poor, working-class backgrounds, traditionally defined class differences among them were relatively narrow and posed little problem. Where there were, in fact, class differences—as with those few women from middle-class backgrounds—they did not always affect the formation of associations and friendships, perhaps because they were washed out by the commonality of circumstances, or because there were so few middle-class women that, if they were to have friends at all, class must cease to be a barrier.[12]

Ages ranged widely, from 18 or so to the mid-70s, and age boundaries, too, were often crossed. Women in their teens and early 20s, however, did show a preference for their own age

---

[12]See Chapter 6 for a more detailed discussion of race and social class differences.

group, and it sometimes appeared as if the older one was, the less relevant age became as a factor in friendship.

Background characteristics of race, class, and age, then, provided only very rough and blurred guidelines to the formation of friendships. Similarly, friendships seemed not to be based primarily on narrow utilitarian or instrumental considerations, although these were certainly an important part of many associations. People did borrow and lend a few dollars or cigarettes here and there, or someone with a car might give this or that person a lift. But by and large there was not a lot the women could do for one another in the way of material exchange.

Friendships occasionally developed out of previous acquaintances. Ginger and Bonnie had first met at the Special Olympics a few years earlier, where they competed in the 100-yard dash. Ginger said that Bonnie beat her out for first place by a hair but that she could beat her now. Bonnie laughed derisively. "We used to be like this," said Ginger, holding her middle finger and forefingers in the shape of a V, "but now we're like this," and she wrapped the fingers around each other: "At each other's throat." They both laughed again as they sparred in mock battle. For many of the several months Ginger remained in the shelter, she and Bonnie were inseparable, their relationship strengthened by this previous encounter and their similar below-average intellectual functioning.

But previous encounters could just as easily work against a friendly relationship. On Deborah's first night at The Refuge, she immediately recognized Betty from three years before, at Mount Carmel shelter in D.C. They had some words. "You never liked me from the beginning," Deborah reminded Betty. "You're right," said Betty. "Let's keep it that way." And so they did.

Similarly, Cora recognized Bonita from two years earlier, when Bonita was an ambulance assistant and Cora was a nurse at Holy Name Hospital. Mostly, however, like Betty and Deborah, the women recognized one another from other shelters, mainly in downtown D.C., and sometimes their paths had crossed at Alcoholics Anonymous meetings or at the state mental hospital. Most of these previous encounters carried no valences; they were simply a matter of recognition. With the exceptions noted, few of them seemed to count for much, one way or the other.

Of far greater importance to building a relationship was what the women could do for one another emotionally and psychologically. Who can comfort you when you hurt and encourage you when you are down? Who can play the fool and make you laugh? Who will seek you out to pass the time? Who will stand with you against the other women or staff? Who will listen to your complaints and tell you her own? Who will exchange histories and intimacies with you? Who will support you in what you do and not call you crazy or dumb? Of such stuff were friendships made.

No one person could offer all these things all the time, so there was much reaching out to one another. The ability to deliver encouragement or solace at a critical moment could almost instantly deepen an ordinary relationship into friendship, but failure to deliver at a critical moment of need could downgrade a friendship to something less than it had been. In one instance, these happened simultaneously; Evelyn's loss was June's gain, suggesting that "best-friends" friendships can be a zero-sum game.

Peggy asked me to drive her and her best friend, Evelyn, to Fort Lincoln Cemetery in D.C. She wanted to visit the grave of a close friend who had just died. June, friendly with both Peggy and Evelyn, said she'd like to go along for the ride. Peggy and Evelyn sat in the back of the car; June sat up front next to me. On the way to the cemetery, Peggy talked movingly about her close, non-romantic relationship with Cliff, whose death made her feel as if she had lost an older brother.

At the cemetery, we left the car and walked over to Cliff's grave, still covered with raw dirt and identified by a temporary hand-lettered sign. Peggy started to cry, softly at first, then ever deeper sobs. Evelyn, standing next to her, seemed ill at ease and did nothing. After a minute or so, June walked over to Peggy and wrapped her arms around her as Peggy continued to sob. Evelyn and I, embarrassed by this intimacy and wanting to give them some privacy, drifted away to read some of the nearby gravestones. For several minutes, June and Peggy, locked together in each other's arms, swayed back and forth in unison. Finally, Peggy let go of June and signaled that she was all right and ready to leave. This time, June and Peggy climbed into the back of the car, and Evelyn sat up front, as if to confirm in space the change that had already occurred in sentiment. From that time on, and for three years thereafter, Peggy and June were good friends, even after Peggy moved out of the shelter. Peggy and Evelyn grew slowly apart.[13]

Spontaneous gift-giving was not a commonplace but, given the circumstances of the women, it was impressive when it occurred. "Look at this," said Grace one evening to the group of us sitting around the table after dinner. She pointed to the cup she was drinking from. It was a lidded porcelain cup with a bright-colored rainbow on the lid. The body of the cup was covered by brief quotations from the Bible. "Judy and Abigail gave it to me," she said proudly, holding it up and admiring it at arm's distance. "We saw it in the store," said Judy, "and we both said 'Grace!' at the same time. We couldn't resist it."

Much of the time these friendships were symmetrical and reciprocal; that is, friends exchanged more or less equal amounts of comfort or encouragement or loyalty with one another, but not always. On a few occasions, friendships took the form of age-appropriate family relationships. Melissa and her husband, John, "adopted" (retarded) Bonnie who called them

---

[13]Evelyn was black and in her early 30s; Peggy was white and almost 50. It is possible, I suppose, that the race and age differences in Peggy and Evelyn's best-friend relationship made for a kind of tension that was resolved when June took over from Evelyn, but all three would surely deny this if asked to analyze the situation.

"Mom" and "Dad." Shortly after Elsie came to the shelter, she joined them as "Grandma." Similarly, several of the young women were "adopted" into Natalie's real family and called her "Mom."[*]

Since most women had so few resources, the obligations of friendship could be draining. Sometimes friendships appeared to observers to be one-sided, as when Elsie seemed to sacrifice her own needs for the sake of others.[14] Reluctantly, Elsie had to pull back. She said she had gone to the hospital that evening to see Melissa but she was not permitted onto the maternity ward. "I left her a note asking for forgiveness. I explained I wasn't angry with them [Melissa, John, and 'daughter' Bonnie], I just needed a little breathing room, a little space for myself. I have to find a job and I can't do that and take care of Bonnie all day."

"You were helping them, weren't you?" asked Dorothy. "You were keeping them going?"

"Do you mean financially?" asked Elsie.

Dorothy said yes.

"No," said Elsie. "I helped physically [Elsie had a car] but not with money."

"Melissa!" sneered Hilda. "Melissa's been having a baby every day since November first and she still hasn't had the baby."

"But the pregnancy isn't phony," said Dorothy.

Hilda ignored that and turned directly to Elsie.

---

[*] DIRECTOR: *The volunteers had great difficulty in not interfering with group dynamics. Watching Natalie and her network of women "swoop" over a new and vulnerable young guest at the shelter was reason enough for the journal to be full of concern and advice that this new woman be told that she was being set up (for money, sex, drugs) in the guise of support and care.*

[14] There was much suspicion, by staff and women alike, that these "family" relationships were fundamentally exploitative—that Bonnie, for example, was being sexually exploited by Melissa and John and perhaps exploited for her (SSI) money as well; that Elsie was being exploited for her money and her car; and that the young women such as Terry were exploited for money by Natalie and her family. But these were suspicions. Whatever the facts, Elsie, Bonnie, Terry, and the other women took much satisfaction from their putative family relationships while they lasted, even if the material exchanges were unequal.

"They were sucking you dry," said Hilda. "Melissa tries to suck everyone into her orbit and suck them dry. She did the same thing with Louise last year." Rachel, standing nearby, shook her head in silent confirmation.

Hesitantly, Elsie agreed. "I love them to death," she said. "I really do love them to death, but I was always meeting their needs. I have needs, too. Right now I need some breathing space to get myself together. I need to get myself a job and a place to live."

At any given time, there was a great discrepancy in personal capacities. There were women whose intellectual functioning and competence were at an exceptionally high level, and there were women who were commonly in a funk, or a deep and chronic depression, and always a handful who drifted in and out of their own private worlds. Some women were always ready to offer emotional support, and others seemed to have none to offer at any time. If the latter performed a service, it was in allowing others to help them. Commerce in emotional support between these two groups of women was not at all symmetrical: comfort, encouragement, caring flowed one way—from the strong to the weak. It is less clear what flowed back.

Thus Betty, who had "been there," went out of her way to befriend alcoholic Pearl, to encourage her to eat, help her shower, deflect any racial slurs that might be directed at her, engage her in conversation, and so forth. Similarly, Betty was a self-designated protector of Flora, who spent much of her waking life asleep or depressed, with her head cradled in her arms. Betty not only helped her wash, eat, and change clothes but occasionally stroked her hair or touched her face to comfort her and bring her back in touch with the world. And once, when Flora, her remaining mental energies spent, neglected to return to the shelter and spent three days on a park bench instead, not eating or drinking and defecating in her clothing, it was Betty who found her and half carried her, with Phyllis's help and mine, back to a shelter where Betty washed her and found her some fresh clothing.

In much the same way, June would regularly go out of her way to engage Lily in long conversations about clothing design and fashion as a way of piercing Lily's unremitting preoccupation with the husband who had abandoned her and their children years before. For Lily, these conversations were among the precious few ordinary, person-to-person experiences available to her, and she grabbed for them eagerly.

In this way, Betty and June and Grace and many of the other women often found themselves in asymmetrical relationships in which various forms of assistance and emotional support went in one direction only. To Pearl and Flora, Betty was clearly a friend, perhaps a best friend. To Betty, Pearl and Flora were women she cared for and protected and had befriended, but it was less clear that they were friends in the same sense Elsie was. Her friendship with Elsie was a quid pro quo arrangement between equals, with the sentiments and acts of friendship moving in both directions.

Finally, there were critical moments that generated sudden intimacies that did not necessarily build on a preceding relationship nor lead to anything beyond the closeness and good feeling that came from that one shared experience.

Elsie had had a terrible day. It was the due date for her car and insurance payments, and her hearing aid had had to be turned in the day before for repairs, leaving her with no anchor for the earpieces of her eyeglasses. Just before dinner, Elsie learned that the job she had fasted and prayed for had gone to someone else. "Oh, God!" she sobbed, waving her arms and shaking her head at the helplessness of it all. "What will I do? No money, no job, no car!"

It took Elsie several minutes, with the help of Betty and some of the other women, to settle down enough to take her seat at the dinner table. Then, as Elsie bent her head over the bowl of chili in front of her, her glasses slid from her head into the bowl. Elsie let out a howl of rage and flung the bowl across the table and against the wall, then collapsed into her chair and gave herself up to great sobs of defeat. Everyone fell silent as Elsie's massive chest heaved and jerked. Kathleen, who was sitting next to Elsie, put one arm around her shoulder and held her hand with the other, and they sat there like that, almost motionless except for Elsie's now silent sobbing and Kathleen's alternate squeezing and stroking of Elsie's hand. The others resumed eating, accompanied by forced and phony dinner talk. Eventually, Kathleen was able to disengage from Elsie, who left the table to lie down on her cot, and the talk relaxed to normal.

Kathleen and Elsie had no prior special relationship and no noticeably different relationship thereafter, although one must assume that, afterward, even the most mundane and casual meeting between them triggered a remembrance of a once-shared intimacy. That it was Kathleen who comforted Elsie was pure accident; Elsie had happened to seat herself next to Kathleen, but it could just as well have been Betty or June or Lisa or half a dozen others who could have done, would have done, what Kathleen did.

This generalized readiness to be helpful was ever-present, along with a generalized readiness for hostility. For Betty, a willingness to help others was the test of friendworthiness. "Why are you friends with Cora?" she asked me. "Have you ever seen her do anything for anyone?"

Even without friends, a woman could usually take aid and comfort from her peers in time of need. You could say something about the Bible, or curse husbands, doctors, lawyers, social workers, or shelter rules, or make some provocative comment about anything at all to no one in particular, and find someone prepared to take you up on your invitation to talk.

Shelter life, then, not only held out the possibility for real friendships but also offered a more transient but no less genuine human contact to all who reached out for it. For those who could not reach out, there was always someone ready to befriend them, and they had only to let themselves be befriended. By themselves, however, human contacts and personal friendships were not enough to make shelter life bearable. In addition to the help they got from one another, the women also required the aid and comfort they got from God. Finally, they also had to look within themselves to overcome despair and conquer homelessness.

• • •

For homeless women, religion was more than an opiate, more than a cry of the oppressed. For them, there really was A Balm in Gilead. Religious belief was typically unquestioning and un-complicated. It had the simplicity and finality of the bumper sticker: "God said it. I believe it. That settles it." Belief often took the form of a nonspecific fundamentalism. Typically, it was something the women brought with them from childhood, but adult failures and woundings seemed to have raised their awareness of God and their intimacy with Him to new levels of intensity.

Religion was not a separable compartment of life reserved for Sundays, holidays, and life-cycle markers. Talking about God was a commonplace, everyday affair, striking in its ordinariness as it took its place with the weather, gossip, work, or health as a topic of conversation. Almost any subject could serve as a lead-in to a discussion of the Bible and God.

It was a midweek afternoon. Peggy, Evelyn, June, and I were in a booth in a McDonald's restaurant. Evelyn reported that Kim had tried to kill Yolanda by putting rubbing alcohol in her drinks because she had discovered Yolanda masturbating and said it was sick. Peggy said that masturbation was a sin and she cited the injunction against "casting your seed upon the ground," but as for its being sick, she didn't know, and a dis-cussion of sin and sickness followed. Seamlessly, the discussion slid into Revelation.

"Ministers don't usually deal with Revelation," said Peggy. "They're afraid to deal with it because it's too hard to under-stand."

Evelyn agreed, but added that W. W. Armstrong was an exception. He came on TV at six o'clock Sunday morning and he often talked about Revelation, she said. The others stayed away from it, however, "because it's too deep. Revelation tells it like it is."

June said she had read that Revelation was John of Patmos's letter to the persecuted Christian churches of the time, and that the letter was in a code that only contemporary Christians could understand. The letter didn't really talk about the distant future, she said, only about the problems that were facing the Church. Revelation wouldn't seem mysterious at all if we knew how to decipher the code.

This was beyond Peggy and Evelyn. Evelyn said, "There are earthquakes almost every day now, and there's fighting in Jerusalem. We're in Revelation right now."

"It's just too deep to understand," said Peggy.

June graciously let that be the last word on the subject and turned back to her french fries. The conversation turned to the relative merits of the various translations of the Bible. No one liked the Good News Bible. All agreed that the King James version was the best, and the conversation turned again to gossip.

What made religion so central to social life was that whenever people searched for common ground, they could almost always fall back on the Bible, God, or their own religious experiences. Since one took it for granted that everyone believed in God, conversational gambits among strangers often began with that subject as a way of feeling the other person out and perhaps starting a relationship.

It was Regina's first night at the shelter. She heard Hilda, in a casual conversation with some of the women, mention God. "I believe in God, too," said Regina, pulling Hilda's attention to herself. She told Hilda how, two weeks earlier, when she was living in her car that was about to give up the ghost and she was about to do the same herself, she turned to God. "God," she said, "Here I am. You said you are my Comforter and my Redeemer. Well, I need comforting and redeeming. Quick." The next day, Social Services gave her an emergency grant and she was able to get an oil change and fill her tank with gas.

Hilda nodded understandingly and reached back into her own past for a similar experience to exchange with Regina, and Regina was no longer a stranger.

Jeanette used much the same technique on her first night at the shelter. She approached Maude and told her she had heard her mention J. Oliver McGee, the radio evangelist, earlier at the day shelter. She'd always liked him, she said, but she hadn't been able to find out when and where he came on. Maude told her he came on at 4:15 to 4:45 weekdays, on station so-and-so. Jeanette thanked her and their bond to J. Oliver McGee became a springboard to a wide-ranging discussion of religion and to a budding acquaintance.

Religion helped the women connect with one another as peers, since they saw themselves as equals before God. When the conversation dealt with religion and personal values, conversation with staff could also take on the characteristics of talk between equals. Regina and Mrs. Hilyard, one of the newer volunteers at The Refuge, soon found common ground in the Bible. Both agreed that putting a baboon's heart in Baby Faye's body was sacrilegious. Regina said that if she had the power, she would blow up every laboratory and hospital where animal experimentation or abortions were being carried out, and she applauded the day's news about the bombing of local abortion clinics.

Mrs. Hilyard and Regina speculated about Revelation and whether John had foreseen helicopters and such. Regina asked if President Ronald Reagan didn't carry the Mark of the Beast—there were six letters in both of his names, she noted. Mrs. Hilyard said she was shocked the other day when the number 666 was pulled out of the lottery hat, and only a short time ago the same number had been fraudulently named the winner in her home state of Delaware.

Regina asked Mrs. Hilyard if she was Protestant.

Mrs. Hilyard was waiting for that one. "No," she said, "I'm a Presbyterian. I don't protest anything. I affirm my Presbyterian faith. I protest nothing." Puzzled, Regina changed the subject.

Sometimes, knowledge of religion and the Bible could be used to assert status difference. Once Regina was wearing a Star of David around her neck; inside the star was a crucifix. Grace admired the pendant and there followed a discussion of things religious. Grace told Regina about the Friday night services of the B'Nai Messiah ("Jews for Jesus") that she used to attend, and the Friday night services of the Conservative synagogue that she now attended regularly. She explained to Regina that the B'Nai Messiah are Jews who believe in both the Old and New Testaments, but the "regular" Jews only believe in the Old Testament—"So far," she added with a broad, knowing smile.

"You mean they don't believe in Jesus?" asked Regina.

"Not yet," said Grace knowingly. "Not yet."

"Jesus was an ordinary man," said Regina.

Grace started to object and Regina quickly corrected herself. "I mean, He hung around with ordinary people. You know, with poor people. Ordinary people like us."

"He was God's only Son," corrected Grace. Regina agreed heartily and tried another tack.

"I don't like those services where people talk in tongues," she said. "Jesus didn't mean for people to do that. When He said, 'talking in tongues,' He only meant that people from Africa and Asia and different countries like that talk different languages. Like someone from a foreign country and you can't understand him. That's what He meant."

"No," said Grace, with a tolerant smile. "I speak in tongues, too. I've been doing it for 13 years. It's called 'glossolalia.'"

"Well, what language is it?" asked Regina, near defeat.

"I don't know," smiled Grace. "I do it, but I don't know I'm doing it. Read the Book of Acts."

"I've always wanted to read Acts," said Regina, "but I never got around to it. I'm going to read Acts."

Grace nodded her head. "Chapter Two," she said, and Regina repeated, "Chapter Two."

Regina made one last attempt at parity. "When I pray, I pray in plain English, just like I'm talking now."

"That's fine," said Grace. "I do the same thing."

Regina had no place to go. "I'm going to read Acts," she said. "I've always wanted to read Acts."

There were a few women who did not believe in God, but if they valued the fellowship of the women around them, they were wise not to say so. A handful of others, like Louise and Edith, said publicly they had no use for "that kind of stuff." But Louise and Edith were essentially loners and had no apparent desire to be liked or respected by the others. Jane, on the other hand, kept her beliefs to herself in public; in private, she conceded that her father was an agnostic and that she herself was inclined toward atheism. She was not yet sure what she did believe, "but I certainly don't believe in a God who looks like Zeus."

Elsie, like most other women, did believe in an anthropomorphic Living God. Elsie was embroidering her excellent freehand drawing of the Crucifixion. She pointed out some of the details: the nails had to be through the wrists, not the palms of His hands where the nails would never have supported His weight. "Elliot, can you imagine His pain? Can you imagine His agony, with the weight of His body pulling down on the nails in his wrists?"

There were times, too, when faith wavered. Ginger and Cheryl were having a heated discussion as they walked down the steps of the day shelter. Ginger said she wasn't sure she believed in God any more, and Cheryl kept reassuring her that God loved her. "If He loves me," said Ginger, fighting back her tears, "why doesn't He give me back my dead mother?" Stalemate. Cheryl could only repeat that God loved her, and Ginger could only cry for her dead mother.

Although belief in God, and more particularly membership in a community of believers, was an important enhancement of social life, the major source of spiritual aid and comfort lay in the direct relationship between the women and God rather than among the women themselves. Some of the more devout women did not need preachers—certainly not TV preachers and especially faith healers—to intercede with God on their behalf. The TV in the day shelter was trumpeting Oral Roberts' public appeal for millions of dollars lest God strike him dead.

"I don't like faith healers," said Peggy.

"Why not?" asked Phyllis.

"I just don't believe them," said Peggy. "There's only one healer and that's God. Only God can heal."

Phyllis nodded in agreement. She said she didn't like any of the TV preachers because they shouted and waved their arms too much. "That's not Christian," she said. "I don't know what it is, but it's not Christian."

The women's relationship with God was personal and immediate, pulling Him into their ordinary, everyday life. On the surface, it appeared that the women sometimes invoked God's participation on some fairly trivial issues, irreverently entangling the sacred with the profane. But a tank of gas for someone living in a car, or a job for someone jobless, or guidance on which town or shelter one should go to next—ultimately, these are transcendental issues because they are issues of survival, of life and death.

Prayer, fasting, reading the Bible or Bible-inspired literature, talking and thinking about God—these were the usual ways of relating to God, and one did these things matter-of-factly, as if they were all of a piece with the rest of one's life. After dinner, for instance, Elsie and Patty and two other women remained seated at the table, and Elsie had a Bible in front of her. "Come on, Elliot," she beckoned. "Let's have a Bible reading." Lisa, sitting in the park on a sunny afternoon, waiting for the day shelter to open, was reading a paperback, *Prayer, Stress and Inner Wounds,* and did not look up for passersby.

Grace was one of the few women with whom God communicated directly. Once again, it was after dinner and several of us were seated around the table. Abigail (who sometimes said she was Jewish, sometimes half Jewish, sometimes Christian), was comparing Bar Mitzvah with confirmation. Elsie quoted something from what she said was First Corinthians about a boy becoming a man. Someone else said something about people who hear voices. Cora said that "from a therapeutic perspective," hearing voices meant that the person was struggling with a very difficult decision around some kind of separation, usually from someone very near and dear. But it could also be a job or something else.

"It all depends," said Grace. She said she heard voices, too, but so did Joan of Arc and Saint Francis and lots of other sane and effective people. "God doesn't speak in a human voice, though," she said. "He doesn't speak in words and you don't hear it in your ears. You hear it inside your head."

For many women, belief in God invested homelessness with meaning. Since everything in this world happens only because God wills it, the women were homeless because God wanted them to be, and He must have his reasons, even if the reasons were to remain forever hidden.[*] This kind of thinking did not, as many supposed, lead to a fatalistic or passive acceptance of homelessness. It certainly did no such thing for Grace.

Grace knew that she was homeless because God wanted her to be, but she was bewildered as to why He should want this for her. She knew it was not for punishment. Through prayer, meditation, and periodic fasting, she struggled to divine God's purpose in making her homeless. Suddenly, after three months of

---

[*]DIRECTOR: *The shelter staff was generally uneasy with the women's willingness to turn things over to God. While the shelter was sponsored by a mainline church, the staff members came from all religions and walks of life. We were uneasy that by turning things over to God, the message of self-help and free will was lost.*

But perhaps the director need not have been uneasy: "Fatalism has not bred passivity in Moslems, nor has determinism sapped the vigour of Calvinists or Marxists. . . . Practice sometimes belies profession, no matter how sincerely held." Isaiah Berlin, *Four Essays on Liberty*, page xvii.

living in the shelter, it came to her. God wanted her to start her own Home for Emotionally Abused Adults. He wanted her to experience homelessness firsthand so she could model her home on personal experience rather than on existing shelters, which are insensitive to the real needs of people. Thus, for Grace, her belief in God gave not only meaning to her homeless life, but purpose as well.*

Crucially, belief in God made it possible for many of the women to adopt a religious rather than a scientific or commonsense basis for calculating the probabilities of their escape from homelessness. The outside observer, basing judgment on an objective assessment of the difficulties and likely opportunities, might estimate that this woman has one chance in 100 of getting her own place to live, that woman one chance in 50, and that one, one in 1,000. The homeless woman, in contrast, knows that God loves her and knows that she wants a place of her own. With God on her side, she sets her own estimate for getting out of homelessness at, say, one chance in five, or one in two, or even at dead certainty. Thus, by substituting a calculus of faith for one based on reason and common sense, she is able to transform a dismal and disabling statistical probability into something she can live with and work for.[15]

---

*GRACE: *I'm here [out of the shelter] because God wants me to be here. My destiny was cut in stone. Unfortunately, I had a lot of learning to get me to where I am today. Learned some good stuff, too! How it feels to be hungry, to work when you slept only two hours that past night. What it's like to have friends and family turn against you because they think that now there is something wrong with your mind. What it feels like when you are completely alone and broke and you don't feel physically well. My shoes got a lot of dust in them and my face was dirty with my tears, but by golly, I got an education!*

[15]Unfortunately, those same fundamentalist religious beliefs that brought aid and comfort to homeless women could work to their severe disadvantage in the workplace. In the largely middle-class world of corporate employers and daily commerce, God is assigned His own special place and time (outside of the workplace and not during working hours), the Bible is not understood to be literally true, God does not speak directly to people, and He does not look like Zeus. Sometimes, when trying to reenter that world, Grace and some of the other women boldly carried their beliefs before them. In that world, however, their faith, proclaimed, made them suspect and unwelcome.

Belief in God, then, could invest homelessness with meaning and purpose and hope. Through the aid and comfort one got from belief in God, together with the aid and comfort one got from staff and other homeless women, shelter life was rendered almost bearable. There was still a gap to fill, however, whenever these resources failed. To fill it, the women had to look within themselves.

• • •

Among the greatest threats to survival were discouragement and disappointment. The women struggled mightily against them, using mental tricks, humor, religion, and whatever other psychological and emotional resources were available to them.

Perhaps the most useful and widely used strategy in this struggle was to expect as little as possible from life and minimize disappointment thereby. The women appeared to rely heavily on Thomas Carlyle's formula for maximizing happiness: one sets life's realizations as the numerator of a fraction; in the denominator are one's expectations. When one carries out the division, the result is one's happiness quotient. Clearly, the numerator—what one actually gets out of life—is typically beyond one's control and not easily changed. But the denominator—what one expects from life—is subject to manipulation. By lowering the denominator—that is, by expecting less from life—one minimizes disappointments and discontent, and one's happiness quotient increases accordingly.[16]

It is this kind of thinking, I believe, that accounts for the extraordinary modesty of the women's expectations, a modesty born of a fear of asking for too much. It is important to note, too, that the women did not always make fine distinctions between

---

[16]"[The] Fraction of Life can be increased in value not so much by increasing your Numerator as by lessening your Denominator. Nay, unless my Algebra deceives me, Unity itself divided by Zero will give Infinity. Make thy claim of wages a zero, then; thou hast the world under thy feet." Thomas Carlyle, "The Everlasting Yea," in *Sartor Resartus,* pp. 241–42.

KIM: *I think the "happiness quotient" is a valid theory.*

what they expected to get from life, what they would settle for, and what they hoped for; expectations, wants, and hopes were usually all of a piece, and all clustered around the most elemental needs. Not once over the years did I hear a woman say, seriously, that she was waiting for Prince Charming to come along and carry her off to Suburban Paradise or Domestic Bliss, and not once did anyone—sane, crazy, or just confused—say she wanted to be an astronaut, a brain surgeon, or even a lawyer or teacher.

Although the women frequently talked about jobs and making a living, very seldom was there talk about careers. The few references to career aspirations were appropriately and realistically modest. Elsie and Martha talked about career training for office work. Regina said she wanted career training that would enable her to avoid the periodic unemployment that she was experiencing as a housekeeper/companion. Of course, economic security was her chief goal, she said, but that wasn't enough. "Life isn't worth living if you don't shoot for the top," she said, and that's why she wanted career training as a psychiatric aide. "I want to make my own security," she said. "I can't wait for Mr. Right to come along."

Elementary security was the paramount concern for most, especially the older women and those who had no immediate prospect of escaping homelessness. Rose looked back on 50 years of working in other people's houses. "It's been a long time that I've been wanting to have a little place to myself, and just be able to live comfortable to myself and all."[17]

"A little place to myself," "safety," "a job I can live on"—in exactly these words or words very much like them, the women talked to one another about their aspirations for the future. In the day shelter, 62-year-old Maude was speculating about where she might go when The Refuge closed the next month. "My major concerns right now," she said, "are safety and housing, in that order."

---

[17]From her transcribed life history.

Whatever her mood, Betty knew exactly what she wanted from life. One evening when she was bad-mouthing almost everyone, I reminded her that she really was paranoid at times. She agreed, but said this wasn't going to stop her from cussing out all those fuckers who were trying to do her in just because she spoke up for herself and her rights and because she wanted to get off the street. "If they think Betty's going to die on the street like a tramp, like a piece of shit, they've got another think coming. I decline that honor. Someone else can have the glory. That's not how it's going to be. Betty is going to have a safe, warm place to live, her own place, and she's not going to have to hit the fucking streets every morning at 7:00 A.M. for 12 hours and 15 minutes."

She paused as if to consider what she had said.

"All I want is my own little cubbyhole," she said finally. "Is that too much to ask for?"

Kathleen laughed at Betty's modest wants. "You'll get bored to death," she said.

"If I had my own little room and my own TV, I'd never get bored," said Betty. "I could spend the rest of my life like that."

Those were Hilda's sentiments as well. When she visited the shelter after getting her own (subsidized) apartment, she said she loved her apartment so much that "I want to die there."

It is difficult to exaggerate the importance of housing in the hierarchy of wants. But "housing" means "an efficiency apartment," "a cubby hole," "my own place," and not a palace or mansion or even a house. Wants and expectations were minimal, elemental. "Housing" did not seem to conjure up physical images so much as impressions of warmth and security and independence.[*]

---

[*]GRACE: *I can remember while in the shelter driving to my destination, looking at the lights in other people's homes and apartments, wishing I had a home too, where I could hang my pictures and set out my little nick-nacks. Writing those words now makes me cry, because it was such a heartfelt wish, something I wanted more than anything. I don't have that wish any longer, it's gone. I've grown stronger and know that just around the corner the Lord has the answer to the promise He made to me over 20 years ago.*

Delores, who stayed at The Refuge only two weeks, often talked about her basic wants. Housing was one, but there were others. "Right now I'm country shopping. Officially. I'm looking at England and the Scandinavian countries. What I'm looking for is free housing, free medical care, and free burial. That's all I need. I'd do anything for the country that gives them to me. I'd wash dishes, I'd be a professor, I'd spy for them. Really, anything. I'm almost 30 and that's the kind of security I need. And you know I'll never get free housing in this country."

In a chair in the day shelter, her head down on her arms, Flora was moaning. Betty helped her raise her head and asked her what she wanted. Still in a funk, Flora said that she wanted to get her children back, to get a job, to live with her children and support them. Betty asked her if she knew where she was. Flora shook her head no. Did she know when she got out of the hospital? Again, no. Unaware of time and space, Flora still wanted from life exactly what the other women, those separated from their dependent children, said they wanted.[18]

Vicki, too, put housing at the top. Everyone was talking about the man who was holding several hostages in the Mormon Temple. Vicki asked me what I would demand if I were holding the hostages. I said I was old enough to settle for peace and quiet. "How about you?" I asked. "What would you demand?"

"An apartment," she said, without a moment's hesitation. Then, as an afterthought, "And a water bed."

"That's it?"

"A good-looking man," she said, laughing.

"What would you do with him?"

"That would be at my discretion."

"Are we talking marriage or a one-night stand?"

---

[18]Women known to have dependent children typically said their main goal in life was to get their children back and live with them. Perhaps they said this, in part, because they were expected to. But Flora was in no condition to censor what she said. It came from the depths.

"For the duration," she said, and laughing, hugged herself at the thought of it.

Another time Vicki put having a job and a place to live at the top of her list, but she was young and allowed herself to dream of more. In the park, I excused myself from a group of women, explaining I had to go to Montgomery Ward to exchange a faucet. Vicki asked to come along. She said she loves to browse in department stores. She does it all the time. "What's your favorite department?"

"Furniture," she said.

I exchanged my faucet and we wandered over to the furniture department. With her good hand, Vicki stroked some drapes.

"I dream when I do this," she said.

"What do you dream?"

"I dream about having a good job and my own apartment," she said. Then, blushing, as if embarrassed at her own extravagance: "Sometimes I even dream of being married and having children."

We moved to kitchen wares, comparing likes and dislikes. "Teflon wears off, you know," she said. "I prefer an old-fashioned iron skillet."

And so it went, down the line. Security, a cubbyhole, a place of one's own, a job one could live on—these elements, singly or in combination, encompassed the wants and hopes of almost every woman. Despite the modesty of these goals, not all the women were likely to achieve them. Indeed, only a few would get jobs that could support independent living, and a few more would eventually come to the top of the waiting list for subsidized housing. The main point about these expectations, however, is that the women were not asking God or Fortune for miracles (for example, their own house); that would only guarantee disappointment. Their wants were modest and reasonable.[19]

---

[19]"A room with a kitchenette was something many of the older women talked about and hoped for. . . . Living on the street could be tolerated because the belief that such a room would become available, was strong." Marsha A. Martin, "Strategies of Adaptation: Coping Patterns of the Urban Transient Female," p. 87.

The women knew, for example, that Jenny had escaped home-lessness by coming to the top of the housing list, and Grace had gotten this terrific job, and "if it happened to them it could hap-pen to me." What made these life goals so reasonable, then, was not that the individual women had a good chance of achieving them, but that it was reasonable to want them and even to ex-pect that eventually, with a little bit of luck and God's help, one might have them.

Carried too far, avoidance of high expectations could lead to chronically low expectations, pessimism, and perpetual dis-content. Betty seemed to thrive on discontent, always ready to denounce the treatment of homeless women, violations of their rights, and so on, often in very creative ways. Isaiah Berlin would have been proud of Betty's analysis of the way Social Services was violating her negative freedoms.[20] One Friday, at the end of the month, when her expected public assistance check failed to arrive, Betty was outraged at having to face Saturday and Sunday with no money at all. They were fucking with her constitutional rights, she said. Where was her freedom of religion if she didn't have bus fare to get to the church of her choice? Where was her freedom of association if she had no money to visit her family and friends but had to stay around the shelter, forced to associate with people not of her choosing? Where was . . . and on and on she went.

To some women, Betty was a champion of the rights of the homeless. To others, and often to the staff, she was the incar-nation of negativism and a genuinely destructive force. When Betty was expelled for 24 hours for proclaiming, "This shelter's a hell hole," Jeanette thought this was too light a sentence. She said she didn't like Betty, mainly because she was always run-ning down the shelter and everything associated with it. This made the women there feel even worse than they already did,

---

[20]I am deprived of "negative" freedom or liberty "if I am prevented by oth-ers from doing what I could otherwise do." Isaiah Berlin. "Two Concepts of Liberty," in *Four Essays on Liberty,* p. 122.

and that was bad enough. "If there's one thing they don't need, it's being made to feel worse than they already feel. We need to believe in something to keep going."[21]

Vicki felt the same way about Betty, and used almost the same language to say so. Indeed, so strong was Vicki's aversion to what she called Betty's negativism that she avoided the day shelter where Betty was a regular. Vicki said she would avoid the night shelter for the same reason—she couldn't stand the belittling that went on all the time—but she had no alternative.

The fear of negativism was strong and steady. *The Power of Positive Thinking* and other feel-good and self-help reading material were exceptionally popular, perhaps too popular. It sometimes seemed as if the women went too far in avoiding negativism and pessimism by closing their eyes to real-world difficulties. When I tried to point out to Jeanette the practical, real-life difficulties and costs that stood in the way of retrieving her car from the abandoned car lot, she cut me off as politely as she could, saying she didn't want to hear about them. Grace did the same repeatedly, reminding me that nothing is too difficult for God.[22] And once, when I tried to talk Kim out of attempting to do something that had no chance of success and every chance for tragic consequences, she said that a true friend would support her in whatever she wanted to do and that if I insisted on talking about why it couldn't or shouldn't be done, we would no longer be friends.

So strong was this apparent avoidance of negativism, especially among those women who otherwise seemed "to see things clearly and see things whole" (that is, as Matthew Arnold and I

---

[21]The switch from third person to first person might suggest the ambivalence some of the women feel. They would like to disassociate themselves from the others but quickly realize—and cannot escape the fact—that they are also talking about themselves.

[22]I once presented Grace with the hoary riddle of how, when God created the world, there could have been three days and nights if God didn't create the sun and stars until the fourth day. Grace didn't see any problem. "He's God. He can do anything."

saw them), that I could only conclude there was more to it than met the eye: that the apparent avoidance of reality in selected circumstances was a conscious, purposeful strategy for freeing oneself to reach for a desirable but low-probability outcome rather than a true inability to see or face up to the real world.

Another important strategy for avoiding discouragement and disappointment was to take life "one day at a time." This was the advice the women gave to one another and themselves. There is no doubt that this strategy helped many of the women over some rough spots, but it also had its costs. Once, when the women were talking about the imminent closing of The Refuge for the year, a staff person asked Dorothy what she was going to do. Dorothy said she didn't know. Did she have any plans? Dorothy shook her head no.

Staff people were constantly puzzled by the failure of the women to plan, even in the face of imminent catastrophe. They attributed this failure to an inability to plan, or an unwillingness to face reality, or as evidence that the women really didn't give a damn, not even for themselves, so no wonder they were where they were. Grace, however, saw things differently. Dorothy had made no plans because "none of the women think that far ahead. I take things one day at a time," she said, "and so do all the others. There's no other way."

Failure to plan, then, was one of the costs of "taking it one day at a time." It is not clear, however, that this strategy was fundamentally incompatible with planning for the near future. Certainly there were women, including Grace, who did plan, even while they were telling themselves to take things one day at a time. But this strategy, useful and perhaps essential for getting through from one day to the next, must partly explain the surprisingly small amount of energy and time that the women gave over to planning.[23]

---

[23] It is possible, even likely, that the women engaged in more planning than they talked about. Maybe it was OK to plan, but to talk about one's plans was to invite disaster.

Other forces also worked against planning. One of them was discernible behind the extravagant language Betty used on one of her not-so-good days. She had been talking about being invited to a retreat at a nearby convent. For three days, she said expectantly, there would be no talking except at mealtimes and no radio, no TV, no newspapers.

"That's great," I said. "It should give you plenty of time to make your plans for the coming months."

"Plans!" she said. "I'm not going to waste my time making plans! That's useless. There's always some asshole around the corner or behind a tree just waiting for me to make a plan so he can spoil it. But that won't keep me from thinking of ways to trick those assholes."

Betty may have been paranoid, but this was not the language of paranoia so much as the language of powerlessness. At the very heart of planning is the assumption that one has the power to control or influence the future.[24] If one is truly powerless to influence events, planning makes very little sense. Even contingency planning requires a sense of options and outcomes and of one's own ability to take effective action. None of the other women were as eloquent as Betty on this subject, but it is difficult to avoid the conclusion that they, too, were deterred from planning by their own sense of powerlessness. From their perspective, it was not only useless to engage in planning; in the extreme case planning was to be actively avoided, for down that road lay failure and disappointment and still further confirmation of one's own impotence.

These survival strategies were often overlaid with personal philosophies and tactics that set the women apart from one another even while they pursued the same goals. When she was working, which was most of the time, Grace took a motel room once or twice a month. From Saturday noon to Sunday noon, Grace luxuriated in a bubble bath and sipped Manischewitz

---

[24]"The Power of a Man . . . is his present means to obtain some future . . . Good." Thomas Hobbes, *Leviathan,* p. 62.

wine (OK for sacramental purposes so it can't be too sinful) and watched TV. "I have to do that to keep going," she said. When Betty learned about this, she began using part of her public assistance check for the same practice (without the wine).[25]

Kathleen had only recently changed her approach to life. She had been more or less homeless for over three years, she said, and always had the feeling she was living in a minefield. She had lived these years in fear of stepping on a mine, but no matter how softly and carefully she stepped, something—a job, a relationship, a place to live—always blew up on her. Since things were going to blow up no matter how careful she was, she decided she might as well stop pussyfooting around and walk hard and fast to wherever she wanted to go. She had a better chance of reaching her goal that way than if she tried to mince her way through the minefield.

Joanne was a regular at the soup kitchen. Her technique for keeping her spirits up was to insist that there was always more than one way to get where you wanted to go, however rocky those ways might be. "There are always alternatives," she said. When she was suspended from a shelter and all the others in the area were full, I offered her $5 and suggested she go downtown to CCNV. She refused the money, saying she didn't think she could handle CCNV, and anyway, "there are always alternatives."

"Such as?" I asked. She said she could always find a hallway to sleep in or a building under construction. I said those were lousy alternatives. "I said there were always alternatives," she reminded me. "I didn't say there were always good ones."

Queen, on the other hand, found the strength she needed in the sheer absence of alternatives, in the need to do what had to be done when she had to live on the street. "I didn't 'adjust.' I had no alternative."

---

[25]When one's wage or other income is so small that it is not likely one can ever save enough to move out on one's own, it does not matter much how one spends it. But when a woman in this situation chooses to take a motel room for a day, or to buy some trinkets, observers are shocked by this apparent inversion of priorities, this childishness, this irresponsibility.

Kim had her own distinctive strategy for lowering her expectations. While others extolled the energizing virtues of optimism, Kim saw it as the mother of disappointment. Optimism, looked at retrospectively, was a trap to be avoided. "All my life," she said, "I've tried to be realistic, to see the world as it really is, but everything always turned out worse than I expected. That means I was optimistic, not realistic." Henceforth, she would make allowances for this slippage. "From now on, I'm going to be pessimistic. Maybe that way I'll end up being realistic."

Regina had her own formula for avoiding being overwhelmed by circumstance. "You have to fight for your religion and what you believe in or the world will walk all over you," she cautioned. Louise used startlingly simple strategies. Staff threats to kick her out of the shelter had no teeth, she said. "That's one good thing about not having children. You don't care about tomorrow. You don't care about the future." And on those days when she did care, she refused to be distracted by abstract beliefs or other irrelevancies. "When you're trying to survive from day to day," she said, "there is no Good or Evil. There is only survival."

For most women, one-on-one relationships with friends, with God, and with themselves had lightened somewhat the crushing weight of homelessness. There was hope now along with despair, and the sense that, most of the time, life was worth living. Homelessness, however, was still an unnatural and detested way of life, and the women were still in danger of being crushed by it, of losing their hope, and with it their humanity. But the women had come as far as they could on their own. All their personal resources had been used up to bring them this far, and there was still much more to overcome. So the women turned to the sole remaining source of potential support—homeless women as a group. Solidarity with one's fellows meant that one did not always have to fight alone.

6
Making It Together

S helters are dynamic social systems whose moods are in a constant state of flux. If, for a moment, the system appears to be in a steady state, it is a stability born of a temporary balance of forces rather than a state of rest. The forces are many. They operate at different levels and pull in different directions. At the individual level, personalities clash and personalities mesh, producing smaller groups and cliques within the system. Superimposed on these are a variety of system-level forces, some of which enhance group solidarity, some of which work against it, and some of which can go either way.

It is unlikely that staff people and shelter rules by themselves could have contained the explosive forces generated by racial animosity, social class differences, competition for resources, overcrowding, individuals who were not always in control of their actions, and individuals who wanted to disassociate themselves from the group. But arrayed against these forces, and born mainly out of shared homelessness and common needs, was a powerful impulse to group cohesion and solidarity. Most of the time, the impulse to solidarity was strong enough to hold the negative forces in check, thereby providing that minimum of peace and good order that made social life possible. Indeed, on many evenings, as the women came together in the shelter, there was sufficient good feeling and fellow feeling, when coupled with their common needs and circumstances, to allow a sense of community to sputter into life. For most women, the loneliness of their homeless state was a terrible burden to bear; this fragile bit of community, however small, was precious indeed.

• • •

Race was the most divisive and destructive force in shelter life, although in practice it was usually contained.[*] To some women, racial differences were an unbridgeable chasm; to a very few, they were no more significant than differences in height or weight. The overall impact of race on shelter life is therefore uneven and difficult to summarize. White women seemed more likely than black women to bunch up at both the high and low ends of a scale of racial attitudes; among them were the greatest and the least animosity.[1] At the same time, white women appeared to be freer or more willing to initiate a cross-color relationship than black women, perhaps because there was less racial solidarity among white women than black.

Public expression of racial animosity was against the rules— the informal rules by which the women governed themselves as well as the formal rules that prevailed in every shelter. The formal rules and the informal, working together, generated a

---

[*] Grace: *I never noticed a race problem in the shelter. Maybe it's because I was not looking for problems, just too busy concentrating on how to survive. There were many different cultures in this shelter and once in a while some white woman might call a black one a name but I thought that due to lack of education.*

[1] "If I don't win the lottery," said Jane (white), "I hope a black person does." And another time, "How can we expect black people to behave with justice if we don't treat them with justice?"

strong moral force. Their joint prohibition against the public expression of racism made it fairly easy for those women who were so inclined to form friendships that crossed the color line. The fact that Betty, Kim, Peggy, and others had such relationships made it difficult, in turn, for other white women to talk the talk of racists, even when no black women were present.[2] Similarly, those who said or did things out of racist promptings were pressed to claim quite other reasons for their actions.

Elsie invoked her Christian values and sense of citizenship to explain why she called the manager's attention to Queen's shoplifting of trinkets in People's Drug Store, resulting in Queen's arrest and removal from the shelter. But Elsie's disloyalty to the group—"Queen was one of us"—was seen as a worse "crime" than Queen's shoplifting of trinkets, which was no big deal to most of the women, not to those who shoplifted themselves and not to those who didn't. Although no one took any overt action, everyone—black and white—deplored what Elsie had done, and there was little doubt in their minds that racism was a factor in Elsie's decision to act.

Only Cora (white) confronted Elsie about Queen. In Elsie's presence but pretending to address others, Cora compared a series of her ex-husband's crimes with Queen's theft of a few trinkets: his forging her name to make a loan on Cora's house, "and he lives free" (in the very same house) while Queen is jailed for stealing a few trinkets; his crime of perjury, "and he lives free" while Queen is jailed for stealing a few trinkets; his crime of . . . Elsie got the message and marched off in anger.

The city of Washington, with its large black majority, black mayor, and black city government, was often used to clothe white prejudice in fairly transparent dress. The night before the 1988 Superbowl, Pam (black) asked Peggy (white) who she thought would win. Peggy said she hoped Denver would win because she hated everything that comes out of Washington, in-

---

[2] I can only assume that the black women, among themselves, felt similar constraints.

cluding the Redskins. Pam said, "Your food and medicine and money comes out of Washington. Everything you got comes out of Washington." Peggy shrugged. "I still hate D.C.," she said.

Not everyone dealt in subtleties. There was always a handful of women, mostly white, whose animosities could not always be contained by house rules, formal or informal. The effect of their slurs and epithets was blunted by the fact that these women tended to be more troubled than the others. They were also more marginal in the sense that, whatever the subject, the others were not likely to set great store by what they said. Nevertheless, these women served to keep the issue of race alive and at the forefront of group awareness.[3]

DeeDee and Hilda were typical of racists who spoke out. One evening—it could have been any evening—DeeDee started ranting against "nigger welfare workers." But DeeDee was often treated as the (mental) child she appeared to be, and two black women nearby, who surely heard her, gave no indication that they had. "You shouldn't talk like that," said a white volunteer. "It's not right to talk like that."

"The truth's the truth," said DeeDee, and she pursed her lips and ducked her head as a truculent child might do.

Hilda was a self-proclaimed manic depressive. She was aggressive with the other women and intimidating because of her size. She was one of the least liked women and certainly commanded little respect. In the presence of white people, Hilda spoke of "coloreds." She was proud of her clear-cut racist beliefs; decisiveness was a virtue and a mark of leadership, she said. She willingly conceded that she was widely disliked; that was the price of leadership, she said. One night—it could have been any night—she started in on how black people have taken over Washington, shutting whites out from jobs, housing,

---

[3]Because these women were considered less competent, they were generally held to lower standards of accountability. At the same time, however, there was a poisonous, cross-race suspicion that these women, like drunks, were less inhibited than the rest of us, and dared to say what all the other white women (black women) felt but did not dare to say.

welfare, and so on.[4] A white staff person interrupted her. "You've gone too far," she said, "and I want you to know where I'm coming from."

"And I want you to know where I'm going," snapped Hilda. "I'm not prejudiced," she said. "I see things as they are and I tell it like it is. I don't straddle the fence. A leader can't straddle the fence."[5]

The Hildas and DeeDees strained the system, but it managed to contain them either by ignoring them or by restraining them with occasional threats from staff or the women themselves. Sometimes, however, a woman came along (see page 126, for example) whose shouted racial tirades could not be ignored or tamed by threats. To allow such a woman to remain in the shelter would have put group cohesion—indeed, group life itself—at grave risk.

It is tempting to see white racism and black racism as mirror images of one another, made of the same kind of stuff. But white hatred of blacks appeared to be a purer, self-sustaining emotion that fed on itself. Black hatred of whites appeared to be more reactive, more dependent, feeding not on itself but on white hatred.

For this reason, perhaps, DeeDee and Hilda had few if any black counterparts who went around making gratuitous racial pronouncements. Many black women responded in kind to racial slurs and were quick to introduce race ("You white motherfucker!") in an argument with a white woman, but I saw

---

[4]Hilda and most of the other women who saw the world in similar terms sometimes coupled Jews with blacks, but in my presence, at least, Jews were clearly of secondary importance. To my knowledge, Hilda was the only one to include Catholics in her diatribes. She sometimes contended that "there are no Episcopalians in shelters." This was not true; Jeanette was born and raised as an Episcopalian.

[5]Another time, Hilda sneered when Bishop Desmond Tutu came on the TV screen. He was not a true leader, she said.

"Why do you say that?"

"He got the Nobel Prize, didn't he? He's liked by both sides. Only a fence straddler is liked by both sides."

none who, like the Hildas and DeeDees, would move to a racial attack without provocation. What one did see at the extremes were black women who felt deeply wounded by white hatred and wanted nothing further to do with white people other than to hate or resent them.

Virginia said she used to work as a nurse's aide in a hospital. She was prejudiced against white people, she said, and this prejudice grew inside her for many years until it became pure hatred for all whites, even her white-faced patients. She quit her job because she was afraid of what she might do to the white patients she was responsible for. That was when she decided to build a wall around herself, she said, and let herself be consumed by a hatred that drove all love and all humanity out of her life.[6] In the shelter, Virginia did indeed live with a wall around her, avoiding all human contact except with Ruby, an extraordinarily patient and loving black staff woman.

Miss Tee was a big, raw-boned black woman in her 60s with a broad, open face, high cheekbones, and exceptionally thick legs. Her walking was labored, and she stayed at The Refuge only a week or so, probably because she could not manage the three flights of stairs. At the shelter, Miss Tee refused all food and remained on her cot all night, fully clothed, speaking only when spoken to.

Miss Tee said she had tried to lead a decent Christian life but the white man wouldn't let her. When she dies, she said, she doesn't want to go to heaven. She just wants to die and be dead.

"Why don't you want to go to heaven?" I asked.

"Because the same white people who own this world own heaven. They're the Christians. They own the religion so they own heaven, too."

"It's sad to hear someone so depressed about the future."

---

[6]This conversation with Virginia took place very early in my association with the shelter. She spoke to me conversationally only one more time.

KIM: *Virginia talked to me once too. I felt privileged, somehow honored, special. After about a week and a half, she quit speaking to me as abruptly as she had begun.*

"Well, that's how I feel," she said.

The same women who were so outspoken about black people also talked freely about their hostility to Asians and other "foreigners." In one or another shelter, there were usually one or two Hispanic women but I never heard anything specifically directed against them. They were, perhaps, included in "foreigners."

DeeDee once threw a chair at Lily "because she's a Jap" and Hilda poked hard, racial "fun" at her Vietnamese supervisor in the cafeteria where she worked. ("They hate us all, you know.") But there was not a lot of anti-Asian talk, perhaps because there were so few Asians around to hear it, and what there was lacked the bite of black/white race talk, possibly because it was fired more by resentment than hatred. Indeed, some of this talk was not really racial so much as xenophobic.

In Bridge House, over coffee, Vicki, Michelle, and I were talking about the exorbitant rents in the county and the absence of affordable housing. "If you want to see some public housing go up," said Vicki, "put those government [housing] people in shelters and let us move into their houses. Public housing would go up the next day." After a pause she continued. "There is public housing, but it's all political. It all goes to Cambodians and Vietnamese."

"Oh, come on, Vicki."

"No, really," she said. "It all goes to Cambodians and Vietnamese. You don't see any of them in shelters, do you? Have you ever seen any of them here or in any other shelter? It's political. They [housing officials] give them public housing and put their own people out on the street. [Long pause] That's the American way."

Michelle, who was black, agreed with Vicki that Asians and other foreigners got preferential treatment from the government. She said she had been forced into homelessness when a tenant reported that she was sharing her mother's subsidized apartment, which was rated for one-person occupancy. She lowered her voice. "They let foreigners have as many people as they want. They can have a hundred people in an apartment and no one says anything to them. It's only Americans that have to go by the rules."

"Just black Americans or white Americans, too?"

"All Americans," she said. "Black or white. But if you're a foreigner, you're OK."

It is likely that this prejudice against foreigners, Asians—anyone who wasn't "American" black or white—served to promote much-needed black–white solidarity. In fact, prejudice against "foreigners" sometimes seemed an afterthought. It was as if the women themselves, knowing that black–white racism was the main threat to peace and good order, saw potential in this joint hostility to "foreigners" for bringing blacks and whites together.

• • •

After race, nothing else threatened group solidarity so much as distinctions of social class. Class distinctions were of two kinds: those that distinguished the women from the middle class of the outside world and those that distinguished the women from one another. The first enhanced group solidarity since most of the women identified with the working class and, more generally, with the underdogs and have-nots.[7] When Jane lost her job because her fellow workers learned she was living in her car, she saw this as an instance of class abuse: "Poor people are always being abused by others," she said. "Each class looks out for its own interests and tries to protect itself, mainly from the class just below them. That's why the lower middle class hates the poor."

---

[7] "I won't forget the kindness that was shown me [on the street]. . . . But these people to me are—they don't judge nobody and I feel like that we were all outcasts. And I always felt that they never judged, see. And I felt I belonged with them because they never said, 'What are you doing with that—you think you're better than those,' you know. . . . We were all in the same boat, so nobody was up or down. We was all on the same level." Regina, from transcribed life history.

Virginia explained her difficulties with Social Services in much the same terms. People in agencies try to keep their clients from climbing into the middle class, she said. But they don't realize that in shutting the door on their clients, they are shutting the door on their own aspirations.

Kim didn't want to move up in class. She and I were walking down the street when a woman hurried past us wearing a tailored suit and carrying a briefcase, her heels clacking. I told Kim that with her brains and skills, she could be like that woman. "But she's The Enemy!" Kim protested, laughing. "Do you really want me to join The Enemy?"

In my car, while we were driving to D.C., Betty winced every time we passed a high-rise office building or apartment house under construction. "There ought to be a law," she said. "No more office buildings or apartment houses as long as there is a single homeless woman in the county."

The women identified primarily with other homeless people, but this solidarity was easily extended to poor people generally. They sometimes said that poor people, homeless people, street people, were "the salt of the earth." Not surprisingly, solidarity with the weak, the poor, the underdog, and the unprivileged was expressed most profoundly by those who were themselves the weakest among the weak and the poorest among the poor.

To Angela, people on the bottom were the inheritors of the earth. In the Greezy Spoon, Angela was reminiscing about her army reserve experience 10 years earlier when she was 19. "They put a pack on your back and boss you around. They're so goddamn bossy! I told them I didn't need that shit and I left. Were you in the service?"

"I was in the Marine Corps. In the Pacific."

"When was that?"

"World War Two."

"Woooorld Waaaaar," she repeated slowly, stretching out the vowels. "I shiver when I hear words like that. When was it?"

"Nineteen forty-one to nineteen forty-five."

"Did you actually fight?"

"A little."

"Who was making war?"

"The Americans and the Japanese."

"Who won?"

"We did. The Americans."

Angela was quiet for a moment as if digesting this enormous fact of history. "You know," she said finally, "Some people believe that only the strong will survive. Can you imagine going through life believing something like that?"

Extending their collective identity to encompass poor people and underdogs enlarged the women's circle of solidarity. Allying themselves with the millions of have-nots gave them a greater sense of security. It also gave them a sharpened sense of social justice and encouraged them to see homelessness as only one of many social inequities.

In the day shelter, Della pulled me aside. She said she was going to start a university that would give only honorary degrees.

"Is there a need for a university like that?"

"Absolutely," she said. "Why do you have to be Frank Sinatra or Nancy Reagan to get an honorary degree? Why can't ordinary people get them, too?"

"What will people have to do to get an honorary degree?"

"They will have to be honorable," she said. "Do you know what I'm going to call my university? 'Masada.' Do you know what that means?"

"No."

"It means 'Death before dishonor.'"

In sharp contrast to solidarity-building distinctions between homeless women and higher classes, class distinctions within the group put the women in serious conflict with one another. Among themselves, the women recognized only two classes: a working class and a dependent class, with each group claiming to be the deserving poor. Here, the usual determinants of social class—education, occupation, income—were irrelevant. The only thing that mattered was whether, at any given moment, one was working or on welfare.[8]

The salience of this distinction was not always evident. One could perhaps see the vague outline of these class differences in friendship patterns or hinted at in private conversations. But by and large, they lay dormant and were mostly unacknowledged, perhaps because, like race, they might be too destructive, or because next week or next month, one might find oneself or one's friends in the other camp.[9]

The class character of this major divide among the women, however, was clear-cut: Who was most deserving of assistance, those who worked or those on welfare? Who were the freeloaders, those who worked or those on welfare? Betty had fewer compunctions than most about acknowledging this division. She said she didn't like Grace and other women here whom she didn't care to name because they had full-time jobs and had no business living off the shelter and the county.[10]

Eleanor saw the division among the women somewhat differently. At night, after the lights were out, Eleanor and Louise were in the smoking area talking about women they liked and disliked. Eleanor said she was angry about the number of women freeloading on the shelters. Some of the women here are

[8]It might be more useful, following Kohn and others, to see education, occupation, and income as indicators of social stratification rather than social class. "By 'classes,' we mean groups defined in terms of their relationship to ownership and control of the means of production, and of their control over the labor power of others. We deliberately distinguish social class from social stratification—the hierarchical ordering of society as indexed by formal education, occupational status, and job income." Melvin L. Kohn, Atsushi Naoi, Carrie Schoenbach, Carmi Schooler, and Kazimierz M. Slomczynski, "Position in the Class Structure and Psychological Functioning in the United States, Japan, and Poland," *American Journal of Sociology* 95, no. 4 (January 1990), p. 965.

[9]Not everyone fell cleanly into one or another category. Persons looking for work or unable to work, or those on workfare might, when called on to be counted, join one or another group or simply stay on the sidelines.

[10]But when Grace lost her job a few weeks later, Betty warmed up and began clipping job ads for her.

very educated, she said. They're slick. They're not homeless, but they know how to act homeless, and they know how to get all the things that are really for the homeless.

It was Kim, however, who provided a public and dispassionate analysis of the conflict. At a Wednesday night shelter-wide meeting, the women were asked for their opinions as to why there was so much contention in the shelter.[11] After Judy and Louise volunteered some minor irritants having to do with heat and showers, Kim stood up.

The bickering, said Kim, is rooted in jealousy and resentment between the two major groups here, those who work and those who don't. Those who don't work, she went on, see those who do as freeloaders on a system that wasn't intended for them. Since they're working and earning money, what do they need a shelter for? And why should they get bus tokens and food and other things meant for homeless women?

On the other hand, Kim continued, working women see the others as sitting on their fat asses drawing welfare and food stamps. To them, the nonworkers are not trying to better themselves, don't even want to better themselves, so why should their laziness be rewarded? Help should go to those who are trying to help themselves.

The remarkable thing about this speech was that Kim (who was working at the time) had put the issue so evenhandedly that no one could tell which side she was on. This very impartiality allowed all the women, workers and nonworkers alike, to nod their heads vigorously. "She's absolutely right," said Abigail, and the women nodded agreement, as if they were relieved to hear the issue brought into the open.

At the very next meeting, the issue leaped into life. Jim announced he had a limited number of bus tokens for distribution. Some of the tokens came from the soup kitchen for the express purpose of enabling those who had no money to get there. The rest came from Catholic Charities for those in greatest need.

---

[11]This was at No Name shelter, soon to become Bridge House. Neither The Refuge nor New Beginnings held such meetings.

The main point, he said, was that the tokens did not come from the county so they were not entitlements; they were charity, not rights. Those who worked, he concluded, did not go to the soup kitchen and were therefore not eligible for tokens from either source.[12]

Abigail, who was working at the time, was furious. The women on any kind of public assistance have both food stamps and the soup kitchen, she said, so they don't have to spend money on food. But women who work don't have the soup kitchen, so they must buy their own food—an especially expensive proposition since they must buy food for one day at a time because there's no place to store it. Jim was adamant. It was not the purpose of the tokens to help working people save their money on food, he said.

That was not her point, said Abigail. Her point was that she made almost $300 every two weeks, about $600 every month. "That sounds like a lot of money," she conceded, "and I keep telling myself I should be able to save some money each month, but I can't, no matter how hard I watch myself. There's no way I can save money if I have to buy my food one day at a time."

"I hear you," said Jim. "I hear where you're coming from. But the tokens are not here to help people buy food."

"You still don't understand," said Abigail. "How will I ever get out of here if I can't save any money? I'm working as hard as I can but I can't get ahead."

It was difficult for Judy to accept the reality of class divisions among the women. Judy wanted everyone to love one another. She also had her own relativistic notion of independence. From her perspective, welfare was not dependency but the road to independence. In a four-way discussion of the subject, Judy said that she was going to apply for SSI. She said she was determined to be independent; her doctor told her that was her greatest

---

[12]During this period, when No Name shelter had not yet become Bridge House, it did not have facilities for hot food and served only cold snacks rather than meals. The nearest soup kitchen served dinner from 3:00 to 5:00 P.M., thereby excluding most working women.

strength. "I could have given up a long time ago and gone to an institution and let them take care of me," she said. "But if I get my SSI, I'll decide for myself when I get up, what I'll wear, and everything else."

Judy conceded there were differences among the women but insisted that the hostility among them was neither natural nor necessary. "It's the meetings," she said. "It's the meetings that set women against one another."[13]

Betty did not work but identified herself with the women who did. For her, the crucial divisions among the women were determined by what they wanted from life. She argued repeatedly for a two-track shelter system: one for those who were content to live out their lives in shelters and another for those who wanted "a higher standard of living," who could make it in the world and wanted a place of their own. Other times, she argued for a three-track system, further separating out those who, for whatever reason, were unable to work.

In general, then, class divisions among the women—and these were not always in evidence—were almost always manifest in terms of their relation to the work force: those who could work and did, those who could work and did not, and those unable to work.

On a few occasions, class and race were mixed with politics and patriotism, and it was difficult to sort out the proportions of the mix. Politics were seldom the subject of sustained discussion but the women often made casual comments, sometimes to one another, sometimes to a TV newscaster.

Clearly, Presidents Reagan and Bush were uniformly disliked by the black women and by most of the white women. Those who were against Reagan and Bush seemed to base their

---

[13]Judy was partly right; the meetings did contribute to hostility. In the name of honesty, openness, and "letting it all hang out," things got said at the meetings that ordinarily would have been suppressed by good manners or a simple reluctance to hurt someone's feelings. It is not at all clear that such meetings enhanced the solidarity of the group or the well-being of the often fragile individuals.

judgment on the administration's presumed hostility to (black and) poor people and favoring of the rich. On the surface, at least, supporters of the president seemed to be less ideological, believing that whoever is president deserves respect and support because he is the elected head of state and has a very difficult job. Among the supporters of the administration were women who seemed to be relatively free of race bias. But also among them were women who were not. All of these perspectives seemed to be in play in an argument that developed in the day shelter.

The TV set was reporting that Colonel Oliver North and Admiral John Poindexter had again invoked the Fifth Amendment. "Why don't they leave Reagan alone?" said Peggy. "He didn't know about the money and he's got to run the country." Phyllis shook her head in agreement. From across the room, Holly said Reagan was not a compassionate person and didn't care about poor people. He just wanted to make the rich richer.

Peggy was incensed. She said Holly should go to Russia if she didn't like it here. Holly said she didn't like Russia either and anyway, she didn't have any money.

"You don't have to go to Russia," said Peggy. "You can go to England or Scotland."

"They're as poor as I am," said Holly. "They don't have any money either."

The argument expanded to include normally quiet Phyllis on Peggy's side and Shirley, who said her family had been radicals in the trade union movement, on Holly's side. Both sides soon got down to fundamentals. While Peggy kept repeating, "Why don't you go to Russia," Holly kept repeating, in singsong, "Yah, yah, right-wing Reagan sold out, right-wing Reagan sold out." They were going at this hot and heavy, shouting at each other across the room, when Lily snatched the small American flag from its usual place alongside her carpetbag, stood at attention, held the flag up high, and began to sing, "My country, 'tis of thee, sweet land of liberty . . . " Lily drowned out Peggy and Holly, both of whom, along with everyone else, stopped to look and listen and laugh in amazement.

However brief, the antagonism between Peggy and Holly, Phyllis and Shirley (all white) was real enough. And while Holly and Shirley were certainly arguing from a class perspective and identifying themselves with poor people and underdogs, Peggy and Phyllis seemed to be talking patriotism, not ideology or even politics. President Reagan should be supported precisely because he is president. The president represents the country and to be against him is somehow to be against the country. But from things they said at other times, it is probable that the commonly assumed anti–civil rights, anti–black character of the Reagan/Bush administrations was also at work here, although both Peggy and Phyllis were meticulously free of any racist taint in their personal, one-on-one dealings with the black women.

• • •

Like most people, the women shared the perception that many homeless persons are mentally ill. Sometimes, in a self-mocking mood, they used the presumption of mental illness to assert their unity. In general, however, the presumed presence or absence of mental illness was one of the major ways in which the women made invidious distinctions among themselves, though it was usually other persons who were thought to be mentally ill, almost never oneself.

Betty held up a newspaper. "It says here that 50 percent of the homeless are estimated to be chronically mentally ill. I'd have guessed more than that," she said.

"Would you include yourself in that?"

"No, not now. But when I was drinking, yes."

Ascribing mental illness to others was one of the ways the women could enhance their self-image. But since this distinction was made at the expense of the group, one had to be careful about sharing this self-serving judgment. Moreover, only the stronger, more competent women could realistically dissociate themselves from the group in this way and lay claim to being not just different but superior.

Lisa and Elsie were standing apart from the others. Lisa said most of the women didn't have jobs because they didn't want them. Would they be here two, three, four years if they wanted jobs? Elsie was probably flattered at this distinction between "us" and "them." "Why do so many choose that way?" she asked. "Why?"

Grace, in another conversation, thought she knew. "The women here," she said, gesturing to take in everyone, "they've given up. There are plenty of opportunities out there but they're not even looking. I know [tapping her temple] that they've all got something wrong with them up here, but still . . ."*

Grace, of course, had to be very careful about sharing such judgments. Some women, however, were able to distance themselves publicly from others by masking the distinction with humor. In the day shelter, the women were talking about the difficulty of getting to sleep at night and Lisa began to describe, in caricature, the lights-out behavior of the different women. She began by naming five women (four of whom were present) who, she said, kept others awake at night by talking to people who weren't there. Everyone laughed as Lisa imitated herself looking to see whom the women could be talking to and, seeing no one, groping blindly with her outstretched arms to try to touch what she could not see. The women she named laughed as hard as the others.

Women with serious and obvious mental problems were sometimes targets of anger and resentment but almost never ridicule. When these women were involved, even behavior that one might expect to be met with hilarity was more likely to be

---

*GRACE: *This comment of mine was taken out of its original context. My opinion of the women in the shelter was not one of giving up, it was one of being in a circumstance that beats you down, and beats you down, till you can't think any longer.*

met with silence, as when Polly, after an argument with a staff person, walked back to her cot at the far end of the shelter, urinating defiantly all the way.[14]

Everyone else was fair game, however. Indeed, the attribution and denial of mental illness were a constant and principal source of merriment, often arising from the most casual circumstances. Kim said that Nancy was beginning to act strangely. Betty said there were a lot of strange women here, and Kim was one of them. Kim protested to one and all that she was not strange, not crazy, and not a deviate like everyone else.

"Then why are you here?" someone called out. "What's wrong with you?"

"I'm a nonconformist," protested Kim. "nothing more, nothing less. A nonconformist, that's all." And everyone hooted and laughed, including Kim.

At times, it seemed as if the periodic attribution of mental illness to all members of the group was aimed at enhancing group solidarity by pulling back into the group those who had been trying to dissociate themselves from it. Sometimes this solidarity took the general form of "All of us are a little crazy" or "We all have something wrong with us." Other times, the women were more specific and named names.

In the day shelter, Edith and Leslie got into a serious discussion that quickly took on the character of two ships passing in the night.

Edith took the Bible from the top of the piano and began reading. Someone said, "I thought you didn't believe that stuff."

"I want to know about the Bible as history," said Edith. "It's not only religion, it's history, too." As if to prove her point, she announced, "Matthias was Herod's lawgiver."

---

[14]The uneasy, even embarrassed silence that followed Polly's silent rejoinder was much like the silences that often followed what seemed to be an irrational outburst from one of the women. It was difficult to shake the feeling that some of the women were not only embarrassed—after all, Polly was "one of us"—but also, perhaps, afraid that they themselves might sometimes look like that to others.

Leslie, a tall, elegant, black woman in her 30s, who carried herself like the model she used to be, turned around in her chair. "Harrod's?' asked Leslie.

"Herod's," said Edith.

"The London department store?" asked Leslie.

Edith was puzzled. She seemed not to know what to make of this and apparently decided to start over. "Matthias was Herod's lawgiver," she intoned again, as if there had been no interruption.

"Charles   Mathias?"   asked   Leslie.   "Senator   Charles Mathias?"[15]

Edith looked hard and long at Leslie as if, by looking, she could fathom Leslie's intent. "I'm talking about the Bible," she said. "I'm talking about a long time ago."

"What color was Cleopatra?" asked Leslie.

"Who?"

"Cleopatra," said Leslie. "The pharoahs. What color were the pharoahs and their people?"

"They were Egyptians," said Edith.

"But what color were they?" Leslie persisted. "Were they white? Black? What?"

"Well," said Edith, "they were white, but they weren't white-white, if you know what I mean. They weren't white like Englishmen."

"They were black," said Leslie. "Egypt is in Africa. They were Africans."

"Did you see *Inherit the Wind*?" asked Edith, who may or may not have been changing the subject.

"I saw *Gone with the Wind*," said Leslie, who may have divined where Edith was trying to take the conversation.

Edith said something about the movie location of *Gone with the Wind* and her aunt's plantation in Louisiana.

"What about Clark Gable?" asked Leslie.

---

[15]Charles Mathias (R), U.S. Senator from Maryland, 1968–86.

At this point, the women who had been listening burst into uncontrollable laughter. Peggy wiped away her tears and said it would be easy to brainwash the Russians and reduce them to blithering idiots—all we'd have to do was put them in the same room with Leslie and Edith. "And Susan!" someone called out. "And Vivian!" said another. "And Regina!" said someone else. "And Peggy!" said someone, and they continued in this fashion until everyone present had been named, at which point they began naming non-present occupants of the three shelters that fed the day shelter, and everyone laughed and clapped as each name, including her own, was called out.

Mental health problems and homelessness stood in a chicken-and-egg relationship to one another. Homelessness was seen as a cause of mental health problems just as often as mental health problems were seen as a cause of homelessness. Indeed, it was not uncommon for the women to use their homelessness to explain their sometimes ungenerous behavior. Judy and Elsie had a bitter argument and stopped speaking to one another. A few days later, they suddenly embraced, laughing and crying as Elsie apologized, saying that she had been lashing out at everyone recently for no reason, that homelessness was getting to her.

When several women rudely and unfairly spoke against another who was not present and talked about petitioning the staff to expel her from the shelter, I told them, with all the sarcasm I could muster, how impressed I was with their tolerance and loyalty to one another. As usual, Betty again spoke for the group. I don't have the time or energy for tolerance when I come here at night, she said, and you wouldn't either if you had to be on the street for 12 hours and 15 minutes and knew you had to go back on the street at 7:00 in the morning. "When I come here at night," she concluded, "I come for rest and quiet and I'm too tired to put up with anyone's shit. OK?"

Another time, the women were talking about Virginia's permanent expulsion, just announced. I said I was sorry to hear it, that (staff person) Ruby was the only one Virginia could relate to and her only human contact. Sneering, Louise asked me if I was trying to get the staff to reverse that decision. I told her I didn't make policy or suggest policy to those who made it.

"Then why did you say it?" she demanded. "If you feel sorry for Virginia, why don't you take her in?"

"I'm not a shelter," I said.

"Then make yourself one," she said, "and Virginia will have a place to stay. But don't try to put her in here with me. She assaults me, throws things at me, and wants to kill me, and you want them to let her back in to do the same things to me all over again." Louise marched out. The argument continued among the women, with Kim and Betty taking up where Louise left off.

Kim said that Virginia was crazy. "Her brains have turned to shit and she is sick, sick, sick." Lisa, who had been arguing against the expulsion, said, "We're all a little sick or crazy, that's why we're here." Kim denied this, and the argument continued heatedly, with Lisa and Cora siding against Kim and Betty.[*]

When I got a chance to speak again, I said how touched I was by their patience, tolerance, and sisterly solidarity. This angered Betty. You'll never understand until you have to live in a shelter, she said. You spend time here but you don't live here. You go home to your sweet little wife and your own house. Do you think a shelter is a place where you learn to be tolerant or patient? Do you think you learn those things living on the street? And even if you were taught those things as a kid, how long do you think you could hold on to them, living as we have to live?

The general argument was straightforward: Homelessness is an unnatural way of life in which people are forced to betray their own values. It puts such extraordinary stress on those who have to endure it that they cannot always think straight or

---

[*]Kim: *There are usually a few nut cases. Too many times, behavior is tolerated from, and allowances are made for, them at the expense of the sane majority. Occasionally, staff couldn't decide who was or wasn't "off." Marjorie (100% sane) lamented the double standard: "I'm crazy when it's convenient for them. I'm getting all of the penalties, without any of the benefits!"*

behave rationally. Importantly, the argument held that any sane person in a condition of homelessness would behave in much the same way.

Louise put it most simply. Normally, she did not identify with the other women, but one night she called me out to the smoking area, saying that she had something important to tell me. "You talk to us as if we are normal people who can hold a normal conversation. That's naive. *No one can live this way and be normal, no matter how they were when they first came."*

I heard this argument from others in many different forms, including its obverse: People who did not have to live "this way" (that is, people who have homes) are (should be) normal and clear-thinking. Thus, when a miscommunication resulted in some confusion among the staff directors, Grace was annoyed. "There's no excuse for Jim and Rachel getting mixed up," she said. "They should be able to think straight. They have homes to go to, and families and bedrooms with real beds and mattresses."

There was also the corollary that only crazy people can adjust easily to homelessness; sane people explode. Gwen, after a bitter verbal attack on a staff member in which she lost control of herself, saw this loss of control as confirmation of her sanity. When she calmed down, she sought out the staff person. "I'm not blaming you, Trudy. It's not your fault, but I've been sleeping on the floor for six months and I just had to get this off my chest. Only crazy people can take all this in stride, and I'm not crazy."

• • •

While race, class, and mental illness issues cut across the group in different ways, sometimes working for solidarity, sometimes against it, there were other, steadier forces always working to bring the women together. The most powerful force for group cohesion and solidarity grew out of the realization that "we're all in this together," that for better or worse, we share our lives, and for the present at least, we share a common fate. This collective self-image was brought into even sharper focus by the sense that the non-homeless world is against us, whipping us with stereotypes and jabbing us with contempt.

At the heart of this group identity was homelessness itself: every homeless woman in the shelter was a member of the group, and every member of the group was a homeless woman. Indeed, so central was homelessness to the definition of the group, and so greedy was the group to make all the women members, that it declared all women in the shelter to be homeless whether they wanted to see themselves that way or not. Thus, the answer to the question "Are you homeless?" was always yes, for everyone.*

In this important respect, "Are we homeless?" contrasted sharply with a question such as "Are we mentally ill (or lazy or failures)?" to which any woman could always reply, "Maybe you are but I am not." Since it was the collective judgment of the women that to live in a shelter was to be homeless, it was almost impossible for any individual to define her situation differently. Struggle as she might against defining herself as homeless, she was homeless whether she wanted to be or not. In this way, the group ensured both its membership and its integrity.

Once in a while, someone tried to climb out of the category of "homeless" by arguing, as Abigail sometimes did, that she was not homeless, the shelter was her home—she had her own cot to come back to night after night, at least one meal a day, and a roof over her head. But this argument was quickly overwhelmed by the Kims, Graces, Vickies, and Bettys, all strong voices that, when they spoke in unison, clearly spoke for the group, either as its representatives or shapers of group opinion.

Whenever someone called the shelter "home," Kim, for one, would demand to know who had ever heard of a home that you must leave at 7:00 in the morning and can't return to until 7:00 at night, or a home from which you can be evicted at any mo-

---

*KIM: *The Housing Opportunities Commission defines "homelessness" as "lacks a fixed regular or adequate nighttime residence (and/or) living in a temporary shelter." Most people are out and about during the day, looking for work, shopping, and running errands. WHO WE ARE IS DEFINED BY WHERE WE SLEEP AT NIGHT.* [Emphasis added.]

ment, with no notice whatever, on someone's whim. At a gas station, a mechanic filled out a work order for Grace's car, then
asked for her name and address. Grace gave her name but de-
murred on her address, saying simply she'd rather not give it.
Later, she explained that the shelter was not her home. "It's just
a shelter. I don't *live* there."

Vicki was downright contemptuous of shelters. In the midst
of a discussion about homelessness, she waved her hand and
announced, "Of course I'm homeless. We're all homeless here.
A shelter's not a home. A shelter is a dumping ground. Shelters
are dumps created by the government so they don't have to
provide low-cost housing."

Occasionally, someone would try to define herself out of
homelessness with a semantic end run. On her first night in The
Refuge, Elsie said that earlier that evening a minister had apologized for not being able to get her a place to sleep because
"they don't accept homeless people."

"Homeless," sneered Elsie. "Who are they calling 'homeless'?
How can anyone with a brand-new car be called 'homeless'?" (A
1981 Chevette "brand-new"?) And when Bonnie kept insisting that
Ginger was homeless just like everybody else, Ginger denied it,
saying that there were lots of homes she could go back to if she
chose, so how could she be homeless? Within a matter of weeks
or even less, however, both Elsie and Ginger fell into line and identified themselves as homeless along with everyone else.[16]

The group was more flexible around the labels of "bag lady"
and "street person," but here too the consensus was affirmative. Women who tried to disavow these labels did not fare well.
Here is Vicki again. She was sitting next to Louise one summer

---

[16]It must be noted that women who regularly identified shelter living with
homelessness when dealing with the question directly, sometimes forgot
themselves and spontaneously referred to the shelter as "home." When
Evelyn was discharged from the hospital after a two-week stay, Peggy
announced, "Evelyn came home today. Isn't that wonderful?" "Do you mean
to her mother's?" "No! To Bridge House! She'll never go back to her mother's."

day, and Louise, in white shorts, blouse, socks, and sneakers, looked as if she had just stepped out of a fashion magazine. Vicki was complaining that, to the outside world, all women in shelters were bag ladies, and the world was right to think so. I pointed to Louise and laughed. "She sure doesn't look like a bag lady, and you don't either. Are you a bag lady?"

"Of course I'm a bag lady," Vicki snapped, with an implicit reprimand in her voice for my seeming to make light of the subject. "I live out of bags, and if you live out of bags, you're a bag lady." Louise was wearing her Mona Lisa near-smile and nodded in agreement. Vicki did not speak for everyone: one woman insisted that bag ladies lived on the street, not in shelters. But majority opinion sided with Vicki.

The question "Are we street people?" was mainly answered in the affirmative, and in one instance by a collective, eloquent silence. Dinner was over, and Edith stood up and stretched. "I'm tired of hanging around shelters and street people," she said, loud enough to be heard by everyone, and probably to introduce some excitement in what had been a routinely quiet evening.

Sara, who was at the ironing board, took the bait, if bait it was. "We're homeless," she conceded, "but we're not street people. Homeless and street people are not the same thing." She appealed to the group at large. "Are they the same thing?" Silence. She tried again. "Are they the same thing?" Still silence. Sara shrugged her shoulders and returned to her ironing.

Peggy, June, and Evelyn were certain that all the women were both bag ladies and street persons. "We're definitely street people," said Peggy. "We're on the street from 7:00 in the morning till 2:00 in the afternoon.[17] We may have a place to sleep at night but we're definitely street people during the day."

"And we're bag ladies, too," she went on, looking at June and Evelyn as if to make certain she was speaking for them as well. "Carolyn carries a bag and she's a bag lady. Cora is a bag lady.

---

[17]Peggy, June, and Evelyn were regulars at the day shelter, which opened at 2:00 in the afternoon.

And we're bag ladies, too, even if we don't always carry bags."
For Kim, the "bag lady" test was a simple one: Are the front and
sides of your legs black and blue?

Wherever she went, Maude pushed all her earthly belongings
ahead of her, strapped to a two-wheel grocery cart. She conceded she was a bag lady but objected to the label nevertheless. Bag lady, she said, is just a name people use to generalize
about other people, and different people mean different things
when they call someone a bag lady. "You never know what people really mean when they use that name."[18]

There was even less agreement in answers to the question
"Why are we here?" In one form or another, the question often
arose in the course of routine, casual discourse, but only a few
women answered this question the same way each time, and others insisted on making the distinction "why I am here" and "why
the rest of you are here." Most women, if pressed, would probably have agreed with Grace that they were homeless because
God had willed it, but unlike Grace, they chose to deal with the
question in terms of more proximal, more mundane causes.

Surprisingly, those who consistently blamed "the system"
were in a minority, as were those who blamed themselves.
("We're all failures here," said Shirley. "The only thing I ever ac-
complished was raising my two children.") Most women
blamed someone or something other than themselves, citing
mid-level explanations for their homelessness, such as job loss,
eviction, divorce, not being able to get along with one's family,
or simply having no money for a place of their own. Only rarely
did the women see "the system" as a higher-level explanation,
or their own personal inadequacies as a lower-level explanation
for their homelessness.

---

[18]Perhaps half the women sat down to watch a television movie featuring
Lucille Ball as a bag lady. There were expressions of disgust as the actress
went through garbage cans scrounging for food. Most of the women sympa-
thized with this portrayal—or rather, caricature—of a bag lady, but no one
seemed to identify with her. Indeed, after the first few minutes, most of them
turned away in boredom. Only one woman watched the program to the bitter
end. She said she was a Lucille Ball fan.

For Vicki, the issue was clear-cut. "The women are here mainly for two reasons, medical or economic. It's one or the other for almost everyone here." Not so for Lisa. In the day shelter, she argued vehemently that "it's always parents and how they treat you" that puts you here or in some other kind of trouble or unhappiness.[19] As the discussion went on, Lisa remained adamant and found strong support from two other participants in the discussion.

It is likely that Holly, too, would have agreed with Lisa about parents. One evening, she and Bonnie were having still another argument over how to operate the washer/dryer. "God damn it!" Holly screamed. "Let me do my own laundry! You're just like my stepmother! She wouldn't even let me make Rice-a-roni because she said I couldn't do it."

Betty was the most vociferous exponent of the popular explanation that "it was a man that brought us here." Most of the time, the "man" referred to was a husband or lover; but it might also be an employer, a judge, a landlord, or, not infrequently, a father. One day when Betty announced, again, that "every one of us is here because of some man," Elsie and Martha agreed vigorously. Elsie was surely thinking of her ex-husband, but Martha's "man" was her father. "Yes!" she said, almost shouting her agreement. "My father! I was put in my first foster home when I was 10 and they took me away from my father when I was 15."[20]

Kathleen did not hold to a one-factor theory. She was prepared to accept some of the responsibility for her homelessness. "I must get out of here," she said to Grace and me one evening. "I lie awake at night trying to figure out how I got here and how I'll get out." She went on to concede that she was partly

---

[19]This assertion does not square neatly with her life history. Since this remark was spontaneous while the life history was more likely to include elements of impression management, I suspect there was more parental involvement in her homelessness than she admitted in the taping session. See Appendix B.

[20]A reference to Martha's claim that she was raped by her father when she was a teenager and removed from her parental home. See Appendix B.

responsible for her own situation but said that it was not entirely her fault. She had no control over some of the things that had happened to her and no control over some of the decisions made by other people. "And I can hear those same people repeating, over and over, 'You blew it! You fucked up!' Excuse the language, but that's what they say."

What is striking about these public, general theories—"medical or economic," "men," "parents," and so on—is that, unlike the private attribution of mental illness to selected individuals, they point no fingers at the women themselves. The cause of homelessness is seen as situational rather than something that inheres in the individual. Even on those few occasions when the "blame" was placed on the women themselves (such as Shirley's contention that "we're all failures here"), it was applied to everyone equally, thereby avoiding invidious distinctions within the group.

Real and perceived abuse by the non-homeless world strongly reinforced group cohesion. Much of the talk in shelters centered on fighting off the negative stereotypes of homeless women and the mindless insensitivity of the citizens at large. Because we see ourselves largely as a reflection of how other people see us, popular value judgments and generalizations of the outside world directed at homeless persons had to be fiercely resisted.[21] By sharing with one another the daily wounds that came their way, and exposing them to the laughter, ridicule, or outrage of the group, the women could blunt or turn aside the taunts and insults of the day.

Kim returned to the shelter one night, wearied and angered by the day's routine assaults. On the street, on the subway,

---

[21]See David A. Snow and Leon Anderson, "Identity Work among the Homeless: The Verbal Construction and Avowal of Personal Identities," *American Journal of Sociology* 92, no. 6 (May 1987). This article offers an excellent discussion of how homeless people "carve out a modicum of self-respect given their pariah-like status." One respondent stated the problem very simply: "It's real hard to feel good about yourself when almost everyone you see is looking down on you" (p. 1340).

wherever she happened to be, she said, people talked about her. "'Look at that bag lady. Why can't she get a job?'" she mimicked in a falsetto whine. "[They talk about me] as if I'm deaf or a dog or something, with no understanding of what they're saying."

Peggy said she was so sick and tired of being pointed out and jeered at as a bag lady that she had been leaving the shelter with two purses instead of her usual one purse and a carryall because "I can't take it anymore."

Louise was well known around the courthouse where she spent so much time. She often complained about the well-dressed lawyers who spoke in stage-whispers for her benefit, saying things like "Why do you think she doesn't get a job?" or "I wonder how she does it," or "I wish I could have a life-style like hers." What made her especially bitter, she said, was that it was lawyers like these who made her homeless in the first place.

Betty was outraged when Elsie, crying hard, came into the shelter to report an especially crude attempt to pick her up. "Everybody thinks they can say or do anything they want to homeless women," said Betty. She shook her right fist in the air. "I'll fix their ass."

In the park, a group of women were beweeping their outcast state. They talked about how unfairly the homeless people in this country are treated. "One day I was a productive and respected citizen, the next day I was dirt," said Shirley. "People treat the homeless as if they had a communicable disease. They treat them worse than cats and dogs," said Bernice. Julie said she wished she could have a cup of coffee out of her own cup, not a styrofoam cup, a real cup that was hers alone. Bernice said that most cats and dogs have their own plates to eat out of, and some even have their names on them.

Clearly, it was essential for their mental health to reject the judgments of the outside world. Alone, it would have been difficult for any woman to do so. Together, however, they were sometimes able to defend themselves and one another. This was, perhaps, one of the major contributions of the group to its members. For the women to have passively accepted the harsh treatment and degrading generalizations of the outside world as reasonable or just would have been to collaborate in their own demoralization.

As one might expect, forces in support of group cohesion and solidarity did not work for all the women all the time, and some women were, indeed, demoralized.* Louise had more trouble than most in considering herself part of the group or of anything else. "There is no place for a homeless person. I always feel out of place, no matter where I am. I feel I shouldn't be there, I'm not wanted there. . . . I feel I've lost my citizenship. I have no rights and no responsibilities. No one cares what I do. I have no connection with the society I grew up in."[22]

Not everyone experienced such profound desolation. Certainly no one else expressed her alienation so eloquently, but several of the women, especially older ones, sometimes tried to say the same thing.

One of the most striking aspects of shelter life, however, was the extent to which the dynamics of solidarity did manage to reach out to include persons on the margins. At any given time there was always a handful of "breathers"—observers of shelter social life rather than participants in it.[23] "Breathers" ranged from loners who fiercely resisted almost all overtures for human contact to very gentle, very shy women who shrank from personal involvements but took great pleasure from the goings-on around them, listening to dinner table talk, laughing at the jokes and horseplay, silently mouthing the words to Christmas carols in the day shelter as other women belted them out,

---

*DIRECTOR: *It was the women without hope who were the easiest to work with in the shelter. Indeed, the aggressive or assertive women were the very ones who caused some staff difficulties. There was an attempt between the staff members to caution each other to be grateful that a woman still cared enough to fight.*

[22]Telephone conversation, May 1991.

[23]"Breathers" is my term, not the women's. I first heard it many years ago on the streetcorner. It referred to men who silently stood around, observing a crap or card game but not otherwise participating in it.

watching warily and in silence as a shouting match threatened to erupt into something more, and so on.

Taken together, the many levels of involvement made it possible for almost everyone, including "breathers," to be a part of shelter life. This inclusiveness gave rise to a sense of camaraderie that, in itself, exerted a powerful attraction for the women. It seemed to have its source in elements that ignored or transcended the differences among them. Sometimes, when dinner was especially good, followed by good talk and easy laughter, with everything going just right ("We had a party! We had a party!" exclaimed Dorothy), the sense of sisterhood was almost palpable. But such camaraderie required that things go well, that people get along with one another, and this was often not the case. People did offer aid and comfort to one another, and entertained one another, and there was often an aura of good feeling; but just as often they snarled at and avoided one another and threatened and bullied and sometimes fought.

At these times, the sense of community disappeared, only to expose an underlying and ever-present remainder of enormous importance: the simple presence of one's own kind, fellow human beings—so close you could touch them—whose every sound and movement gave life to the shelter and all who were in it.

It was this elemental proximity to fellow humans, and not just the sometime camaraderie, when contrasted with the solitary character of living in one's own room or efficiency apartment, that made some of the graduates look back at shelter living with a feeling of loss, especially those who were not good at making or keeping friends. Elsie got her own place and never looked back, swearing she would never again be found alive in a shelter. Similarly, Jeanette never returned to the shelter once she got her own place, but she admitted she missed the shelter sometimes. Betty returned for an occasional visit the first month or two, then stopped. Regina continued to visit the shelter long after she had her own apartment. "One is such a lonely number," she explained.[24]

Agnes was an exception unto herself. She was a tall, thin, bitter woman in her 50s who hated blacks and Jews a little bit more than she hated everyone else. She kept mainly to herself except to hiss at people who came close to her, but occasionally she enjoyed some human contact with one or another homeless woman or some talented staff person who struck her fancy. In January 1990 Agnes was given her own subsidized apartment, but she continued to return to the shelter every night. After a week, she was told she could no longer come to the shelter, that her cot would have to go to someone who had no other place to sleep. The next day, Agnes gave up her apartment. Homeless again, she returned to the shelter.

Thus it was that shelter life sometimes made it possible for the women to be part of a human community in which one could give and take aid and comfort—from each according to her ability; with luck, to each according to her need.

But character and personal values sometimes overwhelmed the tendencies toward cohesion. Theft of one's money or belongings, for example, was a constant threat and generated a constant level of suspicion and distrust. One night someone stole $15 from Kathleen's purse. Kathleen herself felt a special obligation to the women she lived with in the shelter and thought the other women should feel the same. Her anger at having the money stolen gave way to sadness and a sense of betrayal. Loyalty to the group, not honesty, was the issue. "People

---

[24]Having left the shelter and gotten a place of her own, Regina could all too easily romanticize shelter life in retrospect. Here she is, talking on tape, almost a year after leaving the shelter, and saying things completely at odds with things she said and did while she was homeless: "There was warmth there [in homeless living] and that's why I go back now and then to the [soup] kitchens because a part of me is on the street. You can never take that away. . . . Part of me is buried in the streets. . . . My parents had brought me up in such a heaven-like world [!!] I didn't know this side existed until all this happened. And then I realized, 'Hey! This is life! Where have I been?'"

with problems should leave them outside, not bring them in here with the people they live with," she said.

Two days later, in the shower, Martha found a purse that contained $20 and an airline ticket to Los Angeles, and turned it in. Unfortunately, from the perspective of the group, these two events did not balance one another. It is possible, if not likely, that Martha's honesty was more representative of the group's values than the theft. But the increased mistrust resulting from the theft of Kathleen's money could not, even remotely, be offset by Martha's return of the purse.

Personal character and values could also support group integrity. At a Wednesday night meeting, Cora—normally a quiet person who went her own way—passionately denounced the eight women who had ganged up on Virginia the other night, subjecting her to merciless teasing "like elementary school children." Betty, as spokesperson, tried to defend the group, arguing that "that person" had it coming. Cora brushed Betty and her defense aside, saying that the women ought to be ashamed of themselves and that she was going to speak out against this kind of behavior whenever she saw it. Chastened, Betty conceded that she didn't believe in ganging up like that but added, weakly, that if someone chooses to act different, they have to expect to be treated different. As the meeting broke up, Kathleen sought out Cora to commend her for "bravery."

Honesty and dishonesty, courage and cowardice, greed and generosity, and all the other universal virtues and vices were probably distributed among the homeless women much as they are in the general population. Most of the time, however, it seems that it is much more difficult for people at the bottom of society to be virtuous than for those in the middle or the top— much harder, for example, for Martha to return $20 than for her middle-class counterpart to do so; and much harder for people who are weak and powerless to take risks and act bravely. That they sometimes did so bears eloquent witness to the fact that, however degrading their living conditions, some of the women were as virtuous as the best of us. That the same or other women were sometimes cruel or selfish or cowardly is only further evidence that most of these homeless women were really very ordinary people.

And yet, there is something about these women that makes them seem larger than life. This is certainly not because poverty ennobles us or because people at the bottom of society are stronger or more virtuous than others. What sets these homeless women apart is that, sane or crazy or physically disabled, they are all engaged in a titanic struggle to remain human in an unremittingly dehumanizing environment. Most of them are successful, and it is in this sense—the sense of remaining full and complete, even ordinary, human beings—that one can say that they are "making it."

7

Some Thoughts on Homelessness

There are many homeless people in America and that is a shame. Shame on you, shame on me, shame on America. Shame because it is the result of choices we have made; shame because it does not have to be.[1]

To begin at the beginning, let me offer Proposition No. 1: Homeless people are homeless because they do not have a place to live. I do not offer this as a tautology but as a statement of cause.[2]

People are not homeless because they are physically disabled, mentally ill, abusers of alcohol or other drugs, or unemployed. However destructive and relevant these conditions

---

[1] "Homelessness is the *sum total* of our dreams, policies, intentions, errors, omissions, cruelties, kindnesses, all of it recorded, in the flesh, in the life of the streets." Peter Marin, "Helping and Hating the Homeless: The Struggle at the Margins of America," *Harpers,* January 1987, p. 41.

[2] *"The cause of homelessness is lack of housing,"* Jonathan Kozol, *Rachel and Her Children,* p. 11 (emphasis in original). See also James D. Wright, *Address Unknown: The Tragedy of Homelessness in America:* "I have come increasingly to look on homelessness as fundamentally a housing problem" (p. xiv).

may be, they do not explain homelessness; most physically disabled people, most mentally ill people, most alcoholics and drug addicts, and most unemployed persons do have places to live. Moreover, when mentally ill or physically disabled or alcoholic homeless persons do get a place to live, they are no longer homeless but they remain, as they were before, physically or mentally disabled, drug addicts, or whatever. Clearly, then, there is no *necessary* connection between these conditions and homelessness. Homeless people are homeless because they do not have a place to live.

My second proposition derives from the most fundamental fact about homelessness: Homelessness is rooted hard and deep in poverty. Homeless people are poor people, and they come, overwhelmingly, from poor families.[3] Proposition No. 2 holds that homelessness is no longer a matter—if it ever was—of a few unfortunate winos or crazy people falling through the cracks of our vaunted safety net. Indeed, homelessness is not an individual matter at all. *Homelessness today is a social class phenomenon, the direct result of a steady, across-the-board lowering of the standard of living of the American working class and lower class.* As the standard of living falls, individuals and families at the bottom are plunged into homelessness.

The connection between homelessness and poverty points to major system failures at the lower and sometimes middle levels of our wage-labor hierarchy. The major failure is the inability of the system, even in the best of times, to provide jobs for all who are able and willing to work. Every day, many millions of would-be workers are told that our society has nothing for them to do, that they are not needed, that they and their dependents are surplus.[4]

---

[3]"[Homeless people] are very poor. Indeed, other studies find few differences between homeless people and other very poor people." Martha R. Burt. *Over the Edge: The Growth of Homelessness in the 1980's,* p. 21.

[4]The discussion of unemployment in this section draws heavily from my chapter "The Human Costs of Unemployment," in *The Battle Against Unemployment,* ed. Arthur M. Okun.

Another major system failure, equally destructive, is the fact that a growing number of men and women—individuals and heads of families—are workers but remain poor. They work or seek work year-round, full-time. They work as salesclerks and checkers and servers in Ames and K mart, in McDonald's and Roy Rogers; they clean houses and mop floors in hospitals and nursing homes; they work as casual laborers, telephone solicitors, receptionists, delivery men and women, file clerks, even as data-entry clerks at IBM. What should no longer come as a surprise, however, after all is said and done, is that even if they can get these jobs, many workers cannot live on what they earn.[5] These workers file the papers, mop the floors, clean the tables, or guard whatever needs guarding. At the end of the day, they say "OK, I've done what you asked me to do. What am I worth?" And our society answers, through the employer, "Not much. Not even enough to live on."

What goes on here? How can this be? Are these workers not entitled to an honest day's pay for an honest day's work? Admittedly, "an honest day's pay" is a very fuzzy term. At the very least, however, can an honest day's pay be less than it takes to live on?

"Don't look at me," says the employer. "I'm paying them what they are worth. If you force me to pay my employees more than they are worth, I will have to go out of business." In the long run, he is probably right.

Perspective is critical. Unemployment, underemployment, and substandard wages are system failures only when viewed from the bottom. Looking from the top down, they are seen as

---

[5] Increasingly, the jobs themselves are hard to find and the competition is fierce. See, for example, Stan Hinden, "Ad for Janitor's Position Draws 350 Applicants," *The Washington Post*, August 13, 1991, p. C1. It should also be noted that the official poverty line, based entirely on income, leaves a lot of poor people on the unpoor side of the line. "In terms of residual income remaining after rent, such [high] rent-to-income ratios are sufficient to create and maintain de facto poverty among those who are 125% above the poverty line." Karin Ringheim, *At Risk of Homelessness: The Roles of Income and Rent*, p. 223.

"natural" processes essential to the healthy functioning of a self-correcting market system. From that perspective, it is as if the market system requires human sacrifice for its good health.

One result of these system failures is wide and deep poverty and a growing number of working poor, of working yet homeless men, women, and families, and many discouraged workers. Then, through welfare programs, through shelters and soup kitchens and vouchers and a wide variety of purchased goods and services, our whole society goes about the business of subsidizing those employers who are unable to pay their employees enough to live on.[6] As if by magic, however, the onus of welfare and dependency is lifted from the system of work and the employers and placed on the workers and the unemployed right in front of our very eyes, and no one is any the wiser.

Most profoundly affected by the falling standard of living are those who would be dependents if their families could continue to support them. Among the homeless women in shelters and on the street, for example, are many women who would probably not be sufficiently productive to command a living wage under any conditions of wage labor. Many of them are homeless because their relatives and friends, under the gun themselves because of their worsening economic situations, can no longer afford to care for still another dependent.

· · ·

---

[6]If one traces out the further effects of poverty as they ramify throughout our social system, one sees that they also contribute directly to the cost of maintaining mothers without husbands and children without fathers, a monster-size criminal justice system, and so on through a wide range of social life. The ramifications of deep poverty are not always self-evident. "[The lives of the homeless] slowly fall apart. . . . In this instance, a shortage of housing is reflected as crime and child neglect. In other instances a shortage of housing will show up as mental illness or physical illness. Almost anything can mask a need for shelter. When people do not have enough resources to control their lives, official problem labels do not tell what is wrong or what is needed." Harris Chaiklin, "Soup Kitchens and Shelters: The Private Sector as Safety Valve for Public Sector Irresponsibility," p. 2.

Most able-bodied homeless women want to work and do not need to be whipped or shamed into line. Despite the low pay and low status of jobs typically available to them, many continue to work and seek work. Clearly, the work ethic is alive and well among them, even, surprisingly, among those who cannot work or should not work. It is not the worker but the workplace that undermines the work ethic. Unemployment undermines the work ethic. So do jobs that are dirty and hard and boring and low status and lead nowhere. But the real killers of the work ethic are those jobs that do not pay enough to live on. If such jobs paid a living wage, they would automatically become less dirty, less hard, higher status, and it wouldn't much matter if they led nowhere else.

Identifying low-paying jobs as "entry-level" is, at best, misleading. The occupants of "entry-level" jobs are just as likely to be mature men and women trying to support themselves as young people on their way to the top of something. The label notwithstanding, most "entry-level" jobs are not the first step of a career ladder. They are jobs. Just jobs. Jobs that do not pay enough to live on. Woe to the man or woman who, for whatever reason, must seek them out. And woe, too, to the children and adults who depend on that man or woman for their support.

Much the same can be said for those homeless women who must look to the welfare system for their survival. Designed to push recipients into the work force or shame them for daring to be poor, welfare punishes body and soul.[7] The subsidies are so meager and given so grudgingly that some homeless women forego them, choosing to keep their self-respect, even if it means adopting a standard of living that may forever condemn them to a life in shelters, in soup kitchens, and on the street. Then, too, there are many homeless women physically or

---

[7] "Welfare has also been deployed to regulate labor markets by manipulating work incentives . . . goading working-class men and women to labor hard for low wages by frightening them with the prospect of a subhuman and stigmatized descent into the ranks of paupers." Michael B. Katz, *In the Shadow of the Poorhouse: A Social History of Welfare in America*, p. xi.

otherwise disabled who cannot work. Welfare strategy is wasted on such persons, punishing them and shaming them for not doing what they cannot do.

We talk increasingly about an "underclass" as we try to put more and more distance between ourselves and the very poor. "Underclass" suggests that they live outside (under) the system in which the rest of us live.[8] But homeless women do live in the same real world that most of us live in, where security and housing and jobs are major concerns. Perhaps because we do not know how to deal with jobs and housing for the poor and homeless, or do not want to deal with them, we excuse our do-nothing job and housing policies by telling ourselves that homelessness is Oh, such a complex problem! whose many causes lie deep within the homeless people themselves. What is needed first and foremost, we say, is an array of treatment programs to help them straighten out their heads or their habits.[9]

Since most homeless women are much like everyone else, many of them would agree that that is what the other homeless women need, but most homeless women would also agree with Claude, a bright young man in his early 30s. Claude had just moved into a subsidized high-rise after years of living in shelters. We had just finished watching an account of the "Housing Now" March on Washington on television news.[10]

---

[8] "Each state of transition and marginality exists within, not outside of, the very same social system defining the valued, settled, and intact categories. Both the less and the more valued are cut from the same cloth." Constance Perin, *Everything in Its Place: Social Order and Land Use in America,* p. 125. Herbert J. Gans makes a different point: "[The term "underclass"] hides within it all the moral opprobrium Americans have long felt toward those poor people who have been judged to be undeserving." "Deconstructing the Underclass: The Term's Dangers as a Planning Concept," *American Planning Association Journal,* Summer 1990, p. 273.

[9] "It is apparently easy to be mystified by homelessness. Perhaps it is out of fear that we seek to find personal characteristics that would clearly distinguish the poor and the homeless from ourselves." Karin Ringheim, *At Risk of Homelessness,* p. 229.

[10] October 7, 1989.

"That 'Housing Now' march was right on the ball," he said. "Those people know what they're talking about. The homeless need housing, not that psychological bullshit that puts the blame on the homeless themselves." He slapped the brace on his withered leg. "Sure, some of us are imperfect, but we live in an imperfect world, so what's the big deal?"

Claude is mainly right, but he may be overstating the case. Some homeless people could probably benefit from what he calls "psychological bullshit," and it may even be an essential first step for a few of them. For most homeless people, however, even those who could benefit from them, such services are not necessarily the first order of business. Trying to deliver services to people on the run is typically inefficient if not futile.[11] For most homeless people, the first order of business is to help them stop running. The first order of business is to get homeless people out of the crazy-making and destructive world of homelessness. The first order of business is housing.

Crazy-making homelessness produces a world of paradoxes and contradictions: citizens with homes are afraid of the homeless and the homeless are afraid of the citizens and one another and everyone is right to be afraid; people in situations they cannot tolerate another day find they have no alternatives; problems abound that have no solutions.

When Betty was evicted from the shelter and spent the night in some bushes in the park, she called me in the morning to say she had broken no rules and had a right to remain in a publicly supported shelter. I called the shelter director and told him I didn't think Betty could make it on the street.[12] He consulted with his staff and agreed that Betty could return to the shelter on a probationary basis.

---

[11] "Without solving the homelessness problem, we don't even have a shot at trying to solve some of the problems of mental illness." Dr. Robert Okin, Chief of Psychiatry, San Francisco General Hospital, on the "MacNeil-Lehrer NewsHour," April 27, 1992.

[12] To my knowledge, this was the only time I interfered directly between shelter staff and the women.

That evening, at the shelter, the staff person who had evicted Betty pulled me aside. Maybe you did Betty a favor, she said, but you didn't do me one. She conceded that Betty had broken no rules but said that Betty was a chronic malcontent whose constant bitching upset everyone and lowered the morale of the shelter. Yes, Betty had a right to be in a publicly supported shelter but she, Jean, had rights too. "I need this job," she said. "I have a child to support. When I get ready to come to work my stomach is tied up in knots because I know I'm going to have to deal with Betty. Maybe she has a right to be here, but I have a right to do my job without having my stomach tied up in knots, day and night."

Again, Jean is right and Betty is right. Everybody is right and we are forced to make practical and moral choices among contending parties, all of whom may be right and none of whom can afford to lose.[13]

At another level, we seem to accept or ignore conditions of homelessness that mock the values we claim to hold: people who work full time and cannot live on what they earn; people who are put in jail because they have no place to live; people who feel safer living on the street than in public shelters; people in shelters who walk 11 blocks to use the toilet in Union Station rather than use the toilets in the shelter; shelters in neighborhoods in which the homeless are not permitted to walk, but are bussed in at night and bussed out in the morning; and on and on and on.

Appropriate and affordable housing for individuals and families—houses, apartments, single room occupancy hotels, group homes—would do more than simply reduce the number of homeless persons. It would go a long way toward making life on the bottom more rational, more coherent, especially for

---

[13]When Mr. Shapiro and Mr. Goldberg were unable to resolve their argument, it was agreed that Mr. Shapiro would present the case to the rabbi. The rabbi assured Mr. Shapiro he was right. When Mr. Goldberg learned of this, he ran to the rabbi with his version of the argument. "You are right," the rabbi told him. The rabbi's wife said to the rabbi, "You told Mr. Shapiro he was right and you told Mr. Goldberg he was right. They can't both be right." "You are right too," said the rabbi. (After Sholem Aleichem.)

workers who could once again support themselves and their families. Appropriate and affordable housing would also contribute importantly to the treatment and prevention of a variety of social ills and individual tragedies, including homelessness itself. Surely homeless children who are moved into decent housing are less likely to become parents of homeless children than children who grow up homeless. Surely people who are mentally ill or alcoholic or drug-addicted and have a place of their own are more likely to stand still long enough to profit from a program of treatment than someone living in shelters and on the street.

Most important of all, for most homeless persons and families there is no more therapeutic environment than a place of one's own—a place that is safe and warm, that allows wounds to heal, that allows you to choose your associates rather than have them thrust upon you, that gives you your own unique address, your own place in the world. Indeed, as one looks at the handful of women who were homeless and now have a place to live, it is probably no exaggeration to see the transition from homelessness to a place of one's own as a transition from outcast to citizen.

A very few women were able to make this transition entirely on their own efforts. More women made this transition with the assistance of subsidized housing. Unfortunately, very few homeless women can expect to get jobs that will allow them to support themselves, and very few can expect to come to the top of the list for housing assistance.

"Housing Now" must be the principal goal of public policy for dealing with homelessness. But until permanent and affordable housing for the poor becomes a reality, we need more and better shelters.[14] Many will argue that building more shelters will

_____

[14]And we must stop lying to ourselves. A spokesperson for the Montgomery County, Md., Department of Family Resources explains why there is a county-wide shortage of shelter beds although funds are available to build more shelters. "We want to make sure that people don't freeze to death on the streets in winter, but our real goal is permanent housing, so we don't want to overbuild by supplying a shelter for every single homeless person." Quoted in Mark Moran "Feeding the Poor:

further institutionalize homelessness. Not so. Failure to provide minimally decent shelters institutionalizes homelessness. Pushing people onto the street full time—perhaps beyond the point of no return—institutionalizes homelessness far more than giving people a safe place to sleep. To do nothing, then, is to deepen the institutionalization of homelessness; but to close down shelters, as is being done in Washington, D.C., and other cities around the country in the name of economy, is plainly and simply criminal, self-defeating, and dumb.

Homelessness is indeed dehumanizing, but given a shelter such as The Refuge, it is clear that homeless people can remain human, even in the face of dehumanizing conditions. At The Refuge, in contrast to many shelters, there is no time limit on one's length of stay. The women know they have a place to sleep and eat today, tomorrow, next week, and next month.

This "permanence" gives the women some minimum sense of security and makes it possible for them to form real relationships with one another, to have friends and to be part of a human group. At The Refuge, too, one's psychological privacy is respected: your thoughts and your history are your own, to share or not share as you see fit. At The Refuge, you are allowed to be yourself, and there is no great pressure to push you into "improving" yourself—getting therapy, looking for a job, and so on. You are given as much space and time as you need to rest, to heal, to regain your strength, or simply to save enough money (on rent and food) to get a place of your own once more.

In Your Neighborhood?" *Montgomery County Sentinel,* October 9, 1986, p. 1. There was really little danger of "overbuilding" shelters. That same night, and all other nights that year, about half the homeless people in Montgomery County were without shelter.

One finds that kind of thinking at all levels of government. "Every dollar spent on an emergency shelter is one less dollar available for a real solution." James Forsberg, Director of the HUD Office of Special Needs Assistance Programs, quoted in *Access,* 4, no. 2 (June 1992): p. 1. Every dollar not spent on shelters will be spent on permanent housing? Ha!

Not just any shelter will do. An armory or dormitory or other barn of a shelter that thrusts hundreds of strangers into impersonal intimacy will not do. Shelters that cannot ensure the safety of their occupants, or cannot treat them with minimal decency and respect, will not do. The homeless women themselves point the way for public policy in this respect. The best shelters, they say, are those operated by nonprofit organizations (mainly religious, and mainly local rather than national), and the more volunteers and pro-bono professionals the better. The worst shelters are those operated by municipalities or private for-profit organizations on contract with the city or county. There are many exceptions of course, and it is not always easy to detect the difference between a nonprofit and a private for-profit organization. In general, however, the private for-profit sector, which dealt so harshly with many of the women even before they became homeless, often continues to treat them harshly after the fact.

To summarize: In an important sense, homeless men and women and families are victims of the same system of free enterprise that has been so extraordinarily productive and generous to others. Viewed from the bottom, two of the most obvious system failures are the abject failure of the free market to provide minimally decent jobs and affordable housing for poor people. The recent historical record offers clear evidence that the free market, left to its own devices, cannot and will not do the job.

All along the line then, from the world of jobs and housing to the very shelters themselves, the free market has failed the great majority of homeless persons. Indeed, while capitalism has worked in spectacular fashion for many Americans, it has created many poor people and treated them badly. If we cannot change the rules of the marketplace, then the federal government, the government of all Americans, must itself become a much more active and vigorous player in the job and housing markets on behalf of the poor.[15]

For these things to happen, there must be a wider and deeper understanding of the nature of poverty and its destructiveness. We must stop blaming the poor for being poor and the homeless for being homeless. There will always be people at every level of society whose intelligence, ability, and determination will lift them high above the stations they were born into. But it makes no sense to say, "If they can do it, why can't the others?" Not everyone can be above average. Not everyone can be a hero. By definition, most people are of average intelligence, ability, and determination. It is by its ability to make possible a decent life for the masses—for average people and for those who are below average—that a society is to be judged.

By design, we live in a society that is very competitive. After adding individual differences to handicaps/advantages of race, class, and sex, it turns out that some people run faster than others. Those who run very fast are highly rewarded. Those who run at an average pace do pretty well most of the time. For a variety of reasons, seldom if ever any fault of their own, some poor people and some homeless people like Shirley can't run fast at all.

"I'm 53 years old," said Shirley, an ordinary woman of unremarkable appearance. "I failed at two marriages and I failed at every job I ever had. Is that any reason I have to live on the street?"

A society that answers "yes," that is prepared to treat a large number of its citizens as surplus people, is already in steep decline.

---

[15] As a small first step, we might stop punishing low-income renters while throwing bouquets of tax forgiveness to homeowners. "In 1988, federal outlays for low-income housing assistance were only about one-fourth of the amount of tax-forgiveness to [home]owners." Karin Ringheim, *At Risk of Homelessness*, p. 223. David T. Ellwood makes the elegantly simple, powerful argument that if you work you shouldn't be poor. He would start by increasing the earned income tax credit, raising the minimum wage to its buying power of former years, and indexing it to inflation. "If You Work You Shouldn't Be Poor," *Washington Post*, April 4, 1989, p. A25.

Appendixes

APPENDIX A

Where Are They Now?

Note: With a few exceptions, it was only through housing or other assistance that some women were able to leave the shelters. What follows is as of May 1992.

Betty

Betty's certification for subsidized housing came through in January 1988, authorizing her to find a one-bedroom apartment for up to $550. (Her share was to be 30 percent of her income, whatever the amount or source.) Betty's search seemed to others to be desultory at best. Many women, including staff, thought that Betty, after many years on the street and in shelters, no longer had the capacity, energy, or even the desire for independent living. But Betty did find a place—a garden apartment in an undesirable area—and staff people from The Refuge helped her move in and gave her some basic furniture. Betty took her paranoia with her. The very first week, she complained that the landlord or superintendent was sneaking into her (locked) apartment whenever she was out, and that someone had poisoned the can of beans in the refrigerator. The following week, she complained somewhat more weakly in the same fashion. By the end of the second month, there was no hint of any paranoia, at least to a lay person. Betty talked only of personal things and her real problems around transportation, making her money last, her renewed contacts with her sister and daughter, and so forth.

That same year, Betty's SSI came through (on the third attempt), giving her an income of $405 a month and $21 in food stamps. Her share of the rent went up to $112 a month. By the end of the year, when her lease was up, she decided to move because there was no neighborliness among the neighbors. People walked with their heads down and their eyes averted, she said, and no one said as much as "Good morning" or even "Hello."

Betty moved to another apartment in a more distant suburb, where transportation is her major problem. She seems to be content there, if a little lonely. She especially misses her AA meetings. She has had a partial mastectomy (but blames no one for her cancer). Betty has a full schedule. The county helps her with transportation to a weekly group therapy session and to doctors when she needs them. She attends church every Sunday, driven there by a friend (made at church) who also drives her there and back on Wednesdays, when the church "hires" her to work in the kitchen, paying her $30 for the day's work. This extra $30 a week makes the difference between getting by and not getting by on her SSI. Twice a week, Betty walks the two blocks to a seniors' center where she is served a nutritious lunch. Every third Saturday, she also works for three hours as a church volunteer in the same soup kitchen she used to patronize.

Betty and her sister, who lives in D.C., speak to one another on the phone every day. Betty also sees her sister on Wednesdays, when they work together in the church kitchen.

Just this past Christmas, Betty's daughter and 10-year-old granddaughter came to her apartment and they all exchanged gifts. If Betty ever was a paranoid schizophrenic, she seems to have left that behind her, now that she has "my own little cubbyhole, my own little TV."

Life is pretty good, she says. "At least now, I'm surviving." Betty and Elsie are in occasional telephone contact, and Betty sees several of her old friends from the shelters when she works at the soup kitchen.

Elsie

Elsie left The Refuge in September 1985 to spend a year in a state vocational rehabilitation residential center, where she was trained in typing and hospital record keeping. When she graduated, she went to Texas in anticipation of a marriage that fell through: the man's teenage children resented her, he had no job or prospect of one, he wanted them to sleep together before marriage (not on your life, Elsie told him), and Elsie herself could find no work. Four months later, she drove back to D.C. and immediately registered at a Katherine Gibbs School for Secretaries (with financial aid from state grants and student loans). She moved in with a former co-worker, but when that didn't work out, she moved into a women's shelter in downtown D.C. Elsie graduated from Katherine Gibbs in July 1988 and found a clerk typist job (at $12,000 a year) with a large firm.[1] She also took a part-time sales job in a department store, bought a new car (Chevy Nova), and moved to a place of her own. She remained with those two jobs for two years.

In July 1990, Elsie was stricken with carpal tunnel syndrome, took time off for extensive surgery on her hand, returned to work but could not function properly (her typing skill dropped

---

[1] Her cap-and-gown graduation ceremony was attended by several of her D.C. shelter mates and staff persons and by Betty and me. Elsie's triumph was slightly tarnished when she was given a certificate for having completed the course work rather than the usual diploma.

from 50 words per minute to 38), took unpaid sick leave, went on workmen's compensation, continued with the part-time sales job, and was terminated from the typing job. Elsie is currently awaiting final determination by doctors of her workmen's compensation status. She hopes to move to a full-time job at the department store. Meanwhile, she lives in one room in a county-owned apartment/hotel. Her Assembly of God church has been paying most of her rent ($340) since her workmen's compensation expired, but some church members are beginning to grumble.

Elsie is in occasional telephone communication with Betty and they send each other Christmas cards. Last year, Elsie received "more than 30" such cards, most from fellow church members and some from her department store co-workers.

Grace

Grace worked most of the 11 months she was in the shelters. When she left in the fall of 1985, she had saved enough to rent a room until a year later, when she rented a two-bedroom apartment (for occasional visits from her son). She also got her first credit card in her own name and bought furniture and a car. She had several different jobs and left some on her own, once because she found a job that offered 25 cents an hour more. She believed strongly that she was worth more than she was getting. Intervals between jobs were very costly and Grace found herself falling ever further behind financially. By 1991, she had to give up her apartment, store her (mainly unpaid-for) furniture, and move into a series of rooms or house sharings, none of which worked out well.

For months Grace had wanted to file for bankruptcy to protect her paychecks, but she couldn't come up with the $825 that the Hyatt law firm (As Advertised on TV) required up front in order to file for bankruptcy on her behalf. By the end of 1991, two creditors had already garnisheed her paychecks when, by hook and by crook, she managed to accumulate the $825. And now Grace, after an argument about the heat with her present landlord, must find another place to live before the month is out. She is currently working in the secretarial pool of a large corporation.

Her close relationship with Kim broke down suddenly in 1990 over what Kim thought was Grace's refusal to help her acquire more birds. Grace believes strongly that her faith will see her through whatever the future holds for her.

Jeanette

Jeanette left the shelters in December 1986, when her subsidized housing came through. She moved into an efficiency apartment in an exceptionally attractive high-rise owned and managed by the county. Like Betty, Jeanette is required to contribute toward her rent 30 percent of her income, whatever that happens to be. Five years after moving in, she is still in the same efficiency apartment and is currently paying $163 a month. Jeanette is now 65 and collects Social Security. Until recently, she had been getting typing jobs out of a temporaries agency. She is a good typist, she says, and good at shorthand, too, but she never learned to work with computers or word processors and is finding this a discouraging obstacle to a full-time job. For a while, she worked part-time collecting gasoline sales data over the telephone for a government contractor. She currently works two hours a day as a paid companion to temporarily disabled persons in a retirement community. She has several good friends, mainly from church. She is not in touch with any of the women she knew at the shelter.

Judy

Judy left the shelter system in May 1986 and entered a graduated halfway house program at the bottom. She quickly worked her way to the least restrictive part of the program. She worked regularly in the program's central office and contributed several columns on homelessness to the monthly newsletter. She also applied for SSI (Social Security Insurance) and began collecting $398 a month. In September 1988, Judy went to live with her grandparents in Florida, both of whom were ill and needed her assistance. In Florida, she was put on "cure-all Prozac" for what they said was a bipolar disorder.

Judy returned to the D.C. area in July 1990. She sought out Abigail and the two lived together in a rooming house, where Judy fell in love with Frank, the landlord. Abigail had been working for more than two years as a security guard and through her Judy got a similar position. She decided to quit some four months later when she received a 30-day suspension for she-knew-not-what. Abigail continued to work and Judy "kept house" for the two of them. In May 1991, Abigail said they had to leave the rooming house. Judy is certain Abigail was trying to come between her and Frank and told her so. Abigail told her she was delusional, that this was Kent (the singer she made into an imaginary boyfriend) all over again, and that the only reality was that they were homeless once again.[2]

Judy drifted. She was having a bad reaction to Navane. At a conference with her parents and therapist, it was decided she should check herself into the state mental hospital. This was in July 1991. Judy was discharged the following January back to the halfway house program, where she is now.

Judy knows now that her imagined love affair with Kent was just that, imagined. Similarly, she knows now that neither her father nor her brother had any sexual designs on her. She and her parents are again very close and she knows that they love her. Judy's skin has cleared up completely but she again weighs more than 300 pounds.

---

[2]My conversation with Judy took place over lunch. Just as in the shelter, I had the sense that Judy herself was not convinced about what she was saying. I asked her what the chances were that Abigail was right, that her love affair with Frank was, indeed, "Kent all over again." She thought for a moment, then said, "Ten percent."

In the short term, Judy hopes to get a good office job with the assistance of the Voc Rehab people. Long term, she hopes "to settle down and raise a family."

Kim

When Kim left The Refuge, she spent her nights in an abandoned automobile in a lot owned by a public storage facility where she had sometimes filled in as a back-up to the manager. When the manager left the job a few months later, she recommended Kim as her replacement. Kim got the job and did it well enough to get letters of commendation from the regional office. Some few months later, she quit to spend more time trying to heal the breach that had developed between her and her boyfriend. Thus began a long series of jobs, intermittent unemployment, and repeated round-trip moves from the Washington area to her hometown in Tidewater, Virginia. Despondent over the final breakdown of her love affair with Patrick and having once attempted suicide, Kim turned more and more to her original love for animals. Her insistence on keeping dozens of birds, rabbits, and gerbils with her made it difficult for her to find a place to live. At one point, she lived in an abandoned shack in West Virginia that had no heat or light. During this period, she was more or less supported by a man in his 20s who lived with her. There was no sex between them ("not if he was the last man on earth"), but Bruce seemed to be mesmerized by Kim and could not bring himself to abandon her.

In 1991, they returned to Richman County. Bruce worked in a junkyard and Kim, against the competition of dozens of candidates, had the highest score on a standardized test and won a clerical job with the county that pays her $20,000. She and Bruce pay $750 a month for their two-bedroom apartment. It has no furniture. Bruce sleeps on the floor in one bedroom and Kim sleeps in the other, along with her 105 birds (102 parakeets, 1 canary, 1 parrot, 1 cockatiel), 53 hamsters, 8 guinea pigs, 6 rabbits, 30 mice, 1 gerbil, and 1 turtle (as of December 15, 1991). They are regularly evicted whenever a landlord discovers the menagerie.

Over the years, Kim has kept in close contact with Sara and Terry and has had occasional visits with Peggy. She had also been close to Grace and June after all three were out of the shelter, but has since had a serious falling-out with both of them.

Postscript — "I am no longer estranged from my parents. After 10 years of absolutely no contact with them, we have a much better relationship now than we probably ever had.

"My life from here on out is the attainment of two goals. 1) To expand beyond what I am doing on a personal level to help care for birds and small animals. I buy birds, hamsters, guinea pigs, rabbits, mice, etc. that are unwanted/have handicaps or 'defects' that would make it difficult for them to find a home. I provide them the loving home that they might otherwise not find. My dream is to be part of a nationwide/worldwide animal-rights organization focusing on these special birds and (non-predatory) mammals. 2) To marry the love of my life, Malcolm, who I met on Valentine's Day at the soup kitchen. He is 22 years old, $5'10^{1}/_{2}''$ and 148 pounds, with light brown hair and bright-blue eyes, and he is flawless. He says he loves me, and I believe him; he says we are sexually compatible and I know it for a fact. We are a perfect match!"

Shortly after Kim wrote this postscript, the county retrenched. Kim lost her job, then her apartment. Her world fell apart. Once vital, resilient, optimistic, and tough, she is now more deeply discouraged than ever before, almost to the point of paralysis. She is in deep trouble and I fear for her future and her life.

Lisa

Lisa has been alternating between shelters and good jobs. She does not get fired from her jobs; she leaves them. In December

1991, she called to say she was living at home with her mother and her two children in southeast Washington.

Louise

Louise continues to be homeless. She stays at The Refuge during the winter months. The rest of the year, she lives on the street, sometimes staying with Peggy, who lives about three miles from the downtown area. Most months, Louise is able to draw groceries from a food bank, and sometimes she stores her groceries and some of her other belongings as well in Peggy's apartment. Louise also has secret storage places strategically dispersed around the area. She eagerly awaits the opening of The Refuge every November 1, and lines up hours ahead of everyone else so that she may lay claim to the same partitioned sleeping area she has had for the past several years.

Martha

Martha left Bridge House in the summer of 1986 to live with Antoinette, an elderly retired psychologist volunteer who had befriended her while she was at The Refuge. After two months, Martha was hospitalized for what was to be the first of a series of operations on her neck and spine (degenerative disk disease). After the surgery, and fearful of imposing her ailing self on Antoinette who was herself not well, Martha was placed in a halfway house program. At the time, she was continuing to fight her addiction problem (alcohol and whatever pills happened to be around) and periodic depressions. She was expelled about one year later for getting drunk one day and pushing people around. She was sent to an adult foster home for a week, then on to another halfway house program where she remained five years.

During this period, Martha saw her therapist regularly, attended AA meetings regularly, and took word processing, secretarial, and business courses at the local community college. She had two more hip-to-spine bone graft operations, walked with a walker and a black box (transcutaneous electrical nerve stimulator) around her neck to ease her neck and back pain. She went on Social Security Disability and received the maximum because she had worked more than 12 years as an LPN. Twice Martha sought out her father ("I wanted to find the father in him"), but he wanted to return to the incestuous relationship of Martha's childhood and she has given up on him. On Thanksgiving Day, 1991, she was raped by one of her housemates. The program staff denied it was rape, pointing out that she had gotten drunk that day and had engaged in consensual sex. Bad feelings remained, and in January 1992, Martha left the program to share a townhouse with three other people, strangers to her until she moved in with them.

As of May 1992, Martha remains in the townhouse. She sees herself as a recovering alcoholic. Since Medicare does not cover medications, and she has been turned down for Medicaid (because of her SSDI income), her antidepressant and pain medications are pinching her financially. She walks with a cane when her back is OK—a walker when it isn't—and hopes to work again someday. The doctors are not optimistic that she will.

Peggy

Peggy began seeing Harry in 1987 while both were living in their respective shelters. In 1988, they were able to get housing assistance and they moved into their own apartment only three miles from the shelters. Peggy and Harry each received $240 a month in public assistance, with Peggy going on workfare when she could. They paid $98 a month rent for a one-bedroom apartment and furnished it nicely. Harry was a Korean war veteran and a heavy drinker. When he was drunk, he abused Peggy physically, including beating her with his fists. Sober, he was pleasant to be with, but he was sober only three months out of the twelve, so Peggy considers the marriage to have been a disaster. Peggy still receives $240 a month in General Public Assistance.

She would much prefer workfare, but that is no longer available. Now that she lives alone, her rent has been dropped to $41 a month. She also receives $110 a month in food stamps.

Peggy has reapplied for SSI and is hopeful it will come through this time. She is on medication for high blood pressure, on Dolabet for diabetes, and has arthritis in her feet and legs. She is on a Slimfast diet and has lost 65 pounds, down to 135. She says she feels terrific. "Not being on the street helps a lot."

When Harry died, Peggy's apartment became "a home away from home" for several of her friends from the shelter. Until she died in May 1991, Phyllis had been Peggy's closest friend, sometimes staying with Peggy for weeks at a time. Louise also stayed there days at a time and stored her food and other belongings there. And when Louise was not there, June might move in for a couple of weeks or Winnie would drop in for days at a time when she happened to be in town. Several months ago, Peggy called a halt to this. When Louise ignored her request to remove her belongings, Peggy put some of them in the trash; Louise arranged with a volunteer from The Refuge to retrieve the rest. Similarly, Peggy has let the other homeless women know that she and her apartment are no longer available. "If you don't leave shelter people behind, they'll pull you down to their level," she explains.

Peggy has joined a couple of singles clubs (one for dog lovers, another for horse enthusiasts) and has several pen pals drawn from readers of horse and dog magazines. Since coming out of the shelter, she and her family are once again very close. Her mother lives in Ohio and they call one another almost every day, sometimes two or three times a day. Peggy regularly visits her mother for two or three weeks at a time and is planning to move to Ohio permanently, perhaps this summer. Her son George has moved to the D.C. area and visits Peggy on most weekends.

On the street, Peggy still sees Louise, June, and some of the other women who are still homeless. She also bumps into Evelyn occasionally at the grocery store, and Kim will sometimes call Peggy and invite her to a party or just to visit.

Phyllis

Phyllis spent most of The Refuge's off-season in 1988 and 1989 on the street, sometimes in a motel. On the street, she and Louise often spent the night together, sitting at a picnic table in a park or next to one another on a park bench, as much for security as for companionship. In the spring of 1990, Phyllis was formally declared incompetent to handle her affairs (mainly her pension and Social Security income), and she went to live in a nearby motel where she received a monthly allowance from her court-appointed conservator. The motel was near the shelters and Phyllis regularly saw and was seen by Louise and the others who remained in the shelter. Only one year later, in April 1991, Phyllis learned that she had cancer. She died the next month in the county hospital.

Regina

Regina left The Refuge when her subsidized housing came through, and she now lives in a bungalow not far from Upton. She remains on public assistance but occasionally breaks the rules to take in a roomer or to take a part-time job as companion/nurse's aide. She is moderately content but would very much like to have some romance in her life, preferably a decent, reliable man to marry. Once in a while, Regina visits The Refuge or a soup kitchen for old times' sake.

Sara

While she was still at The Refuge, in January 1987, Sara was fired from her job with Giant Foods. Ostensibly, she was fired for moving without notifying Giant so that she was not reachable when her supervisor tried to call her for Sunday work. But Sara believes she was fired because they learned she had moved to a shelter. Sara then went on workfare. In May, her certificate for subsidized housing came through. She found an apartment and had to pay no rent the first year and only $24 the next, while she remained on workfare and took a variety of training courses, including word processing. In February 1988, Sara was hired at the National Institutes of Health as part of their stay-in-school program. The following August, she was hired as a full-time worker, GS-3 ($16,890). By December 1991, she was a GS-5, Step 3 ($19,798). She also worked part-time (30 hours) in a grocery store, was paying $545 a month rent, and had been joined by her 17-year-old son. "I've made government my career. This is it for me."

Sara remains close friends with Kim and sometimes sees Terry.

Terry

Terry works full-time as a waitress at Pancake Heaven. She has been living with Tommy, a warehouse manager, since shortly after Kim introduced them to one another several months ago. (Kim says Terry has the kind of looks that can get her any man in the county.) Terry is now pregnant with their baby.

Terry is in regular contact with Kim and sometimes with Sara. Her ex-husband is stationed in Europe and has their young son with him. She has not seen or heard of her daughter—born in 1988, while she was living in the shelter—since she was put out for adoption.

Vicki

I last heard from Vicki in January 1990. At that time, she was living in a subsidized apartment and working in a photocopying room in a county office building. She was delighted with her apartment but dismayed at the enormous effort she had to make (using public transportation) to get to a job she hated. To Vicki, her job was a make-work job, not "a real job," and she has surely given it up by now.

APPENDIX B

Life Histories

Note: The following life histories have been greatly condensed from the original tapes. Because I waited a few months before taking life histories, and because I also often waited for the women to volunteer them, most of the histories are of longtime homeless women, perhaps because they or their families were especially dysfunctional. They include most of the women I came to know best. These histories, then, are not offered as a sample of the population of homeless women I studied. I include them for the sake of completeness, and for whatever intrinsic interest and value they may have for the reader.

Abigail

Abigail, 27 years old and white, is of average height and weight. Her hair is black, thick, and wiry. Her teeth are very bad and she is diabetic. Abigail gives an impression of competence and mental quickness.[1]

---

[1] In the immediate present of the real world, and Hugh (her imaginary boyfriend) aside, Abigail almost always made sense. The opportunity to tell her life story, however, seemed to be too great an opportunity for her imagination to pass up.

Abigail was born and raised near Trenton, New Jersey. She was the fourth of five children by one reckoning, the first and only child by another. Her real mother, she says, was her private nursemaid and her father's mistress who lived three miles down the road from the family house, although Abigail didn't learn the identity of her real mother until two years ago. Abigail believes her father was a draftsman. Her "adopted" mother sometimes worked as a saleswoman in a clothing store. Her father was Jewish; both her mothers were Christian.

When Abigail was one year old she was hospitalized for removal of a cancerous kidney. After surgery, she left the hospital and walked the three miles to her "real" mother's house. Her real mother had a beautiful vegetable garden but someone was stealing all the vegetables. Abigail set a trap for the thief and caught him. She took the prisoner before her mother. "Eugenia, this is our vegetable thief. Vegetable thief, this is my nursemaid, Eugenia." Eddie, the thief, couldn't believe Abigail was only one year old. He thought she was a 15-year-old midget. By a remarkable coincidence, Eddie was to become the father of Judy, who, in turn, was to become Abigail's best friend in the shelter years later.

When Abigail was four, her father contracted brain cancer and his wife divorced him "because he wasn't a whole man." Abigail was "my daddy's little girl" and begged him to take her with him, but of course he couldn't. Her adopted mother didn't like independence in children and Abigail had long had "a mind of my own."

Abigail's mother remarried months later. Abigail's new stepfather may have been her father's uncle. He worked in a brewery and had "Pabst" printed on all his work clothes. Abigail liked him a lot.

Abigail did poorly at school but "school was the main part of my life. I dreaded staying home. . . . I enjoyed school only for the reason I was out of the house."

When Abigail was 15, the family moved to southern

California. There, at school, she did drugs—mainly pot, sometimes speed—and was introduced to sex. Just before she was 16, she quit school. Somewhere about this time—1976—the whole family moved to a rural commune of some 1,200 persons. Abigail remained there about two years, picking and canning fruit. In 1978, she "figured I wanted to be out in the world again" and returned to New Jersey to live with a boyfriend. There she worked the graveyard shift at Dunkin' Donuts; her boyfriend was a painter/carpenter. After six months in Trenton they returned to southern California. In November 1978 Abigail discovered she was pregnant.

The following spring, five or six months into her pregnancy, Abigail was "put out" by her alcoholic, woman-beating boyfriend. She went to live with her mother for a few months, then moved back to the farm/commune to have her baby in July. Over the next couple of years, Abigail and her baby lived briefly with her grandmother in New Jersey and on and off with her boyfriend, sometimes in New Jersey, sometimes in California, living on AFDC (Aid to Families with Dependent Children) and food stamps. Meanwhile, she got her high school equivalency certificate and made several attempts at going to community colleges in California but "it was a little too difficult for me." It was during this period, too, that Abigail neglected her insulin shots and had to be hospitalized. Her baby was put in protective custody in a foster home until Abigail's release from the hospital.

In November 1982, Social Services made an unannounced visit to her apartment, found it messy and otherwise wanting, and took her baby from her. Abigail believes her brother and mother set her up for this. She recalls the separation: "I was watching the car go and she was crying and trying to get out of that car and I was crying and waving to her and I called her name and she called mine. From that time on, I haven't seen my baby."[2]

---

[2] The little girl, now six years old, is being raised by Abigail's mother.

Abigail then met a young man working with a carnival that was passing through town. They moved north together to Sacramento with the carnival, and there they stayed from December 1982 to May 1983, when they were evicted for nonpayment of rent. Abigail called her brother, then living in the D.C. suburbs. He sent her a plane ticket and she flew to Washington to live with her brother and his wife and their two children.

In January 1984, Abigail met Judy at a vocational training program and they became bosom buddies. When Judy left her parents' home in July of that year and had no place to go, she moved in with Abigail in the basement of Abigail's brother's house. From this point on, Abigail and Judy had a joint history.[3] Asked to move out of the house two months later, they made a pilgrimage to Indiana with the intention of meeting their make-believe lovers, two real-life members of a Christian rock group, the Pente Kostals; tracked down by Judy's father, they were shipped back to the D.C. area after three days. Unwilling to meet the conditions laid down by Judy's parents or Abigail's brother for returning to either household, the two women went to the Crisis Center which referred them to The Refuge.

Betty

Betty is white and 50 years old. She looks older, perhaps because of her rimless glasses. She is of medium build, but her upper arms are exceptionally fat, forcing her to wear a cape and loose-fitting blouses rather than tailored garments. Betty looks very distinguished and this appearance, together with her assertive carriage and way of speaking, suggests to newcomers that she is an important visitor if not the director of the shelter.

---

[3] See Judy's life history.

Betty was born in a small town in Virginia. Her parents separated while she was a small child. She does not remember her father but knows he was a laborer. When she was five or six, Betty, her seven-year-old sister, and her mother moved to Washington to live with her mother's sister in a hotel in a run-down section of the city. Betty's aunt worked for the phone company and Betty remembers lots of parties and drinking in their apartment in that period. A short time later, when she was perhaps seven, her mother remarried. Betty's stepfather was a cab driver and her mother a sometime waitress. Both parents were heavy drinkers and the family moved a lot, staying mostly in downtown D.C. Money was always in short supply and Betty wore only hand-me-downs from her sister, but their stepfather always made certain that the family had enough food. She called her stepfather Daddy.

Although she liked school, Betty found everything except reading difficult. She enjoyed *Black Beauty* and *Little Women* and "doggy stories and horses and things." She sang in the glee club and was liked by the other kids.

Betty did not get along with her sister or mother. In the evenings, on the front steps, "I used to daydream, even though it was nighttime, about how it was going to be for me when I got away from my family—all those people who made my life miserable." With no encouragement from her parents, Betty regularly attended Sunday School at a local Baptist church. ("I'll never forget how good I felt when I went to Sunday School.") She participated in children's activities sponsored by the Salvation Army, "and this also saved my soul." For a while, Betty had a part-time job preparing a cup of tea and two pieces of toast every evening for an elderly woman in the neighborhood. She liked that very much. "To this day, you know, I enjoy taking care of elderly people."

At 16, in the 10th grade, Betty quit school. "I wanted nice clothes. I wanted money to go out with my friends—to stop after school in some soda place and have a soda with my friends."

She went to work for an H. L. Green 5&10 and was regularly embarrassed when "my mother waited out front every payday. She took half my paycheck." If Betty protested, she was "an ungrateful brat."

Betty was briefly engaged to a military policeman she met in a beer joint. "He was so handsome in his uniform and I was a beautiful young lady at the time." Despite the engagement, Betty "didn't cut myself off socially altogether, OK? But I was the type of woman who didn't go to bed with just anybody."

When she was 18, Betty moved out to live with a girlfriend in a trailer and "we partied almost every night, my girlfriend and me." About a year later, they argued and Betty returned to live with her parents, continuing to pay rent there.

Betty left the 5&10 to work in the record department of Hecht's, a large department store where she remained almost five years. She loved the job and the free records and dinners she got from record salesmen. She also took a part-time job as a waitress in a bar and grill. There she met Richard, a truck driver 15 years older than herself, and "of course we messed around, OK?" Betty was soon pregnant, but they couldn't marry because, as Richard had forgotten to tell her, he had a wife and children somewhere in Virginia. Betty moved in with him and stopped drinking and smoking for the duration of her pregnancy. She had her baby in 1959, and Richard doted on the child. They led such a normal life "that I forgot we weren't married." Betty and her mother reconciled. From the moment Betty's mother saw the baby, "it was Grandma all the way."

Betty and Richard had occasional fights. They drank regularly and heavily. They graduated from beer to hard liquor ("seven and seven—7-Up and Seagram's 7"), and from half a pint to a fifth a day. Soon they were confirmed alcoholics.

From here on, the story is not too clear, even now. Richard begins to miss a lot of work. For a while, his family helps with rent and groceries. Betty discovers she has diabetes but goes on drinking. She is hospitalized for a gall bladder removal and goes on drinking. The years pass—maybe five or six—and the family experiences repeated evictions. Richard works off and on with the same firm but has so many drunk driving charges he can no longer drive a truck and is assigned to some kind of inside work. Betty spends her days drinking and watching soap operas. She falls down a flight of stairs and breaks one or more vertebrae in her back. Later, she is hospitalized again for something or other and returns home to find all their furniture on the street. The family breaks up. The daughter, maybe 11 or 12, goes to live with Betty's mother and Betty goes to live with a girlfriend, with Richard bringing her a few dollars occasionally. Betty and Richard get together again and move in with Richard's sister, but this arrangement is short-lived. Richard inherits a couple of thousand dollars from the sale of a family farm, and he and Betty move to a suburban motel and settle in for some serious drinking. "Every now and then we would eat."

The inheritance spent, Richard leaves, Betty is hospitalized again, then gets a live-in job with an old woman through Operation Match and quickly loses it. Over the next many years, Betty makes her way, sometimes on public assistance, sometimes not; sometimes keeping house and sleeping with one or another man in exchange for his keeping her in booze; forever bouncing in and out of rooming houses, live-in jobs, hospitals, alcohol programs, halfway houses, and on and on, always drinking, always Valium. Betty soon discovers that wherever she is, even in the hospital, someone has bugged her room or telephone. In the late 1970s, she tells a psychiatrist some of her life story and he has her placed in a schizophrenic ward in the state mental hospital where she remained for 33 days. "I'll never forgive him for doing that to me, OK? Especially after me confiding in him."

Betty then goes through two separate alcohol treatment cycles from the state hospital to a farm for homeless alcoholics. On October 31, 1979, at The Farm, something takes hold—

prayer, she believes—and Betty stops drinking. She gets live-in jobs caring for sick or elderly persons, sometimes on her own, sometimes through Operation Match, and alternates working with public assistance. In 1983, on a job, Betty re-injures her back, loses a job as a nurse's aide in a nursing home, spends several months at two D.C. shelters, and after a real or imagined (she herself is uncertain) threat of attack from three men on the street, she leaves D.C. and goes to the Crisis Center where staff persons tell her about The Refuge.

Beverly

Beverly is 23 years old. She is blonde and blue-eyed and has a slight lisp. Everyone says she is very pretty, and Betty makes a standing joke of her offer to be Beverly's "madam" and split the proceeds.

Beverly is the youngest of three children; her sister is 24, and her brother is 26. Both her parents—now in their mid-40s—worked for Safeway. Her father and mother had terrible fights, sometimes breaking the furniture, and Beverly remembers her mother grabbing the children and running to a neighbor's house for protection. Her father also abused her sister and brother but never Beverly because she had been sick from birth ("My esophagus didn't close—it stayed open all the time") and was overly protected. Her father had himself been an abused child. His own father had been a wino in downtown D.C. and was now in a nursing home. Beverly's father visits him occasionally, but Beverly has never met him.

Beverly remembers that both her parents had undergone electric shock treatments. Sometimes Beverly's mother would run away for days at a time, but her father always took her back. As small children, Beverly and her brother and sister were forced to attend a Catholic church every Sunday and to go to Sunday School.

Beverly's father moved out when she was six. He lived nearby and the children saw a great deal of him. In the house, the fighting continued as Beverly's brother "took over where my dad left off." The family drew up sides. "My sister is addicted to my mother. My mother can do no wrong. She doesn't like my father and I don't like my mother."

As a child and young girl, Beverly was shy and quiet. At school, she had no friends and was teased mercilessly about her severe speech problem. Nobody wanted to hear her talk so she never got to finish her sentences. Later she learned "to say everything quick before they had a chance to interrupt me. I taught myself that." People said she had a learning disability but she thinks she was just a very slow learner. For the sixth grade, she was sent to a special school for learning-disabled children. At that time, too, her brother moved out to live with their father. Her brother's only ambition was to get stoned (on drugs) and stay stoned. He was also in trouble with the police. Her sister, she said, "turned out to be the biggest slut in town." Beverly herself never did drugs. "I'm a Goody Two-shoes," she said, who always got along better with older people than with her peers.

When Beverly was 15, her mother remarried. Her stepfather had been a neighbor and longtime family friend, one of Beverly's favorite people. But as soon as he became their stepfather, "he became a jerk and treated us terrible. He was irritable and snotty. He wouldn't eat with us. He ate his meals in his bedroom. . . . His door was always closed." Meanwhile, her father had also remarried.

Beverly lost her first real boyfriend to her own best girlfriend when she refused to have sex with him before marriage. She swore that would never happen again. In her last year at high school, she began dating the boy next door, and three months later she was pregnant. Five months pregnant, defying everyone, she went to her graduation ceremonies and received her diploma.

When Beverly came home with the baby, her mother took

over. "Come to Mommy," she would say to the baby, dismissing Beverly's protests with a wave of her hand. Almost immediately, Beverly's mother and stepfather "became addicted to the baby. They were terrified of losing him. They made me so dependent on them I was more like a prisoner there. . . . My mom and I fought all the time." When Beverly was 19 and the baby a year and a half, Beverly's mother learned that she had secretly applied for public assistance and was planning to take her baby and live on her own. Soon thereafter, the police came to the door. "We have a petition here that says you need psychiatric care," they told Beverly, and she was taken to the hospital in handcuffs. Her mother had told the authorities Beverly was a danger to herself and others, and a neighbor said that Beverly was suicidal because she had heard her tell her father, after breaking up with her fiancé, "I get so frustrated at times, I wish I was dead."

Beverly was released from the hospital the same day, July 17, 1982. She left the baby with a friend while she hunted for a place to live. That was the last time she ever saw her son. Two days later, when she returned to pick him up, she was told, "He's not here. Your mom came last night and took him." Lawyers told Beverly to take her mother to court and she would surely win, but Beverly never had the money to do it. Legal Aid told her to "come back when you get your life straightened out."

Beverly moved in with a friend and spent her days looking at pictures of her son, her nights crying. After four months, she moved in with her father, who had separated from his second wife and was living in a small apartment. In June 1984, Beverly met and started dating a security guard. Three months later they were married in Ocean City and lived there a couple of months before returning to the D.C. area to live with his parents. Her husband took a job as a construction laborer.

Four months into the marriage, the fighting got so bad that Beverly left the house and checked herself into County General Hospital. A week later, when she was about to be discharged, her husband told her he "could not stay married to a crazy person. I'm leaving."

Out of the hospital, Beverly again moved in with a friend while she attended a day program at the hospital. Again she tried to live on her own when she got a stock clerk job at K mart, but she found the job too stressful and again went to live with her father, who had taken a larger apartment to accommodate her. After a terrible fight with him, she tried to kill herself by overdosing on some of his medications. She was released from the hospital as soon as she was out of danger.

In July 1985, she started dating a friend of a friend and soon moved in with him. He was 40 and a drunk, and his 17-year-old son lived with them. Beverly did not get along with the son, couldn't stand the drinking, and several times moved out to stay with another friend. Finally, last fall, she moved out for good and stayed with a friend in Section 8 housing. The rules required that Beverly leave after two weeks. She went to the Crisis Center. The Crisis Center sent her to Social Services. Social Services told her about The Refuge.

Carlotta

Carlotta is a small and dark Latina woman with long, straight black hair. She speaks with a heavy Spanish accent.

Carlotta was born in Bogotá, Colombia, in 1951. She was the third of four children, each a year apart from the next. Her father was an encyclopedia salesman, or maybe a supervisor of encyclopedia salesmen. He worked very hard and the family lived moderately well until Carlotta was 10 years old, when the father moved out of the family apartment. The mother went to work as a teacher in a local school, but the pay was low and the now fatherless family was very poor. "Life was very hard for us because a family should have a father and a mother."

Carlotta was an average student. Her two older sisters were her best friends throughout her childhood. She graduated from high school when she was 18 and went to work in a department

store selling men's clothes. She was very good at selling and remained on that job for more than two years, when she came to
Washington to live with her mother's sister, who was a secretary for the World Bank. It was 1971 and Carlotta was 20. She
came to the States "to begin a new life."

Carlotta stayed with her aunt and her aunt's two children in
a Washington suburb for three years. She and her aunt
got along reasonably well. Carlotta worked mainly as a baby
sitter. When her aunt married and moved away, Carlotta got a
job as a live-in housekeeper with a family in downtown
Washington. She remained at that job for three years, then
moved out to a room of her own and worked as a day housekeeper for five different households. That was hard work, a different house to clean every day, but the pay was good ($30 a
day, plus bus fare) and she was content with her life. She lived
like that for four years. She had a few friends and her friends
had lots of friends.

One day in 1977, at the Greyhound bus station, she met
Jason, a Marine on his way to North Carolina where he was
stationed. They talked, and he asked for her address. They
corresponded, first by mail, then by telephone, then face-
to-face, then they got married.[4] Carlotta went to live with her
husband in Jacksonville, North Carolina, where they stayed
eight (for Carlotta, miserable) months. Then they went to
Jason's hometown in Indiana where they stayed with friends,
and soon thereafter Carlotta gave birth to twins. These were
difficult times, mainly because her husband did not want
to work.

When the twins were three months old, the family moved
back to the Washington area, where Carlotta managed to get on
AFDC. Things were not going well between them, and Jason
took one of the twins and returned to Indiana. Carlotta followed

---

[4]There is a discrepancy here of some four years. I suspect that Carlotta's
year of arrival in the U.S. (1971) and year of her marriage (1977) are correct.
The error (perhaps mine) lies in the years of work at one or another job. Her
speech is heavily accented and I may have misunderstood something.

him there, hoping to retrieve her baby. They lived together again for a while, Carlotta had her third child, and Jason moved out to live with another woman, taking all three children with him. That was in 1981. The twins were then about two and a half; the third child was still an infant.

Carlotta remained in Indiana, hoping to see her children and perhaps get them back so she could "do my life." For four years she worked as a live-in housekeeper earning $40 a week. But her husband kept his whereabouts secret, so she has never seen her children since the day he took them from her, more than four years ago. She thinks the courts may have awarded him the children on the grounds that she abandoned them, but she had no friends there, and there was the language problem, so she's not certain of this. Carlotta believes her husband wanted the children so he could go on welfare. She did go to the police but they told her, "If you have custody you can do anything. If you don't have custody you can't do anything."

In Indiana, Carlotta corresponded with her sister back home in Bogotá, writing to her twice a month. Her sister sent her a plane ticket to come home, but Carlotta will not go. "How can I go back to my country? I cannot see the babies." No, she can't go, even for a visit. Although she married an American citizen, she never became a citizen and has no visa. She would like to become a citizen "but I cannot fix the papers I have for this. I have to find myself first. Then I fix my papers."

Carlotta returned to the Washington area from Indiana a few months ago. When she got off the bus, she found a policeman and told him she had no place to sleep for the night. The policeman told her about The Refuge and she took a taxi to get there. This is the first time she has been homeless.

Elsie

Elsie was born in a farming area of Appalachia in 1941. She is white, about 5'4", and normally weighs about 300 pounds, but she has weighed as much as 327. She looks big rather than fat.

Her gray-streaked and short-cropped hair covers where her ears would be if she had them. She has a developed external ear on one side, a partial lobe and no more on the other. She has no ear canals. The earpieces of her round, stylish glasses are attached to her bone-conduction hearing aid. Under most conditions, one would not suspect she has difficulty hearing. Elsie was also born with a palsy, which shows itself most prominently when she is under stress, curling one side of her mouth and pulling down the same-side eyelid.

Elsie was the sixth of nine children. She has five older brothers, two younger ones, and a younger sister. Elsie's father was a preacher until she was born, when preaching could no longer support his fast-growing family. He became a construction worker who spent most of his time on the road, following the jobs, and was often laid off for months at a time. The family was poor but generally self-sufficient. Elsie's mother made everyone's clothes. They grew all their own vegetables and kept cows, chickens, and hogs.

The family was very religious. Even today, says Elsie, "I can't function unless I have a daily devotional with my Heavenly Father."

Elsie did poorly at school. She did not get her first hearing aid (twice the size of a pack of cigarettes, and many times heavier, with many control knobs) until she was in the second grade. School was a horror for Elsie. The other children teased her mercilessly; the teachers were impatient and often hostile. She remembers one teacher locking her in a broom closet. Elsie had no friends and played only with her brothers and sister. (Two years ago, Elsie realized that she had been repressing the fact that she had been sexually abused by four of her older brothers from her preschool years until she was 14 or 15.)

When Elsie was 16 and entering the ninth grade, her parents pulled her out of public school, probably to remove her from that painful and hostile setting. Elsie spent the next two years at home before being sent to the state Department of Vocational

Rehabilitation. After a month-long evaluation, they recommended that she be trained as a hairdresser. Elsie hated the idea—all her life she has wanted to be "an illustrator, a fashion artist"—but her father wanted her to learn a more practical trade, and Elsie was sent for almost a year to a state residential school where she learned to be a hairdresser. The family, meanwhile, had moved to a small town in Ohio, and Elsie joined them there when she graduated from the school.

Elsie was then about 19 and was forced by her father to go through the same vocational hairdressing training in Ohio so she could take and pass the state boards. Even after passing the boards, however, she could not find a job as a hairdresser. Eventually, she was taken on as a companion to an elderly stroke victim.

Elsie was now 21 and had made a few friends. Through them, she met a young man and began going out with him. Elsie had long felt overprotected by her parents and she chafed at her lack of the personal freedoms enjoyed by her younger sister. Two years later, desperate to become her own person, Elsie got married against the strong opposition of her family. Elsie made her own wedding, but no one came.

Elsie and her husband settled in upstate New York where he had relatives. He was a photographer of sorts, and Elsie soon learned that her parents were right: he was no good. He refused to work and, intensely jealous, refused to allow Elsie to work. Most of the time, they lived on welfare. Eventually, Elsie got a job as a dietary aide in a local hospital. Her husband became increasingly abusive and Elsie grew to hate him. When he was sick, Elsie found herself hoping he would die. Once, when she had had another in her long series of operations on her ears, he beat her still-bandaged head with his fists. After seven years of this, Elsie left him and he filed for divorce on grounds of desertion.

Elsie went to the Washington, D.C., area where one of her brothers lived. He helped her get a job as a nurse's aide in a local hospital, helped her buy her first car, and introduced her to a church singles group where she met the man who soon became her second husband. They were married in 1973 and remained together for two and a half terrible years. Her new husband was a woman-chaser. "After the first year, he ceased being a husband. 'Consider yourself my roommate,'" he told her, all the while encouraging her to leave him. Elsie's pain and confusion at home carried over to her job at the hospital, and her patients suffered for it. Her supervisor asked her to resign and gave her a positive letter of recommendation.

Back home in Ohio, her mother had been hospitalized, and Elsie retreated there to take care of her father who had himself had a breakdown, mainly because he couldn't find any work. "He was too old to hire and too young to retire." Elsie remained there two years, getting occasional private-duty jobs.

In 1976, Elsie was called to a job as an aide with the Department of Human Services in the D.C. area. She did not want to leave her mother. "My mom was my best friend. I could talk to her and know she would not condemn me. She never said, 'I told you so.' She would say, 'How about trying it this way' or 'Have you thought of . . .' If not for my mom, I don't know where I'd be." But at her mother's insistence, Elsie took the job, working first in a home for dependent children, then moving on to a long-term nursing home for the indigent elderly in D.C. Elsie started out as a GS-3. Almost seven years later, when she was a GS-5, Step 4, she had two successive hospitalizations for surgery and was fired for too high a rate of absenteeism. The union took her case to arbitration and lost.

Elsie went on unemployment and moved from one furnished room to another several times over the next several months. In the last place, the woman whose apartment she shared decided to get married and wanted the whole apartment for herself. Elsie had no money and no place to turn. Her brother had long since married and started a family, and her mother had died in 1977. In November 1984, age 43 and homeless for the first time in her life, Elsie moved into a shelter for homeless women.

Evelyn

Evelyn has returned to Bridge House after two months in the hospital where her leg veins were stripped and skin grafts were applied to her leg ulcers. Evelyn is 35, black, and very heavy. Her weight has been a major factor in her life since she was 12. She weighs 370 pounds; she weighed 430 pounds during her last pregnancy. She also has high blood pressure and gall bladder disease, and suffers intermittently from diabetes.

The second of six children, five of them girls, Evelyn grew up in Washington, D.C. Her older sister is retarded, cannot read, has difficulty talking, and spent several years in an institution. Evelyn's father worked for the Salvation Army, and her mother gave piano lessons. The family was very poor, especially during that period early in her life when her parents separated for a few years. They went to church on Sundays and they moved frequently, remaining in the D.C. area. On at least one occasion, they lived without furniture. Evelyn remembers giant water bugs coming out of the faucets and "rats that came up and down the steps like high heel shoes."[5]

Looking back, Evelyn sees large chunks of her childhood and youth as a jumble. She seems to have spent most of her life fighting off attempts by her mother, her sisters, and her teachers to label her and treat her as childish, retarded, irresponsible, and weak. She hated school and was always in "basic" classes. "School was dumb to me because I never learned anything. Seemed like I never moved from one grade to another. Just had a lot of different teachers."

Evelyn was always "the dummy of the family" and a black sheep of sorts. Bitterly, she recalls a big birthday party for one of her sisters "and I got mad because my birthday, they acted like I didn't exist." Although she did not feel close to anyone, fighting dependency on her mother and sisters seems to have been a major theme in her life. (Peggy is the only real friend she's had, she said.)

---

[5] "Water bugs" is a euphemism for roaches.

Evelyn quit school when she was 16 and in the eighth grade. She helped her mother with shopping and housework and made many trips to hospitals and clinics, mainly for (unsuccessful) treatment of her leg ulcers.

At 17, Evelyn got pregnant. After the birth of her son she went into a depression that lasted more than three years; there were long periods when she never left the house. Evelyn's mother reminded her that she also became depressed when her father left the family (Evelyn didn't remember this), but Evelyn traces her depression following the child's birth to the effective loss of her son to her mother and sisters, "who took over my son." They played with him and cared for him, and it was to his grandmother he turned for comfort and solace. The baby learned to call Evelyn's mother "Mama," and Evelyn "Evelyn."

Over the next several years, Evelyn attended a series of rehabilitation and vocational training programs in which she raised her reading ability from third- to sixth-grade level. Importantly, she also learned that she was "more independent than I was pretending to be, and I could do things I didn't know I could do. . . . Then my sisters told me they liked me better when I really didn't know nothing." Evelyn concedes she still has a learning problem. "Today, I'm eager to learn but I have a problem with stayability."

When she was 24, after still another argument with her family, Evelyn moved out on her own (without her son) into a subsidized apartment within walking distance of her mother's place. "It was hard for me because I wasn't used to being by myself. I was always around my family." Evelyn continued with one or another rehabilitation program and "ran from hospital to hospital in D.C., year after year," trying to get relief from her leg ulcers.

Two years later, in 1978, Evelyn was pregnant with her second child, a daughter, and returned to the family home. Again there was a battle over effective custody which Evelyn seems to have lost. Over the next few years, Evelyn moved in and out, at least one time with her son. It was during this period that she got her first taste of shelters, going twice to the House of Ruth in downtown Washington for very short stays. In 1981, she had a second daughter by a man who moved in with her for a while and abused her, including appropriating most of her $600 monthly income in the form of food stamps and welfare and disability payments, and again Evelyn returned to her family where she remained until 1985. For some 14 months, she attended another rehabilitation workshop; other times, she remained in the house because walking was "a pain and a half."

Again, relationships were difficult. "It was a depressive situation. . . . They wouldn't let me have my say and I had my own views. . . . I felt like I was getting smothered and didn't have a chance to prove myself. . . . I felt I was too old to be there." Much of the time was spent "cooking and arguing," mostly about money and whether Evelyn was competent to handle her own income.

Last January, 1986, Evelyn left the house. She got as far as Upton and could go no farther. She called the police and was taken to The Refuge, but after four days she had to be hospitalized because of her legs, and from the hospital she returned home. Then, a week before Thanksgiving, Evelyn left home again, returning this time to Bridge House where she remains, hoping to get herself together physically so she can get a job and live with her children in a place of their own.

Ginger

Ginger is white and 25 years old but looks much younger. She is taller than average, thin, almost lanky, with dark hair and fair complexion. Although she is retarded, her eyes are bright and people think she's very pretty.

Ginger was born in New York City. Both her parents were Jewish, and her father was a white-collar worker. Her mother was a diabetic and Ginger does not remember a time when her mother was not in a wheelchair. Ginger likes to recall how she used to help her mother dress and do things. Her older brother and her mother's mother lived with them, too, and Ginger liked her grandmother very much.

When Ginger was very young—she's not sure when—the family moved to the Washington suburbs and her father worked for the federal government. Later, her mother's leg became infected and had to be cut off at the knee. Shortly after that her mother died and Ginger buried her ashes in a plastic bag in the backyard. Almost every day, she visited her mother, talked to her, and prayed. Ginger thinks she was about fifteen at the time. Shortly thereafter, her father married Megan, who had three children older than Ginger. Ginger liked Megan and her children.

Every Sunday, Megan and Ginger's step-siblings went to church. Ginger wanted to go to church, too, so she and her father were baptized as Catholics at the same time. Ginger remembers being given a necklace (rosary?). The family moved to a new house, and Ginger's father moved her mother's ashes to a cemetery without consulting her or allowing her to help. Ginger has never forgiven him for this.

Ginger went to a special school until her high school years, when she was sent away to a residential school run by Catholic sisters. Ginger always liked school. She had lots of friends there and the teachers taught her "a lot of things about cooking, doing laundry, and uh, and being a better person." While there, she was in the Special Olympics, where she won trophies and ribbons. She remembers her parents "yelling . . . rooting for me, saying 'come on! come on!' . . . and then they took me out to dinner and one of my girlfriends, too."

When Ginger graduated from high school, her father, stepmother, and brother came to the ceremony. She thinks that was a year or two ago, when she was 22 or 23. The sequence of events is not too clear to her. She seems to have returned home to live with her father and Megan, but that didn't work out too well, mainly because Ginger and her father were always arguing.

She was sent to live with her brother and his wife, and from there she went to live with her stepbrother and his wife. While there, Ginger got a job at a local restaurant bussing dishes. She also got herself "mixed up with the wrong guy," who more or less forced her to have sex with him and some other boys, too. They also did drugs, including PCP, and were arrested. Ginger's father was very angry when he came to take her away from the police station and threatened to leave her there.

Ginger also discovered she was pregnant at this time, or rather, her (step)sister-in-law discovered she was pregnant. Ginger wanted very much to keep her baby. She knew she could take good care of a baby. But her sister-in-law said, "You're living underneath this roof. [If] you don't have a job, you cannot have the child," and she took Ginger to a hospital where she had an abortion.

Immediately after the abortion, or shortly thereafter, her stepbrother and his wife took Ginger to The Refuge. That was four months ago. Ginger had to leave most of her clothes behind, and her sister-in-law gave them away. She also gave away all of Ginger's stuffed animals.

Grace

Grace is 44 and white. She is about 5'4" with fair skin, blue eyes, and ash blonde hair that most people take (wrongly) to be natural. Most of the time, Grace wears tailored suits that she makes herself. She is almost always on the verge of thinking herself too heavy, so she often diets and sometimes jogs.

Once, when she had been explaining to Brenda about the difference between a mythical animal and an extinct one and the unicorn as a symbol of Christ, she turned away to get some coffee. "Isn't she beautiful!" said Brenda. "Isn't she beautiful!" In truth, to look at Grace, as with many other women, one would never guess she was homeless. Patty, seven months pregnant, said she wanted her baby to grow up to be like Grace.

"She comes right to the point. She sticks up for herself. . . . She's got a good head on her shoulders and I want my child to be like her."

Grace did not enjoy talking about her childhood. Once, thinking back on it, she said she couldn't remember even five minutes of happiness as a child. "Most of my childhood I can't remember, which is what saves me now from going totally berserk." She was the second of four children. "We were poor. Poor poor." Her father was a house painter with a third-grade education. He drank away most of what he earned, and money was always a problem. Her mother "sewed a lot, and that's how we got by," along with hand-me-downs from relatives. Her mother had to quit school just before entering the seventh grade and "from that time on, she was a child between the sixth and seventh grades all her life. . . . So her thinking— what she was then, she still is now. She never passed to the mature stage."

Grace remembers cowering in the house, waiting for her father to come home from work, wondering if he'd be drunk or sober and whom he would start beating on. She says she had a multiple personality as a child, but this was not a mental problem. There were so many traumatic situations, she said, and when she couldn't handle a particular one, she retreated into another personality. "Because you can't handle it as this, so you handle it in another person, and become this person, and that's what I was, several different people." As she looks back on this now, it's as if it was all a bad dream.

Grace was an average or slightly above average student but had no close friends. She was "very withdrawn and very quiet and insecure." She had always gone to Sunday School at her mother's insistence, but somewhere in those years her mother became an especially devout Baptist and passed this on to Grace. In the ninth grade, Grace decided she would become a missionary, and after graduating from high school she went to a three-year Baptist Bible college. She worked her way through school with the help of several hundred dollars from her local church. Her father refused to contribute anything.

Grace graduated in May 1960, at the age of 20, and was married that August to a working-class young man who had just begun his career as a school teacher. Grace had not gone out with boys before; she thought this one was OK but she certainly didn't love him. About an hour before the wedding, she tried to back out of it, "but I was the type of person that did as I was told. So I got married."

Things did not go well from the very beginning, but Grace did not know at that time what to expect. Her husband managed and controlled all the finances, and Grace had to turn her paycheck over to him. (She was commuting an hour and a half each way to an office job.) He would give her some money for a few personal items, such as stockings, but not until she had begged for it.

Grace knew almost nothing about sex. "He wasn't using anything and I didn't know what you were supposed to do, so I got something at the drugstore that was supposed to help. I thought it was a contraceptive but it wasn't. It was called Norform. [Laughing] It was probably a deodorant."

Grace had five children over the next 10 years and had to manage the household and clothe the children with almost no money. After the fifth child, she had a tubal ligation. Early on in their marriage she and her husband moved to the D.C. area and into a townhouse that quickly became too small for the growing family. The husband more or less disassociated himself from Grace and the children. After 10 years of marriage, she learned he was running around with other women but he refused to talk about it. By that time, Grace had become a born-again Christian. Three times she went back to him ("because that's what scripture says") to discuss things and three times he refused. And the Lord said to Grace, "You're free from this," so she moved out of their bedroom. After a couple of years of this arrangement, her husband stopped talking to her, and they lived like that for another five years or so as the three oldest children grew up and moved out.[6]

In 1983, the court awarded the husband custody of the children, the house, and the two automobiles, ignoring Grace's contention that only God, not a court or state, could take children away from their mother and force a woman out of her own house.[7] Eventually she was held in contempt of court, taken out of her house in handcuffs, and spent the day in jail.

After a few weeks with her sister in New Jersey, Grace returned to D.C. and shared a house with four other people for eight months, working temporary office jobs. But she had to move again when the landlord wanted the house back for himself. Grace went back to her New Jersey sister for four months, returning to D.C. again when that didn't work out.[8] Homeless and broke, she went to Social Services, where the staff told her about The Refuge. That was December 1984.

Jeanette

Jeanette is probably in her early 60s but she keeps her age a secret. She is of medium build, white, with dark hair and fair skin. She is shy and quiet and gives an appearance of refinement, an impression reinforced by her thin voice and precise speech. But

[6]To Grace, her ex-husband was "The Person I Used To Be Married To." He had never been her husband or ex-husband "because . . . my marriage was never consummated. It was consummated by him but it never was by me because I was accustomed to playing pretend. I never knew how to have an orgasm. . . . I have had five children and had sex with this person hundreds of times, and I never felt he was making love to me, which he never did. . . . He never talked to me, ever, in bed. . . . I'm talking about talking, just talking—you know, how you say nice things to each other? I've read stories where people would talk to each other, have a good time at it and all. I've never had any of this. I was just totally being used."

[7]This point of view has a long and honored history; Grace was just behind the times. "[People of the Christian Commonwealth] fetch [their laws] out of the Word of God, making that their only Magna Carta; and accounting no Law, Statute, or Judgment valid farther than it appeareth to arise and flow from the Word of God." John Eliot, *The Christian Commonwealth,* chap. 1, part 2 (London: 1660); quoted in Henry W. Schneider, *The Puritan Mind,* p. 25.

[8]See p. 85.

her coat's fur collar is scruffy and her other clothes are beginning to fray.

Jeanette was born in Wyoming, the second of three children. Her father was a laborer and her mother a beautician. Her father wanted to become an electrician, so the family moved to Michigan where he could get the necessary vocational training. Jeanette looks back on her early childhood with fondness. She liked her brother, who was one year older, and she felt that their parents were caring and loving and understood children. Her mother was a devout Christian and raised Jeanette to be the same.

But when Jeanette was nine, her mother died after giving birth to a retarded child, and the motherless family moved to the west coast. About four years later, their father remarried, and the retarded sister was put away in an institution. Jeanette feels that her sister could have been helped but that her father institutionalized her at the insistence of his new wife.

Jeanette's father and stepmother soon had a child of their own. Jeanette felt her stepmother did not want her around, and after about two years, when Jeanette was 15, she was sent to a town about 200 miles away to live with her stepmother's sister and her husband. They were loving, gentle people with two daughters, both younger than Jeanette, and she still feels close to all of them. Jeanette was a B student in high school but "I wasn't aiming for college because I didn't have the money and I wasn't being encouraged in that way." After graduating from high school, she went to live with her paternal grandmother while she went to business college ("so at least I'd have something"), and from that time on, she felt she was on her own.

Jeanette worked at ordinary office jobs and lived in a woman's hotel run by Catholic sisters, remaining there a few years until she felt she was "ready for my own apartment." At the hotel, she defied the other white women by befriending a young black woman who introduced her to Catholicism.

By this time Jeanette was in her mid-20s and felt she was "an ugly duckling." (In fact, she is an attractive woman.) Even in high school she had decided not to smile because she thought her teeth were ugly, but there was no money to fix them. Increasingly, Jeanette became interested in religious life, partly, she thinks, because she wasn't able to develop any healthy relationships with men. She wasn't dating and was despairing of finding "the right person." She felt that maybe this was God's way of pointing her in the direction of the religious life, that He was giving her a message.

At 33 Jeanette entered a cloistered Catholic order in New Mexico; but after a year and a half she realized this was a mistake, and she agreed to try a less cloistered life with the same order in Virginia. But in the Virginia convent, Jeanette began to suffer from nightmares and decided the religious life was not for her. The sisters gave her some clothes and $20 and Jeanette struck out on her own. She stopped off in the D.C. area to visit the wife of her mother's deceased brother, found a good job as a secretary in a trade association, and moved into a boarding house in Washington to be near her job. At the boarding house, she met a man—a glass installer—and they were married three months later. They both worked, living in an apartment on Connecticut Avenue.

In retrospect, Jeanette thinks the marriage was a wrong decision. Her husband drank quite a bit, was jealous, and insisted on buying a new car every two years ("He was one of the many men who are more enamored of their cars than they are of their wives.") Jeanette thought she could lead him to religion and away from drink, but that was a false hope. For a while, her husband's young son from his first marriage came to live with them, and Jeanette often suspected her husband was still in love with his first wife. Then, one night when Jeanette had to work late, her drunk husband charged her with running around and he struck her. Jeanette "had never been around that sort of thing. I couldn't take that. I moved out." They had been married about four years.

Jeanette remained in Washington, working at one or another office job. In 1973 she took a job as a clerk typist with the federal government. She left after six years, hoping to get a job in private industry and build up her Social Security credits. She also thought she might return to the west coast. But she could not find a job right away, used up her savings, and had to give up her apartment. Finally, through a church in Fairfax, Virginia, Jeanette got a job as a companion to an elderly woman—"the first time I've ever done anything like that"—and remained with that woman for three years, long enough to save some money and buy herself a little Datsun. When her charge had to be moved to a nursing home, Jeanette moved in with a woman friend from church; but she could not find another job, fell three months behind on her rent, and was evicted. This was January 1985, and Jeanette was on the street and broke. That first night of homelessness, she slept in her car. The next morning, "I realized there had to be something better. I went to the police station and told them my situation and they gave me a list of shelters." The Refuge was at the top of the list.

Judy

Judy is white and 23 years old. She is of average height but very heavy, normally weighing about 250 pounds although she gets up to 300 at times. When she's at her heaviest, she is very round. Officially, Judy is a "borderline personality" with emotional problems, learning problems, and may be retarded. Unofficially, she is quick-minded and knowledgeable, the person to go to for expert information on welfare or Social Services or the bus/subway system.

Judy was born and raised in the Upton area. At present, however, the family home is a small neat bungalow in a working-class neighborhood about 20 miles from Upton. Money was always a problem. ("Every time I'd eat something, it was like, 'Do you know how much that costs?' ") Judy's father is a salesman and her mother, presently unemployed, used to work as a teletypist. Both parents are deeply involved in their Amway distributorship.

Judy's parents and two siblings, 19 and 15, are Jewish. Judy does not want to be Jewish so, with the help of Abigail, she devised an elaborate fantasy/life history for herself in which she is Christian-born and her parents become her adoptive parents. According to her new life history, Judy's "birth parents" had a natural talent for singing and performing and "that's where my talent for performing came in." But her "adoptive" parents told her she had no voice and no talent, and "like a ninny I followed their advice." Judy says it was a relief to learn she was adopted into her family and that "trying to model myself after them was a waste."

Judy always did poorly in school. From the second grade through high school she was in special education classes of one sort or another. Both her sister and brother had much the same school experiences. "The first label I wore was for retardation," Judy said. "Then they came up with 'emotionally disturbed with dyslexic tendencies,' and that's what it was for a long time. Still probably goes on now."

In the seventh and eighth grades Judy attended a local school for emotionally disturbed students. She spent her high school years in out-of-state residential placements, which she enjoyed "because they taught me to be independent—to fend for myself somewhat." At 18 she graduated from high school and was sent to the state vocational rehabilitation center for evaluation. All therapists agreed she should not return to her home situation, but she did because there was nowhere else for her to go.

Judy enrolled at the Washington School for Secretaries but lasted only a month because "I wasn't working with the program very well." At 19 she was sent to live with her maternal grandmother in Florida. This was not a great experience because her grandparents and uncles and aunts were always fighting with one another. After two years there, she returned home.

Judy was now 22. It was October 1983, and she enrolled in LEAP (Life Experience for Adults Program). There, the following January, she met Abigail, who had just joined the program—and, wonder of wonders, it turned out that Abigail knew Judy's "birth parents." Judy and Abigail immediately became bosom buddies and constructed interlocking life histories that joined them together from birth.

In July 1984, Judy told her parents, "I can't handle it any more. I can't go on this way. I'm growing up but you're trying to keep me small." She packed some things in a knapsack and left home. At Social Services, the staff promised to help her and "they helped me right out the door." Judy moved in with Abigail, who was living with her older married brother and his family.

Two months later, when Judy and Abigail were asked to leave, they decided to visit their real-persons-but-imaginary-boyfriends, who were members of a Christian rock group based in Indiana. After three days on the road, and traced to Indiana by Judy's father, "we were posted, shipped back to D.C." Unwilling to meet the conditions for returning to either household (get jobs, lose weight, give up your imaginary boyfriends), Judy and Abigail went to the Crisis Center where they were told about The Refuge. That was November 1984.

Kim

Kim is 32. She is white, 5'3", medium build, with red (Vita-Wave Brite Red) hair. Almost everyone considers her attractive. Kim does, too. When one woman called her a prostitute, Kim said, "Look at me. Take a good look at me. If I were a prostitute, do you really think I'd be broke and homeless?"

Kim is extraordinarily bright and quick-witted and a great storyteller. She is powerfully attracted to teenage boys and allows this attraction to dominate her life. She confesses that "I am a very self-centered person. I am a selfish person. I'm a person that is out for myself more than most people that know me realize. Everything I do is usually for ulterior motives. I'm concerned with my own game."

Kim was born and raised in Tidewater, Virginia. Her father is a teacher and her mother a commercial artist. Kim has one sister, four years younger than herself. In her early childhood, Kim says, she was very shy and scared all the time. Her parents, both outgoing people with strong personalities, always seemed to control everything, and Kim felt as if "I was always standing behind my mother, like in her shadow or something." Then came that fateful day, July 26, 1961, when Kim, then eight years old, got her first parakeet. "It was like . . . suddenly I belonged somewhere in the world. Suddenly I had something to bond to. Up until then, I felt like I was lost. When I got that first bird, I finally realized this was where I belonged and all of a sudden, I was complete." If Kim had to summarize herself and her life, she says, she would say, "I love birds."

Kim was "born street." "I never learned to be resourceful," she says. "I learned I *was* resourceful." She says she hated her parents and they hated her. She has always hated and resented authority, and she remembers her parents hitting her and herself hitting them back when she was only three years old. It's weird, she says, because they bought her so many things. "I was spoiled. I was very greedy and I was spoiled." Although Kim was a good student in elementary school, she was very shy and was absent a lot because school scared her. Her mother says that Kim was reading and writing at the age of three.

When Kim was 16, most of her friends were three or four years younger. This and other things troubled her parents and they took her to a psychiatrist, but nothing came of it. She had a 12-year-old boyfriend, Wayne, and no one suspected she was "going into the woods with this boy and getting laid." Kim quit school after the 11th grade. When she was 17, her parents petitioned the court to take custody of her but the judge refused. After the hearing, Kim went to live with her grandmother for about two years before returning home. It was at this time, too, that Kim became a vegan with an uncompromising intensity that persists into the present.[9]

---

[9] A vegan is an extreme vegetarian who eats no animal products whatever— no eggs, milk, honey or anything produced by or from animals. Kim also wears no leather, no wool, no furs, no silk, and uses only "cruelty-free" toiletries, cosmetics, and household products. Many such items, I learned from Kim, are tested for safety by being injected into the eyes of rabbits and other animals.

Two days after Kim turned 21, her parents filed trespassing and other charges against her. At the hearing, a psychiatrist told the court that Kim could not benefit from therapy, that she had "a behavioral problem, not a mental problem." Kim remembers that her father laughed derisively when her lawyer said that Kim was not a danger to herself or anyone else.[10] As a result of this hearing, however, Kim—no longer a minor—was forced out of the house.

Kim maintained her relationship with Wayne until she was 29. They had two "decent" years together, but "11 solid years of depression" followed. Kim worked off and on, mainly as a cashier but also at office and restaurant jobs, while Wayne pursued his own life-style, which included drinking, drugs, and petty crime. Wayne was in and out of trouble with the law, but Kim continued to love him and allowed him to exploit her. "I held the torch high . . . the eternal flame." During large chunks of those 11 years, Kim was unemployed and lived on the street, sleeping in doorways and church entrances, begging on the street or cadging peanuts or potato chips from bar patrons.[11]

In 1982, when she was 29, Kim took up with Jesse, who was 13. Jesse ran away from home to live with her, and she got into a hair-pulling, face-scratching fight with his mother. Kim was charged with contributing to the delinquency of a minor and with assault and battery, but Jesse threatened never to speak to his mother again if she didn't withdraw the charges, and she did.

Jesse was sent to a detention center and came out a changed person. He was now heavily into drugs and car theft, and he was repeatedly returned to detention. Sometimes when he was out

---

[10]To prove his point, her father was allowed to question Kim in court. "So my father said, 'What do you think of me?' I said, 'I think you're a hateful, spiteful, vicious, wretched person.' He said, 'Would you prefer to see me alive or dead?' I said, 'Dead.' He said, 'Would you rather that I die peacefully or painfully?' I said, 'With pain.'"

[11]Kim has never drunk alcohol or tried drugs. "I don't want something to look different or larger or brighter than it really is. I want to see it just as it is." She has also never had sex with anyone other than her three boyfriends.

on holiday passes or escapes he "treated me rotten and put me through hell."

In early 1984, when Kim and Jesse had been more or less together for a year and a half and Jesse was again in jail, Kim fell in love with Patrick, a 14-year-old Asian youth. Kim was then 30 and had known Patrick since he was 11. Patrick's parents ran a retail business in Tidewater. In October 1984, the family moved to a Washington suburb and three weeks later Kim followed them there. That's when she heard about The Refuge.

Lisa

Lisa is a black woman of average height, with dark skin, a round, pretty face, and an infectious laugh. She is 27 but looks older, mainly because she is so big: 300 pounds or more, say the other women. She is very bright and easily dominates a conversation when she chooses to.

Lisa was born in Washington, D.C., the middle child and the only girl among eight boys. Her father was a mechanic and her mother a governess for the children of a white minister and his wife who traveled extensively on behalf of the NAACP, taking the children and their governess with them. When Lisa was about two, the family moved to Virginia or West Virginia. Lisa remembers mountains.

When she was seven, her parents divorced and Lisa was taken by her father to live with his parents on a farm in Georgia. The other children were taken back to D.C. to live with their mother.

Lisa remained in Georgia for five years, attending a Catholic parochial school there, even though her family was Baptist. When she was about 12, she was brought back to D.C. to live with her maternal great-grandfather, who gave her the religious training—Bible reading, Bible classes, prayer classes—that was to remain with her throughout her life. She also lived with aunts and great-aunts. "We went all over," said Lisa of herself and her brothers. She still resents her mother for putting another woman's children ahead of her own, even if it was her job.

At 16, Lisa left home to live with and marry her boyfriend, who did construction work and home repair while Lisa continued high school. Lisa had her first (unplanned) child when she was in the 11th grade. Over the next 10 years, they had three more children. Lisa, meanwhile, graduated from high school and attended Strayer's Business College for two years. She worked off and on as a secretary, bank teller, and cashier, and did clerical work in a hospital for a while. She got bored quickly, and seven months was the longest she stayed on any job, but those 10 years with her husband and their children "were some of the best years of my life."[12]

Those best years ended suddenly when Lisa discovered that her husband had been unfaithful. Still pregnant with their last child, she left her husband, taking the children with her. Or perhaps her husband left her. In any event, Lisa found herself in nearby Virginia where "I couldn't do for me and I wouldn't do for my kids." (Because she was depressed? Things are not too clear here, mainly because Lisa does not like to talk—and has very seldom talked—about this period in her life.)[13]

Lisa had a breakdown and was hospitalized. Her mother came and took the children to live with her in D.C. In the hospital, Lisa remembers, she was depressed and anorexic. She remained there about four months and would have been there much longer had it not been for three very old white women who came to visit her in her room every day. They were very religious women. Nobody else ever saw them because they came only when Lisa was alone. Had it not been for them, Lisa thinks

---

[12] This chronology is not internally consistent. Some time periods seem to have been elongated, others shortened.

[13] "I went through a terrible time when I left him. I ended up in a hospital."

"You never mentioned that [before]."

"No, I don't talk about it."

"Tell me about it."

"I don't like to talk about it."

"Yes you do."

Laughing. "No I don't."

"Well, you don't have to enjoy it, just so it doesn't hurt you."

"That was one of the worst times of my life because of the fact that I do love him so much and still left him. . . ."

she would have died. She concedes they might have been crea-
tures of her imagination, but "to me, they were very real. I never
talk about that. People think you're crazy."

Out of the hospital, Lisa lived again with her children in
Virginia. But when her mother became ill, "she said to me, 'Let's
try living together again.' So we tried it and it didn't work out."

That was about two years ago. Lisa left her children with her
mother (she visits them often; so does their father, who also
makes regular child support payments) and went to live with a
girlfriend for two or three months, then another six months
with a man who had been her teacher at business college, then
to Pennsylvania to stay with a friend who had just had another
baby and needed help. Last summer, no longer needed there,
she took a bus back to D.C. She went to Social Services, which
sent her to the Crisis Center, where she was told about Bridge
House. She's been at Bridge House and now The Refuge about
eight months.

Louise

Louise is white and 42 years old but looks younger. She has long
blonde hair parted in the middle and gathered into a bun at the
nape of her neck. She has an excellent figure and amazes everyone with her knack of looking not only well-dressed but even
stylish, whether living in her car, in a shelter, or on the street.
She has blue eyes and fair skin. Many people think she is pretty,
even sexy, but others think her face too lifeless. Louise spends
a lot of time combing her hair and grooming herself. Given her
concern with dress and her appearance, one might expect her
to welcome the attention of others, especially men, but she is
essentially a loner who shies away from personal contact.[14]

---

[14]Louise was eager to cooperate, but she had a great deal of trouble talking about herself and her past. At one taping session, I tried to stop after a few
minutes because I found myself doing all the talking. Louise was shocked to
hear me say this. She said she had never before talked so much about herself.
I did not fully appreciate Louise's difficulties until I asked her to pick a name

Louise was born in Lansing, Michigan, where her father worked as a tool and die maker. She remembers very little about him because her parents were divorced when she was seven. After the divorce, Louise and her mother went to live with her mother's mother in Athens, Ohio. Louise never saw her father again.

In Athens, Louise's mother worked as a bookkeeper for the county. Louise was not close to her mother and did not like her grandmother at all. She remembers being a good student in elementary school and having a few friends. All this began to change when she was about 12. She did not like high school. She was a terrible student and had no friends, but did enjoy playing the clarinet in the school band.

After Louise graduated from high school her mother got her a few part-time clerical jobs, but this part of Appalachia was in a depression even when the rest of the country was not. When she was 22, Louise visited a relative in Detroit, saw that the job market was better there, and decided to stay. She got a clerical job with an insurance company that paid only $200 a month. "I starved but I was happy."

Louise stayed with that job two years, then moved on to a better-paying job as a credit investigator. Two years later, through a mutual friend, she met the man who was to become her husband. They got married in 1965 and lived in a very middle-class neighborhood in the Washington area, where he worked for the federal government. The marriage was "OK I guess." They didn't go out much, didn't fight much, and had no money problems. Louise worked off and on at office jobs and also served for a while as a full-time (unpaid) secretary for the local civic association.

---

for herself that I would use in the book. She said she couldn't. I said, of course you can, just pick a name, and I rattled off five or six names. I can't do it, she said. In disbelief, I presented her with another set of names. Just pick one, I said. I can't, she said, and she recalled that when she was alone in the house and wanted to name her new cat, she had to go to a neighbor and ask her to give the cat a name. Fortunately, one does not need to understand this in order to accept it.

In 1978, Louise's husband moved out of the house after 13 years of marriage. Louise is not sure why he moved out, but she was not happy that he had done so. He continued to make the mortgage payments and, for a few months, he paid for the utilities as well. Louise remained in the house alone with her cat. She cashed in her life insurance. That gone, she went on workfare for five months, which required her to work 30 hours a month, but after an argument about money, she dropped out of the program. By this time, Louise and her cat were living without electricity, gas, or heat. Some of the neighbors helped them out with food.

Eventually, Louise was evicted preparatory to the court-ordered sale of the house.[15] She had some money then—alimony payments awarded her by the courts in preliminary hearings. Four times Louise found a room for rent but she never remained in any of them more than three or four months. One landlord was a gangster who rented out rooms only as a means of recruiting people into his gang. Another landlord and his family used to hit her and pound on her door all night long, and so it went, one place after another.

In between room rentals, Louise lived in motels. Once she got a job as a live-in companion to an invalid. But Louise could never learn what the family wanted her to do, and every time she decided to do something on her own, they told her not to do it. That, too, lasted about two months.

Broke, Louise slept in her car and ate at soup kitchens, and then moved into a shelter in Northeast D.C. She had no gas money and her car was giving her a lot of trouble, preventing her from going to her suburban post office to pick up her al-

---

[15]While Louise was at The Refuge, in 1984, she confided that she had just received her share of the proceeds from the sale of the house. Spending it carefully on food, clothes, and storage payments, she made this money last about four years. By 1987, for lack of payment, Louise forfeited the furniture from an eight-room house and other belongings that she had stored in two public storage facilities. Her alimony checks had stopped long before, apparently in response to her failure to pick them up and cash them.

imony checks. In November 1983, with its very last breath, her car took her to The Refuge.

Marian

Marian is 33 years old. She is white, 5'6", brown-haired, and weighs 140 pounds. A front tooth is missing. She does not seem especially bright and, with the sometime exception of Kim, seems to gravitate toward women like Bonnie and Ginger who are noticeably slower than the others.

Marian was born and raised in a small town in Missouri. Her mother was a waitress who separated from Marian's father when Marian was about a year old. When she was 15 months old, her maternal grandmother came to the house and found her in the garbage can where she had been discarded by her mother. Marian went to live with her grandmother and her own mother moved away to Florida. Marian seems to have shuttled back and forth between her maternal grandmother and her father's parents. When she was five, her parents tried to live together once more, and she lived with them in a trailer, off and on, for the next five years.

"I didn't have a childhood," says Marian, "because I was always thrown from one parent to another . . . and always got beat by one parent or another." Her mother, she remembers, was a drunk. So was her father. Marian feels much closer to her father (who died three years ago) than to her mother whom she last saw two years ago. At that time, her mother told her she never wanted to see her again and not to come to her funeral, either. Marian feels very close to her one full brother, three years older than herself, but she has not seen or heard from him in six years. She thinks he's in the army, somewhere in Germany.

Marian says she was a good student. When she was 18 and in the 12th grade, however, she got pregnant, and when she learned that her boyfriend had been killed in Vietnam, shot 22 times in the heart, "it blew my mind and I went into a nervous breakdown." No, she was not hospitalized, but she did lose the baby.

When she was 20, Marian went to live with her mother and half-sister in Florida "to try one last time." There she met Walt, a sailor third class, and a month later they got married. It was not a great marriage but they stayed together six years and had three children in three consecutive years. Walt drank a lot and used to beat Marian and the children as well. Once, when Walt, drunk, was beating the kids, Marian knocked him out with an iron skillet to the head. When he came to, she warned him that if he ever beat the kids like that again, "God knows I will kill your ass." Meanwhile, Marian's mother was forever calling Walt to tell him that Marian was being unfaithful "and all kinds of shit." ("My mom never wanted me to be happy.") The family moved around from one base to another, ending up at a base in Tidewater, Virginia.

In Tidewater, in 1977, Walt divorced Marian. He then went to Social Services and "told them a bunch of lies." Marian suspects he paid off the judge because he wouldn't let her defend herself against Walt's lies and they took the children away from Marian, judging her to be an unfit mother (once, she left the children by themselves for a few minutes) when, in fact, she was "the best mother that ever was in this world. I fought for my kids right and left."

With no allotment, no job, no children, Marian ended up living on the street, and that's how she met Kim, with whom she became street buddies. Three years later, in 1980, she met and married David, a shipyard worker, but she divorced him after three months when she found him in bed with another man. "I am not this kind of person," she told him, and she hit the streets again.

Marian returned to Missouri "to forget David." She stayed there about three years, working as a waitress and nurse's aide. She returned to Tidewater where, on the street one day, walking and crying, she met a man who tried to comfort her. This man, Ken, who was to become her third and last husband, was an ex-Marine living on disability. They married in 1982 and divorced in 1984. Marian felt this marriage would have lasted had Ken not been a momma's boy and had his momma not lived just down the street, where Ken could always run to her and tell her momma this and momma that.

Marian went to live with Mike, an old friend who was a security guard. They lived together like brother and sister for the next seven years. Marian kept house and cooked while Mike supported them. There was no sex, at least not between Marian and Mike, but there was a lot of group and kinky sex in the house with Mike often trying, without success, to get Marian to participate.

About two months ago, after getting a letter from Kim, Marian decided to leave Tidewater "where all my troubles started. This is where my marriage ended. This is where my kids were taken away from me. This is where my best friend was shot and killed. . . . I needed to get me a job and straighten out my life." Mike gave her some money and she took a Greyhound to Washington. She came to The Refuge because she knew Kim was there, and "to keep her [Kim] out of trouble."

Martha

Martha is a white woman somewhat taller than average, with fair skin and blonde hair parted in the middle. She was born in New Haven, Connecticut, in 1956. Her father was a machinist. Her mother did not work outside the home and not much inside it. Martha went to a Catholic school for kindergarten; sometimes the family went to Sunday mass. Alcohol combined with violence to make Martha's childhood tumultuous. She and her sister, two years older, and her brother, five years younger, watched their parents drink, get drunk, and battle with one another. When her father wasn't beating her mother, he could often be found beating Martha or her sister. One of Martha's earliest memories is of her mother bringing down the bedroom ceiling with a shotgun blast that went astray. It was meant to be a suicide. Another early memory was of her father holding a gun to her head and telling her, "If you don't say, 'I hate niggers,' I'm going to shoot you." Martha did as she was told. Later, alone, she told God she didn't mean it. (In retrospect, she thinks her father thought he was preparing his children for life by teaching them to know who the enemy was.)

When Martha was six, her mother was sent to a mental hospital and the children were sent to D.C. to live with their paternal grandmother. Her grandmother was a very nice woman and Martha remembers her fondly. When her mother came out of the hospital, about a year later, the family was reunited in a town in Virginia. At school, Martha was a good student, but at home she was given the job of mother to her little brother and resented it. Home life continued to be "bizarre." The drinking and violence continued. Her father "snarled like an animal" when he was drunk. Martha remembers gunshots at different times and several visits from the police, who had been called by the neighbors. Surrounded by alcohol, Martha started drinking when she was seven or eight, smoking when she was 10. Her mother tried to stop her but her father saw nothing wrong with it. Martha made her first attempt at suicide when her mother, being beaten by her father, called out for help and Martha was unable to help her. Martha was 10. She "wanted to kill the crazy beast" but didn't know how, so she overdosed on the many pills in the house.

Martha's mother was hospitalized from one of the beatings and was subsequently transferred to a mental hospital. Her father put an ad in the paper seeking full-time care for his three now-motherless children. An affluent couple in their 50s took the children to live with them. Martha was relieved to live in a house with no drinking, no yelling, no guns going off, but there were other problems. "Aunt" Gladys demanded gratitude and housework from the girls and "Uncle" Vinnie would feel up the girls (as their father sometimes did) and give them a quarter each not to tell anyone. When Martha finally reported this to Aunt Gladys, Aunt Gladys explained that Uncle Vinnie was just testing them, trying to find out if they were good girls.

Again Martha's mother was released from the hospital and again the family reassembled. They went on a picnic, the parents got drunk, and Martha's mother was struck by a car as she staggered into the street. In the hospital, with many broken bones, she lingered in a coma for almost a year before she died. Martha saw that her mother had been neglected in the hospital, and it was then she decided to become a nurse. She was 14 when her mother died. Her 16-year-old sister ran away to New York to become a prostitute. Shortly after her mother's death, Martha's father raped her. She ran to the police and she and her brother were sent to a receiving home. Her brother was soon placed in a foster home, but Martha remained in the receiving home, all the while increasing her consumption of drugs and alcohol. After nearly a year, she was placed in a group home in D.C. with four other girls and a psychologist/housemother. Martha lived there—"the best place I've ever lived"—about three years.

After graduating from high school, Martha tried nursing school but couldn't make the grade because of her alcohol and drug problems. She was then given a full scholarship for an intensive, 12-month practical nurse residential program, and graduated with a course average of 93 percent. At one point in the program, her father tracked her down and telephoned her. Martha became hysterical and had to be hospitalized briefly, but she managed to catch up with her class. After graduating, she returned to the group home and took a job as a nursing assistant. Six months later she passed the exam for a Licensed Practical Nurse, took a job at a D.C. hospital, and moved into her own Georgetown apartment.

A short time later, Martha became pregnant ("a threesome of sex and cocaine on Christmas Eve"), had an abortion, at-

tempted suicide again, and was hospitalized again for deep depression. She returned to her job after a month and remained
there another two years or so. After suffering whiplash in a minor automobile accident, she ruptured a disk in her neck lifting
a stroke patient, went on workmen's compensation for a few
months, returned to work, and again had to go on compensation, meanwhile taking a lot of pills for both pain and depression. Martha switched to a light-duty job in a nursing home.
After a trouble-free year there, she tried a regular hospital job
again and again had to quit. She registered with a nursing
agency, working when she could.

When Martha found herself stealing drugs meant for her patients, she was horrified at herself. "Fuck all this," she said. She
quit working, and a woman friend introduced her to shooting
galleries in downtown D.C. Martha remained in D.C. for the next
two years, working occasionally when her back and the drugs
allowed her to, and homeless and in shelters when she wasn't
in one or another hospital psych ward. (Once, in Holy Cross
Hospital, she had a spiritual experience. "When I told them I
talked with God, it didn't help my case worth shit.")

Martha was ineligible for welfare benefits in D.C. "When I
couldn't work and couldn't get benefits, I gave up on society.
'You can all go to hell,' I said." A friend took her to another friend
across the D.C. line where she learned about The Refuge. That
was the winter of 1985–86, when Martha was 30 years old.

Patty

Patty was born and raised in the same town as the shelters. She
is white, 19, of medium height and build, and very ordinary in
appearance (although she has recently learned to think of herself as bright and pretty). When Patty was only a year or two old,
she and her older brother and sister were placed in a foster
home nearby. Patty has no idea why her foster parents wanted
foster children when they already had four children of their own.

Patty hated her foster parents, who insisted she call them Mom and Dad. Both of them beat her, and her foster father and foster brother each assaulted her sexually when she was about 12 or 13. She told her foster mother, who couldn't or wouldn't believe it. Patty remembers that her foster parents also mistreated her brother and sister but never their own children. Christmas and birthdays were the only good days. Her only friend was her sister, 10 years older than Patty, who moved out of the home as soon as she was 18.

Patty's foster father went to work in a suit and tie, but Patty does not know what kind of work he did. Her foster mother was a government secretary. Patty's real mother worked in a cafeteria, and her father worked in a local gas station. Patty has met her father but is not in touch with him or her brother. Since she was a child, she has visited her mother once or twice a month. She says her mother several times filed suit to recover custody of her but failed each time, mainly because she was not married, Patty believes.

Patty did poorly at school and was placed in a special education program because she was learning disabled. School officials tried placing her in a regular class when she entered junior high school, but that didn't work out. "At that time I couldn't accept it and I thought I was retarded or something. . . . I just kept thinking, kept thinking, 'Why am I in Special Ed?' I felt like I was crazy or something. . . . Kids knew I was disabled. I felt sad. They just looked at me like 'Yuck, I really don't want to get near her, she's disabled. She can't function normally,' and I felt so bad."

Patty was almost 19 when she graduated from high school last June. Within days of her graduation, "I packed up my stuff and was walking out the door and [my foster parents] asked where I was going. I said I was leaving and they would never hear from me again, and I told them I hated them for what they did to me. . . . They just looked at me—'Fine. OK. That's it.'— and they just said 'goodbye and good luck' to me and that's it. I said, 'Yeah,' and I just walked away."

Patty went to live with her mother and remained in her apartment from June to October, 1984. Her mother got Patty a job as a dishwasher (her very first job) in her own place of work. But Patty and her mother argued often, mainly about Patty's late-night hours. In October, Patty quit her job and moved out. For the next two or three weeks she lived on the street, sleeping in hallways and alleys and a couple of times at a girlfriend's house, and eating poorly on the few dollars she had saved from her job along with the few dollars her mother had given her.

One night, a young man she had met through mutual friends invited her for a ride. "He pulled up in his car and said he wanted to talk to me and I got in his car and he raped me. No one was around." Patty ended up in a hospital where some woman (social worker?) asked her where she was staying. Patty told her, "On the street," and the woman told her about The Refuge. Patty left the hospital a few days before the end of October. She stayed again with her mother until the first of November when The Refuge opened for the winter. "Take me to The Refuge," she told her mother.

Patty likes The Refuge. "I met a lot of nice people there."

She's pregnant now and looking forward to entering a live-in program for unwed mothers where her baby will be put up for adoption and she herself will be given job training. She hopes her baby will be a girl and grow up to be like Grace, partly because Grace is so beautiful but mainly because she stands up for her rights.

Peggy

Peggy is white and 50 years old. About 5′2″ with medium-brown hair and fair skin, she is very conscious of her appearance and would like to lose a few pounds. Peggy is seen as a warm, friendly person. She is close to Phyllis, who is 71 and white, and also to Evelyn, who is 35 and black.

Peggy was born in a coal mining town in Pennsylvania. Her natural parents separated before Peggy was born, and she was raised by two maternal great-aunts, Dottie and Zoey. Her aunts were fond of her and good to her. It was just the three of them, and when Zoey died early on, "it was Dottie all the way down the line." Peggy saw her mother once a year or so. She first met her father 10 years ago. She has "no feelings" for either of them.

Peggy enjoyed her childhood. School was fun and she was a good student. But when she was 15 and in the eighth grade, she married a 16-year-old neighbor. The marriage ended almost four years later when her husband didn't show up. "I waited two weeks and then I said, 'I waited two weeks. I ain't pining away. I'll go find me somebody else,' and I did." That was July 1955. In November Peggy became briefly engaged to a construction worker ("I was the only girl in town that was married and engaged at the same time.") The following July, her fiancé was called into the army and Peggy decided she was not going to sit at home and wait for him. She then met her second husband-to-be in a bar ("Oh, Lord, I wish I hadn't met him!"). She got pregnant and they were married in December. That was 1956 and Peggy was almost 20.

Peggy and her husband lived with Dottie the first year, then moved out on their own. Over the next five years, Peggy was pregnant five times and produced three children. But things were not going well. Her husband drank heavily, they fought a lot, and he took no responsibility for the children. "He was cold, very cold. He was there and eating. Big deal." So the children grew up amid constant feuding and fighting. Peggy pushed away thoughts of leaving her husband. She had grown up without a father and was determined not to let that happen to her children.

In 1967, Peggy and the children went to live with Dottie while her husband went to the Washington, D.C., area looking for work. In February 1968, she and the children followed him to D.C. Peggy had been getting bad headaches for a year or so, and a psychiatrist put her on Librium. "Three kids in three years and two kids in diapers and bottles all the time—it was just too much. It caught up with me when they got a little older." In 1972, Peggy was hospitalized and a trial separation was recommended, but nothing came of it.

In 1975, Peggy's two daughters, Roberta and Jennifer, 14 and 15, ran away from home to get away from the bickering. They were quickly found nearby, "drunk as monkeys." Roberta failed the ninth grade and never returned to school. Jennifer quit school as soon as she was 16 to work at McDonald's. Peggy's "nerves" worsened.

In 1975, both Peggy and her husband began running around. Peggy met Charles, whom she was to see off and on for several years. In 1978, when her son George went into the service and both daughters left home, Peggy left her husband to go to Pennsylvania to live with her natural mother. There, in a CETA (Comprehensive Employment and Training Act) program, she earned her high school equivalency certificate and received clerical training. But Peggy wasn't getting along with her mother and returned to the D.C. area the next year to take a clerical day job with the government and a short-lived night job at a 7-Eleven.

By 1980, "everybody was living with me." Son George had come out of the service, Jennifer had left her husband, and Roberta, who had been living with her father, had been kicked out "because she was dating this black dude." In addition, they were joined by an old boyfriend of Roberta's, and Booby, the dog that Peggy had become so attached to. Five adults and a dog, all in a one-bedroom apartment. Then, when Peggy's mother called to say she was also coming to live with her, Peggy told Roberta's boyfriend he had to leave. Jennifer then left to return to her husband, Roberta left to join the service, and George went to live with his father.

Later that year, Peggy's divorce came through. Her asthma, long a nuisance, became much worse. She "retired" and put together a package of money from her government retirement, her mother, and unemployment compensation to go to southern California, where her asthma was much better. She stayed there a year, not doing much of anything and enjoying it, then returned again to Pennsylvania to take care of her sick mother. When her mother recovered, she "started running" with a man 30 years her junior and kicked Peggy out of the house.

Broke, Peggy and her dog somehow made their way back to D.C., and for the first time in her life, Peggy found herself homeless. The dog went to a kennel and Peggy went to the House of Ruth where she remained for nine weeks. Peggy then moved from place to place, sometimes with a girlfriend, sometimes alone, and again returned to House of Ruth which referred her to D.C. General Hospital for an evaluation. The diagnosis included the words "chronic" and "depression" but Peggy is not sure what it was.

During this second tour at House of Ruth, a vocational rehabilitation counselor sent her to "business and finance" school where Peggy met and became friends with Emma. After six weeks at House of Ruth, Peggy moved in with Emma and her sister. Peggy was on welfare all this time, and stayed with Emma and her sister about a year and a half, until July 1985, when Emma died of cancer.

Peggy again took a place of her own, seeing Charles off and on. Then, when Charles refused to give her money to give to son George who was in deep trouble, Peggy said, "Screw this mess," overdosed on sleeping pills, and was hospitalized once more for four weeks. ("I didn't intend to kill myself.") Peggy's social worker helped her find other shelters until September 1986, when Peggy went south to help George who, high on coke, had jumped off the Tennessee River Bridge on a dare. But George, always on booze or drugs, refused to be helped. Money ran out and Peggy returned to D.C. on money sent her by Emma's sister. She slept in the airport the first night, the House of Ruth the second night. The next day her social worker suggested Bridge House. That was November 13, 1986.

Phyllis

Phyllis is white and 71 years old. She is a fairly big woman, taller and heavier than average. She has white hair and very fair skin, with many "age spots" on her hands and neck. Her walking is labored, as if her feet hurt (they do). Phyllis stands tall and erect and seldom speaks unless spoken to. She carries herself with great dignity and is respected and liked by all the women.

Phyllis has spent her whole life in the Washington area. She was born and raised in a town just over the D.C. line. Her father worked for the Patent Office and her mother worked for a firm (now Government Services, Inc.) that provided cafeteria services for the federal government. Phyllis was the only girl and the youngest of three children, each one year apart from the next. She had a very ordinary childhood and a family life that was quiet and pleasant. Phyllis liked both of her brothers and got along well with them. She liked school, too, but she was not a good student, partly, she thinks, because she ran out of energy toward the end of the day and was not able to stay awake long enough to do her homework or study.

When Phyllis was in the fifth grade, the family moved into D.C. and stayed there for two and a half years before returning to their suburban community. In high school, Phyllis took four years of home economics because she wanted to be a dietician. Her mother was a good cook and Phyllis, too, enjoyed cooking. Her graduation from high school was delayed by her difficulty with academic subjects. Her brother had gone on to the University of Maryland but Phyllis decided against college because she feared she "couldn't make the grade." So she did "the next best thing" and went to work for GSI where her mother had worked for so long.

Phyllis started at GSI in 1935 and worked in different cafeterias, mainly as a cashier. In 1937, her father died. In 1941, when her brother married and moved out, her mother sold their house and she and Phyllis took an apartment in D.C. In 1943, after eight years at GSI, Phyllis took a file clerk job with the State Department, believing that the government offered greater job security. She started as a GS-2 and worked herself up to a GS-5 over the next five years. But when she was "bumped" and asked to take a $20 per month pay cut while doing essentially the same work, she quit the government and went back to GSI, where she worked at various jobs including cashier and payroll clerk.

In 1955, after 18 years of widowhood, Phyllis's mother remarried and Phyllis took an apartment for herself. It was in a high-rise building with a rooftop pool. Phyllis loved her apartment.

In 1978, Phyllis was 63 and had worked for 43 years: eight years for GSI, five years for the State Department, and 30 years the second time around for GSI. Her brother had been killed in World War II, her mother had died in 1965, and Phyllis had been living alone in the same apartment for more than 20 years. It was her intention to work until she was 65, which would give her 40 years at GSI, but "I was ready to go till 70 if they needed me."

But this was not to be. Phyllis was back at her cashier's job "and things got kinda crazy at work. . . . All of a sudden my money started coming out wrong. I was $10 short here, $2 short there, $10 short again." Before that, she had always been "right on the penny or within a quarter or 50 cents. It worried me. I thought maybe I shouldn't handle money anymore. So I just decided I'd quit. Retire early."

So Phyllis retired to live on her Social Security and GSI pension, a total of about $700 a month. That was April 1979, and things are not at all clear after that. It may have been days or weeks or months after her retirement when the manager of her apartment house refused to accept her rent check, repeatedly pushing it back at her across the desk. Phyllis thinks this happened more than once. Sometime later, a woman in uniform knocked on Phyllis's door, saying she was from the Department of Welfare and wanted to talk, but Phyllis told her there was nothing for them to talk about and refused to let her in. Still later, maybe days, a man slipped a piece of paper under her door when Phyllis refused to open the door to him. Phyllis thought it might be a subpoena so she put it down the trash chute without looking at it.

And then more people came and said they wanted to speak to Phyllis and wanted to know why she was doing all that screaming and yelling and banging of doors, and Phyllis told them she hadn't been making any noise and anyway the apartments were soundproof so how could they hear anything?[16] Then one of the women showed Phyllis a petition signed by the tenants in the building. Phyllis thinks it said something about her going to the hospital "because of the screaming and everything."

Then some people came and took her to a hospital. Phyllis returned home after a few hours, and the next day or maybe a few days later the police came and took her to another hospital where she was held for several days before being released. Home again, the resident manager asked her when she was going to move out, and Phyllis told him she had no intention of moving. Soon six men forced their way into her apartment and put all her things in boxes, and a welfare worker helped her pack a suitcase with toiletries and a bathrobe.

That night, Phyllis slept in her car, a 1969 Buick Skylark, and she thinks she may have slept there a second night, too. Sometime later, she found herself in the state mental hospital. She doesn't know how long she was there. In the winter of 1982, when The Refuge opened, she was there.

Regina

Regina is 50 years old. She is white, of medium height, thin and wiry, with short reddish-gray hair. She has an upper plate and

---

[16]In the shelters, once a day, Phyllis would close the bathroom door behind her, stand in front of the mirror, and yell. She came out looking perfectly ordinary and relaxed, as if nothing had happened.

lower partial. Her speech announces her English working-class background.

Regina was born and raised in Manchester, along with an older brother. When she was still an infant, her mother had an extramarital affair and her father moved the children and himself to another neighborhood, where he soon remarried. Regina did not learn that her "mother" was her stepmother until she was in her teens. Regina was raised as a Catholic, and attended church regularly. Her father was stern and undemonstrative but she felt he loved her. "I don't remember ever my father coming to me and putting his arms around me. Or my stepmother. The love was done by hard work, by providing."

Regina always did poorly at school. When she was 15, and maybe in the sixth or seventh grade, she left school and went to work in a local lard factory. Perhaps because she had just learned about her real mother, she thinks, or perhaps in rebellion against her stern father, Regina "went on the wild side," running around with so many men that when she had her first baby (she was still 15), she did not know who the father was. She also did not know, while she was in labor, how and from where the baby would emerge.

When Regina returned with her child from a home for unmarried mothers, her parents insisted on raising the baby boy as their son. He learned to call Regina's stepmother "Mom" and Regina "Regina." "It upset me, but that's the way it was." Regina went back to work in the lard factory, and later in a weaving mill.

That was when Regina met Ralph, an American stationed at a nearby U.S. Air Force base. They went out together for a couple of years. In 1959, Regina returned to the United States with Ralph. They married and lived in base housing and trailers over the next several years, and Regina worked off and on at waitressing and odd jobs. In 1967, their son Brian was born. Ralph was shipped off to Europe and Regina refused to go with him. She didn't really love him, she said. When Ralph returned from overseas, Regina continued to run around and Ralph called a halt to their 10-year marriage

("He couldn't put up with my running around and I couldn't blame him"). Ralph gave her their car and $500, and Regina married Tom, a security guard who was 10 years her senior and just divorced.

After a brief trial period, Brian, then about four, was sent to live permanently with his father. Regina and Tom continued to live together for about seven years when they decided to call it quits. Regina was working in an electric parts factory at the time and continued to run around. She lived with a black man for a while, but that didn't work out and she went back to living alone, loving her job and her freedom. ("I could have lived like that the rest of my life.")

In the fall of 1980, in the middle of the night, a stranger broke into her bedroom, beat her badly, threatened her life, and forced her into oral sex. Regina never recovered fully from that experience. She began therapy at that time with a rape crisis center and has continued with therapy ever since. She is terribly insecure physically and dreads being alone.

In the aftermath of the rape, Regina was unable to work and was forced onto welfare for the first time in her life. A nice, undemanding neighbor befriended her and Regina lived with him for the next six months, eventually recovering sufficiently to return to a series of live-in jobs, one of which she held for four years, enabling her to buy a car and the protective security of the first of a series of Doberman pinschers.

In 1984, Regina took a live-in job with an old man who fired her the first week when a misunderstanding escalated into a fight. The man called police and Regina was literally put out on the street with her belongings. For the next three months she lived in her car. One day in November, at a local soup kitchen, she heard about The Refuge and moved in the same night.

Rose

Rose is a 60-year-old black woman, lively and friendly, and almost always in good spirits, at least on the surface. She has worked all her life as a maid in other people's houses.

Rose was born in a small town in Virginia, the middle child of three. Her mother was an only child whose own mother died at an early age, so Rose did not know her grandmother. Rose never knew who her father was. Her mother always worked, almost always at general housework and cooking. Rose started school at the age of six when the family moved to Staunton, Virginia. She had very few friends but doesn't know why. She was somewhat close to her brother and sister but closest of all to her mother.

The family went to church every Sunday and all three children sang in the church choir. When Rose was 12, her mother found her small, after-school housecleaning jobs. She has never minded doing housework because she likes to make things look nice and clean.

Rose did not like school at all. She quit while she was still in the 10th grade and took a job in a local hotel, first as a dishwasher alongside her mother, later as a maid.

In 1946, at the age of 23, Rose got married, and over the next nine years she had five children, only three of whom are still alive. Her husband was a local laborer. They lived in a nice little house that had no running water or electricity but rented for only $4 a month. When her husband's parents decided to move to Washington, he decided to do the same. Rose remained in the house—"It was a house that I could come in from work, you know—it could feel like I could say was mine. I felt very happy in those days." Some time later, Rose's husband returned to pick up the two oldest children and take them back with him to D.C. Rose and her two remaining children, five and six, moved to Winchester to be near her sister, who was in a situation much like her own.

Again Rose worked as a housekeeper, and she lived in a big room (with kitchen privileges) in a large house for which she paid $7 a week. But the landlord soon found her children intolerable, claiming they were destroying his house. Rose's sister suggested that she take them to Washington to live with their father. After all, she reminded Rose, "you didn't get them by yourself." So Rose and her sister took the children to D.C., where there was "a big mess." The children ended up, temporarily, at the Children's Bureau and Rose thinks she was charged with abandoning them, but she returned to Winchester and heard no more about the charges.

Rose remained in Winchester another four years, then returned to Staunton to care for her mother who had had a series of small strokes. In Staunton, she took another housekeeping job and remained with that same family for nine years.

Joanne, the only daughter (now dead) that Rose felt close to, repeatedly asked her to come to Washington and finally prevailed on her to do so. In Washington, her daughter found her a live-in job in the suburbs. Rose stayed with that family for nine years until business reverses forced them to let her go. Almost immediately, she found another live-in job. Rose's social life was minimal, limited to her days off, but Joanne called her twice a week. On Saturdays, Rose would go downtown to get her hair done. Joanne would meet her there, and they'd go to lunch, go shopping, have a few drinks.

Then and now, Rose was more or less estranged from her other children, who are doing very well, thank you. One daughter who lives in an expensive high-rise in Silver Spring, Maryland, refused to let Rose store her things with her for fear—according to Rose—they would mess up her apartment. The daughter who lives in a large house with a large yard in Prince Georges County, Maryland, refused the same request.

One day, Rose took "one taste too many" and not only neglected her work but also took the time to tell her employers what she thought about their "mouthy children." She was fired immediately and told to move out, with all her belongings, by the next morning.

The next day, Rose piled all her belongings in a taxicab, being careful to take her savings and her insurance policy. (She had no family that she cared about, and needed the insurance "for myself, when I pass. I need something to be buried with.")

Driving around in the cab, Rose could not get a motel room because she had no ID. Her purse had been stolen the day before when, still high, she had fallen asleep on a park bench. The cabdriver took her to a couple of downtown shelters. One was closed until that evening; the other was too dirty and smelly. They drove to a church where they were told about The Refuge, and the cabdriver drove her there.

Sara

Sara was 31 when she first came to The Refuge. She is a black woman, short and stout, with a round, pretty face. She moves and dresses with a flair, not afraid of calling attention to herself. There is an air of self-confidence about her, a solidity, that commands instant respect from everyone in the shelter, including the staff.[17]

Sara was born in 1955. Because her sister is 12 years younger, Sara thinks of herself as having been raised as an only child. The family never moved, and her mother and sister continue to live in the same Harlem apartment the family has lived in for more than 35 years. Both her parents were factory workers in the garment district. Her mother's mother also lived with them.

Religion has always been an important part of Sara's life. In her childhood, the family regularly went to church on Sundays and participated fully in church life.

Sara was an excellent student and was usually on the honor roll. She had many friends at school but would not call herself "popular." When she was 15, she began dating a boy in the neighborhood. In 1973, when she was 18 and only six months short of graduation, they married and moved out on their own. Her husband was a young man who found it hard to make a

---

[17]This interview took place in late 1991. Sara had long left the shelter, had remained in close contact with Kim, and was working for the federal government when we ran into one another and she agreed to put her life history on tape. Her first choice for a pseudonym was "Imani." When I asked her for a name more like her real one, she picked "Sara."

living, and they had to move several times for failure to pay the rent. Sara was soon pregnant and in January 1974 she left her husband and moved to Washington, D.C., to live with her mother's sister and her family. She enrolled in night school and received her GED in May. In July her son was born, and the following month Sara went on public assistance and moved into a place of her own.

Sara remained on public assistance for two years, during which time she enrolled in Strayer's Business College, but left before graduating to take a home nursing job with a large firm. She enjoyed taking care of her mostly elderly, always poor patients—bathing them, dressing them, buying groceries, taking them to a doctor, or performing other errands—but after two years she got fed up with five-cent raises that carried her from a starting wage of $3.10 all the way to $3.55. She left that job to take another as a security guard at $6.25 an hour for a private firm on contract with the federal government. Two years later the contract expired and Sara was laid off. She went on unemployment, but her apartment went co-op, forcing Sara and her son into the Pitts Motel, a D.C. shelter for homeless families.

It was now 1986. Sara and her son stayed at the Pitts for a month, then moved down the street to the Community of Hope. She got another job as a security guard, and after six months she was able to save enough money for a security deposit and the first month's rent of $332 for an apartment in southeast D.C. Money remained a problem and Sara sometimes had to choose between paying rent and buying groceries. When the security guard job ended after only a few months, she went on unemployment again and had to give up her apartment. She knew that "if push came to shove" she could go back to one or another family household, but she was determined to make it on her own, remaining in telephone contact with family members in New York and Washington. She took her son, then 12, to New York to live with her mother until she could make another home for the two of them.

Sara returned to D.C. and took a furnished room. When her unemployment compensation ran out, she went back on public assistance and took a part-time job in a nightclub, alternating between checking coats and waiting on tables. There she met and became friends with a woman co-worker who invited Sara to live with her and her mother. This was early September, 1986.

In late October, her girlfriend had a fight with her mother, presumably over Sara's living with them, and the friend, as part of a threat to move out, called and reserved a space for herself in a local shelter. Sara was startled. "This is your home and you're telling me you are going to move to a shelter and leave me here with your mother?" Sara insisted on moving out herself to make peace between mother and daughter, and she took her friend's place at the Port-in-a-Storm shelter.

In December, Sara's "time was up" at Port-in-a-Storm. Just before Christmas 1986, she moved into The Refuge.

Sybil

Sybil is white and 30 years old, a brunette of ordinary appearance. She is a registered nurse with a master's degree in nursing and tends to patronize some of the other women, especially black women—for instance, complimenting them for being "articulate."

Sybil was an illegitimate child, one month old when she was put up for adoption. Her adoptive family was an army major (now a retired colonel) and his wife with no children of their own. At the time, they lived in Washington, D.C., but subsequently they moved around a great deal. Sybil had an older adopted brother, blonde and blue-eyed and the family favorite. Both parents were heavy drinkers and Sybil "grew up thinking that was the norm."

Home was "a hostile and alcoholic environment." There was constant arguing and fighting, and Sybil was often the subject or the target, but there was never any physical violence. Sybil has been "a free kid most of my life." She was given money and credit cards but her parents "did not do things with me. They were not participative parents."

Sybil always enjoyed school. "School was school. . . . School was fun; home was hostility and danger." After high school, Sybil went to a small college in North Carolina where she took an Associate of Arts degree, then graduated as an RN after a two-year nursing program. Her parents did not come to her graduation; they did not want to come and Sybil did not want them to. "[At college] I had been around other people who saw me different than what [my parents] saw me. I liked the way that those people saw me and I didn't want [my parents] down there to ruin it."

Sybil returned to Washington to live with her parents after graduation. She took a nursing job at Walter Reed Hospital and registered for graduate courses in nursing that her parents paid for. But at home, nothing had changed in any significant way. She had never gotten along with her adoptive brother, also a drinker. Now he was married, and to Sybil's dismay, her mother treated the daughter-in-law like the daughter Sybil wanted to be. After a year or so and another bitter argument, Sybil moved out on her own. She also began seeing a therapist.

Since the age of 10, Sybil had wanted to know about her natural parents. Now, in 1981, at the age of 25, she learned about "adoptive research" from a sympathetic social worker. She soon traced her mother to a small town in Delaware, thereby setting off a long train of events around the discovery of her birth family. Sybil's mother was shocked to hear "I am your daughter" over the telephone. She wanted to put off a face-to-face meeting and asked Sybil repeatedly if she was sure she wanted them to meet. A month later, at Sybil's insistence, they met at a hotel in Baltimore, Sybil recalls that her mother was emotional and upset, but she was also a loving person (and here Sybil takes out a picture of a young woman who looks very much like herself). This is her mother, she says, at the age of 22.

Sybil learned that her mother had come from a broken home, had gotten pregnant at 20 by a college student who did not want to get married, and met another man who wanted to marry her if she would agree to put her baby up for adoption. Reluctantly, she agreed. But now, and over the next several months, Sybil's mother resisted introducing Sybil to her half-siblings and the rest of the family, yet Sybil fought to meet them. Meanwhile, she was having trouble on her job. Her superiors said her performance was inconsistent and that she needed to straighten out her personal life. In 1984 she took a leave of absence to prepare for her master's comprehensive examinations. She returned to Walter Reed, but the job situation worsened so she resigned and again moved in with her parents, this time in a separate apartment on the upper level of a big house in Arlington, Virginia.

It was now the spring of 1985. Two or three non-nursing jobs didn't work out, but since she had saved up quite a bit of money, Sybil decided to take things easy, spending much of her time working out at spas and going out on dates. Her father repeatedly asked her to find a job. When Sybil refused, he asked her to leave. "Where would I go?" she asked, and her father said he didn't know but he wanted her to leave. Again she refused. In December she received a letter from her parents' lawyer. "Due to domestic problems, please leave immediately." Sybil packed her car and left.

Through a minister, Sybil got a job as a companion, giving her charge "$6,000 worth of care for $125." Then she quit and went to North Carolina for a few days to stay with a friend. She returned to D.C. where another friend took her to the Crisis Center. There the staff told her about New Beginnings. "I'm 30," she said, "and I don't feel like the whole world is ahead of me. I feel like I've been ripped off."

APPENDIX C

How Many Homeless People?

H istorically, the very poor were more or less contained in
our ghettos, poorhouses, orphanages, "hospitals," and
other institutions. More recently, our policy of containment has
faltered and many of the poorest among us are extraordinarily
visible. They are now in emergency shelters and on the street,
and present us with an in-your-face poverty that confronts us
wherever we turn.

This visibility notwithstanding, reliable statistics on homeless persons are hard to come by, partly because there is continuous movement in and out of that status, partly because
many won't stand still long enough to be counted, partly because many don't want to be counted, and partly because there
is no accepted definition of homelessness. Given this softness
of statistics on homeless persons, answers to the question of
how many there are, and what percentage are mentally ill and
what percentage are this or that, are often determined in large
part by what one wants the answers to be.

Some people want the numbers to be large, others want them to be small, because public attention and the allocation of money and other resources to aid the homeless depend in large part on the number of homeless persons. This politicization of the numbers question has led to some bizarre differences of opinion. In the mid-1980s, for example, the U.S. Department of Housing and Urban Development, apparently not looking very hard to find them, decided that the total number of homeless persons was about 250,000. Outraged at this low number, advocates of homeless persons, including providers and researchers, went before congressional committees with a counteroffer of 2.5 million to 3 million.[1] Similarly, when Peter Rossi and his associates, using sophisticated sampling techniques, concluded that, on any given night, there were about 2,700 homeless persons in the city of Chicago, local service providers and advocates denounced the study, arguing that Rossi and his associates had somehow missed the great majority of the city's homeless population. There were 20,000–25,000 homeless persons in their city, they said.[2] Meanwhile, estimates of the mentally ill among the homeless, bedeviled by definitional and methodological problems, ranged even more widely.[3]

Predictably, politicians, advocates, service providers, and

---

[1] U.S. General Accounting Office, *Homelessness: Implementation of Food and Shelter Programs under the McKinney Act,* p. 2.

[2] Peter H. Rossi, "No Good Applied Social Research Goes Unpunished," *Society* 76 (November/December 1987): p. 78. A part of the discrepancy may lie in the difference between the number of persons homeless on any given night and the number of persons who are homeless over the course of a year. Martha R. Burt and Barbara E. Cohen suggest that the number of people homeless during the course of a year is approximately double the number of homeless on any given night. *America's Homeless: Numbers, Characteristics, and the Programs That Serve Them,* p. 2. Quite apart from this issue, however, gross differences remain.

Overheard at a conference on homelessness: "If Pete Rossi can't count them, no one can."

[3] See Cynthia M. Taueber and Paul M. Siegel, "Counting the Nation's Homeless Population in the 1990 Census," pp. 93ff. This volume offers an excellent analysis of the definitional and methodological problems involved in developing a statistical picture of homelessness in America.

others will go on using numbers that serve their interests. It is possible but unlikely that they will all eventually settle on a consensus number, perhaps something like the 600,000 developed by Martha Burt and Barbara Cohen from a national sample.[4] For the present, however, that number, or even twice that number, is considered far too low by those who cite the Department of Education's estimate of 450,000 homeless children in the country,[5] to say nothing of the Children's Defense Fund's estimate that there could be as many as 2 million homeless children alone.[6] So much for numbers and hard data.

On average, single women comprise about 12 percent of the homeless population.[7] It was not always so. Homeless women seem to be a relatively recent phenomenon. An estimated 25,000 to 30,000 homeless women were "riding the rails" during the depression years of the 1930s, but "the story of women on the road ended in the 1940s" with America's entry into the war and absorption of these women into the work force.[8] Studies in

---

[4]Estimate for total number homeless on any given night during 1987. Martha R. Burt and Barbara E. Cohen, *America's Homeless,* p. 2.

[5]National Law Center on Homelessness and Poverty, "Small Steps: An Update on the Education of Homeless Children and Youth Program," p. 1.

[6]Lisa Klee Mihaly of the Children's Defense Fund, quoted in "Homeless Children: A National Tragedy," *USA Today,* July 30, 1991, p. 9A.

[7]U.S. Conference of Mayors, *A Status Report on Hunger and Homelessness in American Cities: 1991,* p. 2. But Peter Rossi estimates that single women comprise from one-fourth to one-fifth of homeless persons in Chicago. *Down and Out in America: The Origins of Homelessness,* p. 118. However many there are, the great majority of homeless women live in shelters rather than on the street, as suggested by Kathleen H. Dockett's study of street homelessness in Washington, D.C., which found that only 5 percent of the homeless people living on the street were women. *Street Homeless People in the District of Columbia: Characteristics and Service Needs,* p. ii. Although the Rossi study differs (women comprised 18 percent of the Chicago street sample), it makes the same point: homeless women are overrepresented in shelters, underrepresented on the street.

[8]Dodee Fennell, "Uncommon People," unpublished paper, University of Pittsburgh History Department, 1974, p. 42. Cited in Marsha A. Martin, "Strategies of Adaptation: Coping Patterns of the Urban Transient Female," p. 28. See also Howard M. Bahr and Gerald R. Garrett, *Disaffiliation among Urban Women.*

the 1950s and 1960s noted the striking absence of homeless women in those decades.[9] It was not until the early 1970s that homeless women began to appear on the streets of our cities in growing numbers.[10]

The United States Conference of Mayors' 28-city survey suggests that homelessness is increasing along a broad front. The Conference reported that overall requests for emergency shelter increased by an average of 13 percent in 1991 over 1990. For the same period, requests for shelter by homeless families increased by an average of 17 percent. Meanwhile, the supply of services fell far short of the demand. On average, 15 percent of all requests for emergency shelter were unmet, and 78 percent of the cities' shelters turned away families due to lack of resources.[11]

All cities were expecting requests for emergency food and emergency shelter to increase during 1992. The number of homeless persons is surely going up.[12] And just as clearly, supportive public sentiment toward the homeless is going down.[13] This failure of conscience contributes mightily to the problem of homelessness. It is also a dark and ominous sign in its own right.

---

[9] Peter H. Rossi, *Down and Out in America*, p. 118.

[10] Kim Hopper and Jill Hamburg, *The Making of America's Homeless: From Skid Row to New Poor*, p. 38.

[11] U.S. Conference of Mayors, *A Status Report on Hunger and Homelessness*, p. 2.

[12] Not everyone is convinced of this. Burt and Cohen (*America's Homeless*, p. 27) cite studies that suggest little or no growth in selected cities. Also see Sar A. Levitan and Susan Schillmoeller, *The Paradox of Homelessness in America*, p. 9.

[13] U.S. Conference of Mayors, *A Status Report on Hunger and Homelessness*, p. 3. See also National Law Center on Homelessness and Poverty, *Go Directly to Jail: A Report Analyzing Local Anti-Homelessness Ordinances*.

APPENDIX D

Social Service Programs

F or the homeless women I knew, the Richman County
 Department of Social Services—about a 30-minute bus ride
from the shelters—was the starting point for applying for most
official social services.[1]

A few of the women were over 65 and drew Social Security
(the age is 62 for reduced benefits). Social Security automatically qualified them for Medicare as well. Women who were permanently disabled, physically or mentally, and women 65 or
over who were not eligible for Social Security could receive SSI
(Supplemental Security Income). Successful applicants had to
pass a needs test and submit medical documentation of their
disability and much more. In the mid-1980s, SSI benefits were
about $350 a month. In those years, however, applicants were
lucky to be approved for benefits on the second or third reap-

---

[1] I am indebted to Tom Rosser for most of the information in this section.
He is the Office Manager of the Department of Social Services, Richman (pseudonym) County.

plication, which may have been two or more years after the initial attempt.

A few of the disabled women with solid work histories were eligible for SSDI (Social Security Disability Insurance). Benefits were based on lifetime average earnings.

General Public Assistance (GPA) was available to those who could not work for at least 30 days and could provide medical documentation to that effect. Monthly benefits were about $180 in 1984 and climbed, in steps, to $220 about three years later.

Workfare (GPA-E, General Public Assistance–Employable, discontinued in April 1991) was for able-bodied persons who could not find work. Participants were required to work at assigned public sector jobs for at least 30 hours a month, for which they received about $45 more than those on GPA. Under GPA-E, "all of your assets are considered available to you [and} . . . will be deducted from your GPA-E grant. For example, if you have a savings account of $40.00, we must reduce your grant by $40.00 for as long as you have the $40.00 available to you."[2]

Most persons in these programs were automatically eligible for food stamps. Other low-income persons could apply for them as well. In 1986, a woman with a net income of $148 a month could qualify for $66 in food stamps (good for domestically produced edibles only—no imports, and no paper goods, toiletries, tobacco, or alcoholic beverages).

Medical assistance, like food stamps, was automatically available to most people who qualified for any of the above programs, and other low-income people were eligible as well. A major problem, however, was that many private sector providers refused to honor medical assistance cards. The reimbursements, they said, were too low.

Housing assistance was especially hard to come by. Most housing programs are administered by the Richman County Housing Authority (RCHA). The two major programs are the

---

[2]Income Maintenance Division, Richman County Department of Social Services, mimeo, November 1990.

Federal Public Housing and the Section 8 Rental Assistance programs. The RCHA is owner and landlord of public housing; tenants pay 30 percent of their gross annual income for rent. Participants in the Section 8 certificate/voucher program find their own housing units in the private housing market. They, too, pay 30 percent of gross annual income for rent; federal funds make up the difference between the renter's contribution and the actual rent.

Eligibility and waiting lists are major hurdles. For either program, single applicants (as distinct from families) must be "disabled or handicapped or over 62 years of age." Women with a child in temporary foster care are considered a family. Eligible persons are assigned places on the waiting list according to a point-preference system: five points for living in a shelter or car or substandard housing, for being involuntarily displaced, or for paying more than half one's income for rent; two points for living in the county; and one point for being a victim of domestic violence or for having a family member in foster care due to lack of housing. Even for the most qualified applicants, waiting time for an efficiency apartment under either program is a minimum of two years. For eligible persons with less than the maximum preference points, however, waiting time is "indefinite."

Some smaller, non–federally assisted programs are also available through RCHA, but they pose the same problems of eligibility and waiting time for single, homeless women. Other assistance programs are trivial (for example, Operation Match, a "roommate referral service").

Finally, there is a network of voluntary community services. Chief among them for homeless persons are soup kitchens (the nearest is in another town, 25 minutes by bus from downtown Upton), surplus food and clothing distribution centers, individual churches, and Community Ministries where, with a referral from a shelter or other agency, one can get various kinds of personal assistance. Such aid might include up to $50 cash (but no more than once in a six-month period).

In general, both the formal social services and the voluntary community programs tend strongly to discriminate against single individuals in favor of families with children. In theory, emergency assistance cash grants were available from Social Services.[3] Such assistance, however, was targeted at families with children. In practice, single adults could almost never meet the requirements. Similarly, no emergency housing assistance is available through RCHA; applicants are referred to shelters. Community housing assistance programs are similarly restricted. Clearly, public policy at all levels assigns needy individuals a much lower priority than needy families. But there never was too much assistance available for anyone, individuals or families, and every day there is less and less.[4]

---

[3]Emergency assistance from Social Services to help with payment of rent or utilities required a court eviction notice or utilities cut-off notice before the grant would be made. This credit-destroying prerequisite surely put many individuals and families on the road to the street.

[4]In May 1992, GPA (General Public Assistance) was replaced by DALP (Disability Assistance and Loan Program). On July 1, 1992, payments were scaled back to $205 a month (1986–87 levels), and no earned income—such as part-time work—was permitted. To be eligible, the applicant must have a doctor certify that he or she cannot work for three months (instead of one), a DALP physician must concur, and the recipient must sign a promissory note—yes, sign a promissory note!—to repay the full amount of the benefits if the disability is projected to last from 3 to 11 months. After 11 months, the individual will be taken off the state/county rolls and moved to SSI if the federal government agrees.

There is more: workfare has long been discontinued, and state medical assistance no longer covers hospital in-patient or out-patient services.

Research Methods and Writing

The purpose of these few pages is to give those readers who are not familiar with participant observation research some sense of the mechanics of how one goes about doing it. I assume that most participant observer researchers would go about it in pretty much the same way, although most people today would make far greater use of computers for organizing and perhaps analyzing their notes than I was able to do. Also, most researchers would probably start with a clearer idea of what they were looking for and proceed in a more systematic way. But as I explained in the Preface, I backed into this study, with the result that some of the major elements of the research process were not carried out in the more usual, more logical sequence.

• • •

When I began this study, three of the more or less routine admonitions for doing this kind of research seemed to me more important than others, so I recast them into more personal

terms and elevated them to Basic Principles for Myself: (1)
Some do, some don't; (2) Ask me no questions, I'll tell you no
lies; and (3) Change it into eggs.

Some do, some don't — Several years ago, in a humorous book
of rules, I came across "Dibble's First Law of Sociology: Some
do, some don't."[1] Suddenly I realized the significance of
something I had learned as a child from an elderly man in my
neighborhood:

> Some do, some don't.
> Some will, some won't.
> Some can, some cain't.
> Some is, some ain't.
> I is.

"Some do, some don't" is an important truth about human behavior and a testament to human individuality. It is a reminder
that, even under identical circumstances, not everyone be-
haves the same way. In the social sciences, there is always the
danger that the need to see patterns and make generalizations
about human behavior will dictate the research enterprise.
There is always the danger of going too far in smoothing out
data curves by ignoring important outliers, or of underreport-
ing exceptions because we believe they are, indeed, exceptions.
Only exceptionally do we use exceptions to prove (literally,
test) the rule.

"Some do, some don't" is a reminder that exceptions—even
one or two cases—may not be exceptions at all. They may be a
different way of doing things, a different way of behaving, and
instead of "proving the rule," they may be evidence of a different rule, a different pattern.

In any event, I found it useful to rely on "Some do, some don't"
as a general principle, thereby discouraging me from trying to
force-fit all the women into a single mold and seeing uniformi-
ties that were not there. Of course, this way of thinking makes

---

[1] Paul Dickson, *The Official Rules*, p. 37.

writing more difficult. One is always resorting to qualifiers—"on the other hand," "however," "almost," "some women," "some of the time"—and this makes it difficult to write a straightforward sentence. So be it.

Ask me no questions, I'll tell you no lies—A second principle that I adopted for myself was also something one often learns in childhood: Ask me no questions, I'll tell you no lies. This principle is especially salient for the participant observer. It would probably raise troubling epistemological issues for survey, interview, and other question-based research methodologies, and is probably of limited utility for short-term time-limited participant observation.

In the present instance, however, I was under no time restraints. So far as I was concerned, the whole study was open-ended, to be conducted at my leisure and terminated at my leisure, and I was under no pressure to bring ready-made questions into the study situation. I did ask questions, of course, but these were not questions I brought with me from the outside. They were "natural" questions that arose spontaneously and directly out of the social situation. They were the same sorts of questions that everyone else asked. They were situation-specific questions, not research questions.

In practice, then, I understood the principle to be "Ask me no (research) questions, I'll tell you no lies." For participant observation, the value of this injunction has more to do with questions than with lies. Lies may be a problem for the participant observer but not a major one. In participant observation studies, one returns day after day and month after month to the study situation, and lies do not really hold up well over long periods of time, and even if they do it's no big deal. The main value of the injunction lies in the first part, "Ask me no (research) questions," in that it discourages the researcher from contaminating the situation with questions dragged in from the outside. It allows the different situations under observation to

But EL. gets reviewing involved in the lives of these women!

develop according to their own inner logic and according to the needs of the participants, not the needs of the researcher. In this way, one comes closer to the ideal of observing behavior as it would have been had the observer not been present.

Change it into eggs — My third principle comes from someone else's childhood. Many years ago, I worked on a construction crew. At lunchtime, a little boy came to have lunch with "the men." Over sandwiches, we exchanged names and ages. He said he was eight years old and in the third grade. I asked him what his favorite subject was.

"Arithmetic," he said. "Ask me a question."

"OK. How many three-cent stamps in a dozen?"

"Twelve," he said without hesitation.

"That's terrific. How did you do it so fast?"

"It's easy," he said. "Whenever I hear a question like that I just change it into eggs."

What a wonderful principle to do research by! "Change it into eggs!" Don't allow yourself to be bedazzled or confused by all the irrelevant elaborations that invariably attach themselves to problems. Reduce the problem to its simplest, real-life terms, to smooth, bounded, lovely-to-handle units. Change it into eggs.

Unfortunately, most problems are not reducible to discrete units, and even when they are, it is usually very difficult to ferret out the relevant units from the maze of growth surrounding the problem. Nevertheless, the principle is a valid one. "Change it into eggs" can be a useful ideal and guide to writing, to analysis, and to problem solving.

. . .

I typed my notes on a computer after I got home at night or at my NIMH office the next morning. As best I could, I tried to remember conversations, or parts of conversations, verbatim. With practice, one does this pretty well. When I couldn't easily remember a given conversation, I tried to reconstruct it out of the bits and pieces I could remember. If I was certain that the reconstruction was so close to the original that the speaker herself would not have known the difference, I retained quotation marks. If I could not achieve this certainty, I used indirect quotation.[2] Sometimes I also used the form of direct quotation without quotation marks to indicate something short of a verbatim quotation.

Very occasionally, I was able to take down what people said at the time they said it without drawing undue attention to myself. In the day shelter, for example, it was commonplace for people to write personal letters, notes to themselves, or whatever else struck their fancy. Also, in the night shelters, after dinner, people sometimes remained at the dinner table or sat on their cots to write personal letters. Sometimes I joined them in this activity. Sometimes I wrote letters. Sometimes I took notes.[3] At such times, my notes consisted only of neutral descriptions—who was present, who was doing what, and who was saying what everyone could hear. Very occasionally, someone looked over my shoulder to see what I was writing, and I made no effort to conceal it. No one took much notice.

To make sense of my notes was, in effect, to write the book. This was far and away the most difficult part of this study. For me, to make sense of my notes meant to organize them and order them, along with my own ideas about them, into a more or less coherent whole that told a story. A true story, I hoped.

My first step was to rearrange my chronological notes by subject matter without knowing precisely what the subject matter would be. This commitment to organization by subject matter

---

[2] See p. 46, for example. The problem here was that my notes had Lisa saying, "Suppose . . . suppose . . . suppose . . ." followed by a line in which I said that Kim dismissed all of Lisa's "what-ifs." Reading my notes, then, I did not know whether Lisa said "suppose" or "what if." I decided to change the "supposes" to "what if's" and to keep the quotation marks on the grounds that Lisa herself would not have known whether she said "suppose" or "what if."

[3] The conversation between Edith and Leslie on p. 207 was recorded in this manner at the day shelter.

raised the terrible problem of how to keep the individual women intact, how to allow them to remain whole, recognizable persons across subject matter categories. I had no satisfactory answer (and still don't), but I knew I did not want to write life stories of individual homeless women, of which there were plenty.

I sorted the chronological notes into some 40 categories suggested by the notes themselves and drawn from a variety of levels and universes, such as work, violence, lawyers, religion, food, holidays, values, sex, problems in shelters, problems with staff, money, friendship, killing time, health, and so on, with many overlaps. Eventually, I switched from line-numbered computer print-out sheets to 3″ × 5″ cards that could be shuffled and sorted into different experimental groupings. Each card was headed by the relevant line numbers and the category name. On the rest of the card I copied enough text to remind me of the content of the original note, thus enabling me to shuffle the cards to my heart's content and allowing me to return to the full text of the note at will. However tedious, this procedure of moving from sheets to cards gave me an additional and valuable familiarity with my notes.[4]

It is quite possible that in taking many notes over a long period of time, I bit off more than I could chew. Although I studied my notes many times over, I could never digest them all at once. I had the feeling, while writing, that I was dealing with them piecemeal; that because of the volume, I could pick up only one corner of the notes at a time. I felt that I could, perhaps, connect one piece with another, but I never had the feeling that I could embrace them all at once, or that, all together, they made a special sense of their own. To me, the substantive chapters,

---

[4]An anonymous reviewer describes this "fussing" with my notes as "dinosaur-like" in view of all the computer software available for dealing with qualitative data. My problem, however, was not retrieval or even organization of my notes but rather seeing how they related to one another and integrating them, and I did not know how to make the software do this for me. Sometimes we do better by sticking to what we think we know.

taken together, have a linear structure of sorts but not the connectedness of each part to every other that gives one a sense of rounded wholeness.[5] Part of this problem simply reflects my own limitations, but part, I believe, is traceable to the fact of too many notes.

When I began to write, I still had no order, outline, or structure in mind. The first draft chapter was on work and jobs. The second was on family. The third was on the women's relationships with shelter staff and other public agencies. But these were just discrete chunks that bore no logical or other relationship to one another. I had plunged ahead for many months without knowing where I was going, hoping and believing that some kind of structure and story line would eventually jump out.

My original intention was to write a flat descriptive study and let the women speak for themselves—that is, to let the descriptive data and anecdotes drive the writing. In retrospect, that was a mistake. Ideas drive a study, not observations or unadorned facts. "All observation must be for or against some view if it is to be of any use," said Charles Darwin, and I needed something to be for or against.[6]

I shuffled my remaining cards again and discovered that many cards wanted to be grouped under Problems in Day-to-Day Living, so I undertook to write that chunk. The first paragraph asked the question, How do the women survive the inhuman conditions that confront them? After I wrote that paragraph, it occurred to me that most situations, experiences, and processes could be seen as working for or against the women's survival and their humanity—that the question of

---

[5] Herbert Gans, in a personal note, dryly observes that "only traditional anthropologists, with their fix on culture, can believe in a rounded wholeness." I would like to note the possible irrelevance that I have not used the term "culture" even once.

[6] Charles Darwin, letter to Henry Fawcett, quoted by Stephen Jay Gould in a review of Donald O. Henry, *From Foraging to Agriculture: The Levant at the End of the Ice Age, New York Review of Books* 36, no. 22–23 (January 18, 1990), p. 26.

survival might serve as the opening and organizing theme of the book as a whole and give the enterprise some kind of structure. I could start with the day-to-day problems, move on to other problem areas, and conclude with chapters that would focus on the resources the women drew on for survival. And that, for better or worse, was how it turned out, in a bare-bones sort of way.

. . .

I made many mistakes, some of which are noted in the discussion above. Others were even more serious. Among the most important was the decision to stick closely and exclusively to the women and their perspective. This meant, however, that I almost never got to see things from the point of view of service providers, public agencies, and local officials and policy makers. Given my training and experience, I should have known better. I should have known that homeless people are not unattached to the world we live in, free-floating bodies in a social space all their own. But it was not until after I had started the study that I realized how profoundly the agencies, service providers, state and county officials, and legislation affected the lives of the women. At that point, I realized that the study would be substantially enhanced if I could expand it into a more well-rounded ethnography that took other perspectives into account.

It was not too late to do so, but I chose not to for very personal reasons. When I first retired, I decided that, given my circumstances, I was going to do only those things that gave me pleasure. Working at the soup kitchen and spending time with the women and even taking notes gave me pleasure. Interviewing agency people, service providers, and state and county officials would not, so I didn't. The result is that those perspectives are sorely missing from this study, although I hope that the comments of Rachel, director of The Refuge, will take the edge off this omission.

• • •

As one might expect, I did come up against ethical problems in the course of doing this study, but they do not seem to have been peculiar to the research effort, perhaps because this was not a study of a different culture. In general, I tried to bring the same ethics to fieldwork that I bring to any other part of my life, and this effort seemed to work reasonably well. It would have been wrong for me, for example, to misrepresent myself to the women and to conceal my purposes, but it would be equally wrong to do that with anyone else.

Big issues with real-life consequences were easier to deal with than little ones with no obvious consequences. I treated what I was told privately as confidential except when someone's life or well-being was at stake. When one woman, whom I cared for a great deal, told me of her plan to harm someone seriously, I took her at her word and took steps to stop her, including cooperating with the police, then telling her I had done so, mainly to stop her from carrying out her threat and partly to keep our relationship straight. As much as I hated to do this, there was no question in my mind about what I ought to have done.

A more difficult but perhaps less consequential ethical problem arose around the issue of shoplifting. Pauline was distributing underwear and stockings to the women, explaining that her boyfriend had had a good day shoplifting. Brenda took me aside and asked me what I would say to her if she told me she had been shoplifting. I told her I care very much about what happens to her and I would advise her to stop because it's very dangerous.[7]

"Because a clerk might call the police?"

"Yes."

"Is that all you'd have to say?"

---

[7]In retrospect, perhaps I should have taken a lesson from my clinician friends and answered, "What do *you* think about shoplifting?"

It was clear from her tone of voice that I had failed a values test. I tried to recover the high ground but only made the matter worse.

"Yes. I think it's wrong to shoplift. It's stealing, and I won't do it, but you have to decide these things for yourself. I would just remind you how dangerous it is."

Brenda was clearly disappointed in me. I had patronized her, claiming, in effect, that what was morally wrong for me might be OK for her. I lacked the courage to tell her that I thought it was just as wrong for a poor person to steal as it would be for anyone else. Or perhaps it was not courage but conviction that I lacked. In effect, I was confronted with the choice of holding myself morally superior to Brenda or of taking the morally untenable position that it is just as wrong for a poor and hungry person to steal bread as it is for someone rich and sated.[8]

Although the particular formulation of this age-old problem arose in a research setting, it, too, is a more general problem for which the research setting had no special relevance. At least in one's own society, ethics are ethics.

---

[8] "When a man is destitute of food, or other thing necessary for his life, and cannot preserve himselfe . . . but by some fact against the Law . . . he is totally Excused." Thomas Hobbes, *Leviathan,* p. 208.

Bibliography

Bahr, Howard M., and Gerald R. Garrett. *Disaffiliation among Urban Women.* Columbia University, Bureau of Applied Social Research, November 1971.

Berlin, Isaiah. "Two Concepts of Liberty." In *Four Essays on Liberty.* London: Oxford University Press, [1968] 1991.

Bloom, Allan. *The Closing of the American Mind.* New York: Simon and Schuster, 1987.

Breakey, William R., Pamela J. Fisher, Morton Kramer, Gerald Nestadt, Alan J. Romanoski, Alan Ross, Richard M. Royall, and Oscar C. Stine. "Health and Mental Health Problems of Homeless Men and Women in Baltimore." *Journal of the American Medical Association* 262, no. 10 (1989), pp. 1352–57.

Brodsky, Joseph. "The MacNeil-Lehrer Newshour." Thursday, November 10, 1988.

The National Institute of Mental Health's Office of Programs for the Homeless Mentally Ill, under the direction of Irene S. Levine, has supported a rich and extensive body of research on the chronically mentally ill homeless. Research products and annotated bibliographies of these and other studies on that subject are available from the National Resource Center on Homelessness and Severe Mental Illness, 262 Delaware Ave., Delmar, NY 12054. (800) 444–7415.

329

Burt, Martha R. *Over the Edge: The Growth of Homelessness in the 1980's.* New York: Russell Sage Foundation/Washington, D.C.: Urban Institute Press, 1992.

Burt, Martha R., and Barbara E. Cohen. *America's Homeless: Numbers, Characteristics, and the Programs That Serve Them.* Washington, D.C.: Urban Institute Press, 1989.

——. *Feeding the Homeless: Does the Prepared Meal Provision Help?* Report to Congress on the Prepared Meal Provision. Vol. I (revised), March 1989.

Carlyle, Thomas. "The Everlasting Yea." In *Sartor Resartus.* London: Curwen Press, [1836] 1931.

Chaiklin, Harris. "Soup Kitchens and Shelters: The Private Sector as Safety Valve for Public Sector Irresponsibility." Paper presented at annual meeting, Society for the Study of Social Problems, Washington, D.C., 1985.

Daniels, Sister Veronica. *Affidavit (V) in Support of Plaintiffs' Memorandum of Points and Authorities in Support of Motion for Temporary Restraining Order.* Michael Atchinson et al., Plaintiffs, v. Marion S. Barry et al., Defendants. Civil Action No. 88-CA11976, Superior Court of the District of Columbia, 1988.

Dickson, Paul. *The Official Rules.* New York: Dell, 1978.

Dockett, Kathleen H. *Street Homeless People in the District of Columbia: Characteristics and Service Needs.* Final Report to United States Department of Agriculture, University of the District of Columbia, March 1989.

Ellwood, David T. "If You Work You Shouldn't Be Poor." *The Washington Post,* April 14, 1989, p. A25.

Erikson, Kai T. *Everything in Its Path: Destruction of Community in the Buffalo Creek Flood.* New York: Simon and Schuster, 1976.

Forsberg, James (Director, HUD Office of Special Needs Assistance Programs), quoted in *Access* (a publication of the National Resource Center on Homelessness and Severe Mental Illness, Delmar, N.Y.) 4, no. 2 (June 1992), p. 1.

Gans, Herbert J. "Deconstructing the Underclass: The Term's Dangers as a Planning Concept." *American Planning Association Journal,* Summer 1990, pp. 271–77.

Goetcheus, Janelle, MD. *Affidavit (W) in Support of Plaintiffs' Memorandum of Points and Authorities in Support of Motion for Temporary Restraining Order.* Michael Atchinson et al., Plaintiffs, v. Marion S. Barry et al., Defendants. Civil Action No. 88-CA11976, Superior Court of the District of Columbia, 1988.

Gould, Stephen Jay. Review of Donald O. Henry, *From Foraging to Agriculture: The Levant at the End of the Ice Age. New York Review of Books* 36, no. 22–23 (January 18, 1990), p. 26.

Hinden, Stan. "Ad for Janitor's Position Draws 350 Applicants." *The Washington Post,* August 18, 1991, p. C1.

Hobbes, Thomas. *Leviathan.* Cambridge: Cambridge University Press, [1651] 1991.

Hopper, Kim. "The Ordeal of Shelter: Continuities and Discontinuities in the Public Response to Homelessness." *Notre Dame Journal of Law, Ethics, and Public Policy* 4, no. 2 (1989), pp. 301–23.

——. "Shelterized Syndrome Theory Has Dangerous Flaw." *The New York Times,* June 5, 1990, p. A28.

Hopper, Kim, and Jill Hamburg. *The Making of America's Homeless: From Skid Row to New Poor.* New York: Community Service Society of New York, 1984.

Hopper, Kim, Ezra Susser, and Susan Conover. "Economies of Makeshift: Deindustrialization and Homelessness in New York City." *Urban Anthropology* 14, no. 1–3 (1985), pp. 183–236.

Katz, Michael B. *In the Shadow of the Poorhouse: A Social History of Welfare in America.* New York: Basic Books, 1986.

Kohn, Melvin L., Atsushi Naoi, Carrie Schoenbach, Carmi Schooler, and Kazimierz M. Slomczynski. "Position in the Class Structure and Psychological Functioning in the United States, Japan, and Poland." *American Journal of Sociology* 95, no. 4 (January 1990), pp. 964–1008.

Kozol, Jonathan. *Rachel and Her Children.* New York: Crown, 1988.

Levitan, Sar A., and Susan Schillmoeller. *The Paradox of Homelessness in America.* Washington, D.C.: (Research Report) Center for Social Policy Studies, George Washington University, January 1991, p. 9.

Liebow, Elliot. "The Human Costs of Unemployment." In *The Battle Against Unemployment,* ed. Arthur M. Okun. (Rev. ed.) New York: W. W. Norton, 1972. Pp. 1–11.

——. *Tally's Corner: A Study of Negro Streetcorner Men.* Boston: Little, Brown, 1967.

Marin, Peter. "Helping and Hating the Homeless: The Struggle at the Margins of America." *Harpers,* January 1987, pp. 39–49.

Martin, Marsha A. "Strategies of Adaptation: Coping Patterns of the Urban Transient Female." Unpublished doctoral dissertation, School of Social Work, Columbia University, 1982.

Mihaly, Lisa Klee. Quoted in "Homeless Children: A National Tragedy." *USA Today,* July 30, 1991, p. 9A.

Moran, Mark. "Feeding the Poor: In Your Neighborhood?" *Montgomery County Sentinel,* October 9, 1986, p. 1.

National Coalition for the Homeless. *Safety Network* 8, no. 2 (February 1989).

National Law Center on Homelessness and Poverty. *Go Directly to Jail: A Report Analyzing Local Anti-Homeless Ordinances.* Research report. Washington, D.C., December 1991.

——. *Small Steps: An Update on the Education of Homeless Children and Youth Program.* (Research report.) Washington, D.C., July 1991.

——. *Social Security: Broken Promise to America's Homeless.* (Research report.) Washington, D.C., March 1990.

Okin, Robert (Chief of Psychiatry, San Francisco General Hospital). "The MacNeil-Lehrer Newshour," April 27, 1992.

Perin, Constance. "A Biology of Meaning and Conduct." In *Discourse and the Social Life of Meaning,* ed. Phyllis Pease Chock and June R. Wyman. Washington, D.C.: Smithsonian Institution Press, 1986. Pp. 95–125.

——. *Everything in Its Place: Social Order and Land Use in America.* Princeton, N.J.: Princeton University Press, 1977.

Pullum, Geoffrey K. *The Great Eskimo Vocabulary Hoax and Other Irreverent Essays on the Study of Language.* Chicago: University of Chicago Press, 1991.

Rich, Spencer. "Federal Offices Urged to Hire Temporaries." *The Washington Post,* January 3, 1985, p. A3.

Ringheim, Karin. *At Risk of Homelessness: The Roles of Income and Rent.* New York: Praeger, 1990.

Ropers, Richard H. "The Rise of the New Urban Homeless." *Public Affairs Report: Bulletin of the Institute of Governmental Studies,* University of California, Berkeley, 26 (October–November 1985; published May 1986), pp. 1–14.

Rosenberg, Morris. "A Symbolic Interactionist View of Psychosis." *Journal of Health and Human Behavior* 25, no. 3 (September 1984), pp. 289–302.

Rossi, Peter H. *Down and Out in America: The Origins of Homelessness.* Chicago: University of Chicago Press, 1989.

——. "No Good Applied Social Research Goes Unpunished." *Society* 76 (November/December 1987), pp. 74–79.

Schneider, Henry W. *The Puritan Mind.* Ann Arbor: University of Michigan Press, 1958.

Sennet, Richard, and Jonathan Cobb. *The Hidden Injuries of Class.* New York: Vintage Books, 1973.

Snow, David A., and Leon Anderson. "Identity Work among the Homeless: The Verbal Construction and Avowal of Personal Identities." *American Journal of Sociology* 92, no. 6 (May 1987), pp. 1336–71.

Taeuber, Cynthia M., and Paul M. Siegel. "Counting the Nation's Homeless Population in the 1990 Census." In *Enumerating Homeless Persons: Methods and Data Needs,* ed. Cynthia M. Taeuber. Washington, D.C.: U.S. Department of Commerce, 1991. Pp. 92–109.

U.S. Conference of Mayors. *A Status Report on Hunger and Homelessness in American Cities: 1991*. Washington, D.C.: December 1991.

U.S. General Accounting Office. *Homelessness: Implementation of Food and Shelter Programs under the McKinney Act*. Report to Congress (GAO/RCED-88-63), December 1987.

Wickenden, Dorothy. "Abandoned Americans." *New Republic,* March 18, 1985, pp. 19–25.

Wright, James D. *Address Unknown: The Tragedy of Homelessness in America*. Hawthorne, N.Y.: Aldine de Gruyter, 1989.

Index of Names*

Abigail, 39, 40, 44, 57, 67n, 81, 84,
    155, 156, 165, 200–201, 211, 242,
    242n, 251–54, 278–79
Agnes, 95
Aleichem, Shalom, 230n
Alison, 128n
Anderson, Leon, 216n
Andrew, 95, 96
Angela, 137–38, 153n, 197–98
Annabel, 111
Armstrong, W. W., 171
Arnold, Matthew, 184
Auschwitz, 141

Babs, 87
Bahr, Howard M., 83n, 313n
Ball, Lucille, 214n
Berlin, Isaiah, 176n, 183
Bernice, 141, 217
Beryl, 56
Bessie, 72
Betty, xv, xvi, 17, 21, 28, 29–30, 38, 40,
    43, 46, 61, 75, 76, 83, 106–107, 112,
    114n, 122, 123, 128n, 131, 146n,
    163, 167, 168–69, 180, 181,
    183–84, 186, 187, 191, 197, 199,
    204, 206, 208, 209, 211, 215, 217,
    219, 221, 229–30, 237–39, 240, 241,
    254–58

Beverly, 44–45, 66n–67n, 101–102,
    144, 145, 258–61
Biff, 87–88
Biff Jr., 87
Bonita, 163
Bonnie, 99, 102, 163, 165–66, 212,
    215, 287
Booth, J., 41n
Breakey, William, 39n, 48n
Brenda, 19, 68, 70, 76, 327–32
Brian, 301, 302
Bridget, 107
Brodsky, Joseph, 134
Bruce, 243
Buck, 46
Burt, Martha R., 14n, 224n, 312n,
    313n
Bush, George, 202
Buster, 109

Carlotta, 60, 61, 63, 64, 261–63
Carlyle, Thomas, 178
Carol, 57
Carolyn, 53, 213
Catholic Charities, 154, 200
Chaiklin, Harris, 226n
Charles, 152, 296
Cheryl, 102, 174
Ciserine, 89

*Numbers-only page references apply to text or text and footnotes. Page references
followed by n apply to footnotes alone.

FOR THE BEST IN PAPERBACKS, LOOK FOR THE

In every corner of the world, on every subject under the sun, Penguin represents quality and variety—the very best in publishing today.

For complete information about books available from Penguin—including Pelicans, Puffins, Peregrines, and Penguin Classics—and how to order them, write to us at the appropriate address below. Please note that for copyright reasons the selection of books varies from country to country.

In the United Kingdom: For a complete list of books available from Penguin in the U.K., please write to *Dept E.P., Penguin Books Ltd, Harmondsworth, Middlesex, UB7 0DA.*

In the United States: For a complete list of books available from Penguin in the U.S., please write to *Consumer Sales, Penguin USA, P.O. Box 999— Dept. 17109, Bergenfield, New Jersey 07621-0120.* VISA and MasterCard holders call 1-800-253-6476 to order all Penguin titles.

In Canada: For a complete list of books available from Penguin in Canada, please write to *Penguin Books Canada Ltd, 10 Alcorn Avenue, Suite 300, Toronto, Ontario, Canada M4V 3B2.*

In Australia: For a complete list of books available from Penguin in Australia, please write to the *Marketing Department, Penguin Books Ltd, P.O. Box 257, Ringwood, Victoria 3134.*

In New Zealand: For a complete list of books available from Penguin in New Zealand, please write to the *Marketing Department, Penguin Books (NZ) Ltd, Private Bag, Takapuna, Auckland 9.*

In India: For a complete list of books available from Penguin, please write to *Penguin Overseas Ltd, 706 Eros Apartments, 56 Nehru Place, New Delhi, 110019.*

In Holland: For a complete list of books available from Penguin in Holland, please write to *Penguin Books Nederland B.V., Postbus 195, NL-1380AD Weesp, Netherlands.*

In Germany: For a complete list of books available from Penguin, please write to *Penguin Books Ltd, Friedrichstrasse 10-12, D-6000 Frankfurt Main I, Federal Republic of Germany.*

In Spain: For a complete list of books available from Penguin in Spain, please write to *Longman, Penguin España, Calle San Nicolas 15, E-28013 Madrid, Spain.*

In Japan: For a complete list of books available from Penguin in Japan, please write to *Longman Penguin Japan Co Ltd, Yamaguchi Building, 2-12-9 Kanda Jimbocho, Chiyoda-Ku, Tokyo 101, Japan.*